The Battle for Madrid

IL GARIBALDINO

GIORNALE DELLA BRIGATA GARIBALDI

LA CONQUISTA DI VILLANUEVA DEL PARDILLO

Pasaremos

XI. BRIGADE

...ringt uns den Sieg

VENCEREMOS

ORGANO DE LA BRIGADA "DOMBROWSKI"

UN AÑO DE GUERRA..

!!!ADELANTE!!!

© George Hills 1976
First published in Great Britain 1976
First published in the United States of America 1977

Published by Vantage Books
and distributed by
Robert Hale Limited
Clerkenwell House
Clerkenwell Green
London ECIR OHT

ISBN 0 904545 02 4

St. Martin's Press, Inc.,
175 Fifth Avenue,
New York, N.Y. 10010

Library of Congress Catalog Card Number 76–28035

Design by Behram Kapadia
Layout by John Leach

Photoset, printed and bound
in Great Britain by
REDWOOD BURN LIMITED
Trowbridge and Esher

The
Battle
for Madrid

George Hills

VANTAGE BOOKS · LONDON
ST. MARTIN'S PRESS · NEW YORK

£ 6.50p

Contents

List of Maps

Acknowledgments

The Author and Publishers are grateful to the Spanish Ministry of Information and Agencia Efe for permission to reproduce photographs in this book.

If the Publishers have mistakenly infringed copyright in any illustration in this book, they will be glad of the opportunity on being satisfied as to the owner's title to pay an appropriate reproduction fee.

Preface

This book is about the political and military Battle for Madrid – a detail of the vast and complex panorama of the Spanish Second Republic and Civil War. Within the detail some factors stand out more than they would in a picture of the whole, and others, important elsewhere, are here absent.

This account of that political and military battle – or rather series of battles – will be found to differ in greater or lesser measure from others hitherto published in English. During my research for another book I was allowed access in the middle 1960s to documents previously zealously guarded, and I had the opportunity to question several of the then surviving principal figures, republican and nationalist, of the war. They provided evidence on both its political and military aspects which led to inescapable conclusions at variance with the then available accounts by supporters of either side let alone by those whose object in writing had been to justify their personal actions in the war. In the last ten years many more documents have become available for consultation, and several books have been published in Paris, Mexico, Moscow and Madrid providing fresh evidence which I have taken into consideration in this new attempt to pan the grains of truth from the coarse sand and clay of propaganda in which all contenders in the war, and their allies, hid and enveloped them.

I acknowledge a great debt to Colonel José Manuel Martínez Bande with whom I have exchanged ideas on the Civil War for more than a decade, and whose heavily documented *Monografías de la Guerra de España* I have quarried extensively for facts. Those 'monographs' are the result of half a long lifetime of meticulous research in the mountain of primary documents of both sides which were brought under one roof after the war. However, the assessments here of the relative importance of this or that political or military factor in each successive phase of the struggle are my own, and the conclusions drawn from those judgments are therefore also my own. Coincidences and differences and our personal friendship may all be accounted for by the fact that we were both gunners, but in different armies.

My thanks are due also to Derek Poulsen who cast an infantryman's eye over the manuscript and made some valuable suggestions, and to Asher Lee who answered queries on Soviet and German air force men and machines, and, of course, to the many *Madrileños* and republican and nationalist soldiers who suffered my enquiries into their memories of the period.

G.H.

London and Madrid
January 1976

9

1 Madrid 1931

Madrid in 1931 was a compact city. Almost all its 900 000 inhabitants lived within a half-hour's walk from the popular focal point, the Puerta del Sol.

In the lifetime of those in their fifties – about 200 000 were of that age group and over – the place had been transformed from a dirty and unhealthy conglomeration into a city which compared favourably with other European capitals. Madrid could no longer be justly called, as it had been by Spaniards in the nineteenth century, *la ciudad del polvo y de la muerte*, the city of dust and death. The maze of narrow alleys which dated back beyond 1561, when Philip II had decreed that Madrid should be the capital of his several Spanish kingdoms, had been provided with main drainage, and cobbled. Squares had been turned into gardens. Hundreds of old houses had been pulled down to widen the Puerta del Sol and the road eastward from it, the Calle de Alcalá. There was a new wide diagonal worthy of its name, Gran Vía. There was an even wider avenue – never less than fifty and in parts eighty metres wide – running south–north. The total length of its three sections (Paseo del Prado, Paseo de Recoletos and Avenida de la Castellana), came to four kilometres, and there were plans for its extension northwards. The seventeenth-century Plaza Mayor and Palacio de Santa Cruz, the vast Royal Palace built at the instigation of Philip V's termagant consort, Elizabeth Farnese, and the handful of neoclassic structures inspired by the 'enlightened despot' Charles III, were no longer the sum total of Madrid's fine buildings. Along the Castellana, along the Calle de Alcalá all the way to an enlarged Puerta del Sol and along the Gran Vía there were now public buildings and headquarters of banks and business houses grandiose in size, expensive in materials and of various, even if to subsequent generations not always aesthetic, designs. East of the Castellana there were wide boulevards flanked by tall buildings which, divided into *pisos* (large flats), were occupied by aristocrats, prominent politicians, successful lawyers, doctors and businessmen. For the less exalted professional men, civil servants and service officers, journalists and employees of business houses, there were also new pisos in three, four and five storey buildings mostly to the north of the Palace, between Madrid's principal barracks, the Cuartel de la Montaña and the Cárcel Modelo or 'Model Prison'. North of the prison there was a zone where work was in progress to convert some 360 hectares (900 acres) of steppe-land into a University City for 15 000 students of which 5000 were to be resident.

Within the lifetime of those in their fifties the population had increased, through immigration from the provinces and a falling death rate as much as through births, from under 400 000 in 1880 to

500 000 in 1900 and 750 000 in 1920. In the first 100 years from
Madrid's establishment as a capital it had grown rapidly from a few
thousand to 350 000, but it had then stayed at that figure for the next
200 years through epidemics and the losses of war and civil strife.
Madrid had had a turbulent history: in the War of the Spanish Succession twice captured by the British and Spanish forces of the one side
and twice recaptured by the French and Spanish troops of the other; a
century later occupied by Napoleon's predatory troops against whom
the people of Madrid rose on May 2 1808 with a loss to themselves of
200 on that day in the battle at the Puerta del Sol and surroundings,
and of over 300 before firing squads on subsequent days – the scenes
depicted in Goya's famous set of pictures; further losses as the French
evacuated the city having lost the Battle of Bailén; more death and destruction as in counter-attack Napoleon in person advanced and took
it, and as Wellington recaptured it. During 1812 there was a famine in
which at least 20 000 *Madrileños* died; and after 1814 it was the epi-
centre of sixty years of revolutions, *pronunciamientos, juntas,* the de-
thronement of a Queen, the imposition of a foreign King and rule by
an intellectual oligarchy which called itself a Republic.

It was the peace, or rather comparative quiet, which had followed
the restoration in 1875 of the Bourbons in the person of a young officer
cadet at the Royal Military College at Sandhurst, England, as Alfonso
XII, that had enabled the local authorities, with support from the
national government, to reform the city. The attempt by an anarchist
to assassinate Alfonso XIII and his English wife, Queen Ena, as they
drove from the Royal Chapel of San Gerónimo to the Palace on their
wedding day, May 31 1906, the assassination in 1912 of a Prime
Minister, Canalejas, at the door of a book shop in the Puerta del Sol,
the 'palace revolution' of 1923 to establish General Primo de Rivera as
Dictator, and a number of less important but violent incidents in Spain
had not seriously delayed Madrid's development.

The University City was Alfonso XIII's favourite personal project.
Spanish Universities had declined from the apex of thirty-two establishments with over 50 000 students in the 1620s to twelve with a total
of under 10 000 by the 1820s, though the population had almost
doubled in that time. In 1822 what was left of Cardinal Cisneros' great

foundation of 1498 at Alcalá de Henares had been transferred to Madrid. There it had languished over the next sixty years, and then, like Madrid, revived. In 1931 there were 9000 students in the various and scattered schools which together comprised the Central University. In other professional colleges and centres for further education there were another 70 000. A fair proportion of these, however, were not Madrileños, for it was only in Madrid that studies for certain professions could be pursued.

Much remained to be done. There was primary and secondary education available for about 45 000 children in establishments run by religious orders and for another 90 000 in state schools, which left no schools for about another 60 000. At least one adult Madrileño in five was illiterate.

There were around 100 000 workers in industry, building and other trades, public services and transport, whose wages were enough to provide them and their families with only the simplest fare, cheapest clothing and insanitary lodging. For them meat – even the toughest mutton – was a luxury. Alimentary and lung diseases were endemic. Workmen wore the *mono*, a blue boiler suit of coarse cloth which, buttoned up to the neck, hid whatever clothing, if any, lay underneath. The *mono* was worn so uniformly by workmen that it was almost a uniform. Women wore dresses of coarse black cloth.

Workers lived either in over-crowded tenements, of which there were plenty in the old town towards the Toledo Gate and round Atocha, or in shacks outside the city's official limits. There were slums across the River Manzanares on the road to Toledo. On the road to

The Puerta del Sol; in this photograph taken in the 1930s the Ministry of the Interior can be seen on the left of the picture.

The junction of the Gran
Viá and the Calle de
Alcalá in the 1930s.

Vallecas, just across the bridge over the stream which formed the right-
hand side of the Madrid triangle, there was a concentration, within
half a square kilometre at most, of 80 000 people – a figure higher
than that of several of Spain's more spacious provincial cities. Not all
the poor, however, were residents in the slum tenements within or
shacks outside the city. Every one of the buildings of *pisos*, inhabited
by the upper and middle classes, had its resident porter, and every
block of such buildings its *sereno*, or night watchman. Porters and
serenos were in receipt only of pittances. There were hundreds of beggars. They slept in the streets and church doors where they begged by
day. Glaucoma was widespread.

The poor, the urban proletariat and their families constituted over
half the population. Little better off, since they had to spend more on
clothing and footwear, were some tens of thousands of employees of
shops and clerical workers in business houses and banks. They staved
off hunger with tobacco: the consumption of tobacco in Madrid was
more than double the national average.

Workers frequented taverns, of which there were eighty-eight in the
Calle de Toledo alone. It was not that the workers drank much but that
a glass of wine cost less than the quantity of bread with the equivalent
nutritional value, and that there was usually a newspaper somewhere
in the place. The Madrileños who could read were avid readers to the
extent that the Press was often referred to as 'the fourth estate'. In the
poorer quarters it was a commonplace to hear literate workmen read-
ing newspapers aloud for the benefit of the illiterate. The papers of the
day were the medium of propaganda, monarchist and republican,
Catholic and anti-Catholic, conservative, liberal, radical, communist,
socialist and anarchist – to mention only the main trends. The last two
were the most popular in the taverns.

In the cafes, establishments patronized by the middle class, the
choice was wider. There was at least one cafe in virtually every block in
the town. The clientele often included a handful of the genteel poor,
pensioners, retired army officers of middle rank, and widows. Over a
beverage costing two *reales*, a quarter of a peseta, they could sit there
for hours on end, and enjoy cool in the summer and warmth in the
winter for free. There were cafes with specialized clienteles – literary,

artistic, journalist, police and so on – but the characteristic common to all in the 1930s was that in the late evening they were full of men who would argue into the early hours of the morning. The favourite topic was comment on the latest political news – or rumours. For the more aristocratic or wealthy there were '*casinos*', that is clubs, mostly political in purpose*, and masonic lodges, also centres of political discussion and intrigue. There was the elitist meeting place, the *Ateneo*, for the many with pretensions to literary or political eminence. There were twenty-two theatres, as befitted the capital of a country with such dramatists of the past as Lope de Vega, Tirso de Molina and Calderón,

The Toledo Bridge leading out of Madrid.

and with such contemporary figures as Casona and García Lorca. Straight comedy and tragedy apart, the theatre in the 1930s was also a platform for politics, with works by socialists and communists as well as anarchists.

Taverns, cafes, theatres had kept pace with the multiplication of Madrid's population through the years. Not so churches. There were only 30 parish and 20 other public churches including a cathedral under construction. Madrid had become the seat of a bishop only in 1884. The diocesan boundaries were those of the Province of Madrid, the population of which was 1 400 000, nominally 95 per cent Catholic. The diocese had 600 secular priests and the help of another 400 members of religious orders. The ratio of priests to layfolk (1:1400), might have been sufficient but for other factors. The province stretched 40–60 kilometres in all directions from the city, and totalled overall 8000 square kilometres (2900 square miles). There were within the diocese not only the towns round Madrid (Vallecas, Vicálvaro, Chamartín and Carabanchel), and the more distant Chinchón, Navalcarnero, Escorial, Valdeiglesias and Torrelaguna, but about 400 villages, some of them very isolated. An 'economic' distribution of the clergy would therefore not have been possible – but no attempt had been made at a reasonable compromise. Thus, for the poverty-stricken settlement at the Puente de Vallecas, the parish of San Román, there was only one priest per 16 000 people, whereas in

* The word *casino* in Spanish does not have the meaning of its English homonym.

the upper-class city parish of Santa Bárbara there was one priest per 1250. Not surprisingly, therefore, in the parish of San Román only 7 per cent of the parishioners went to Mass on Sundays, 25 per cent were not baptised and concubinage was as common as marriage. Forty per cent of those who bothered to get married did not know the Lord's Prayer.[1]

The figures for San Román were the lowest, but not all that different from those for any of the working-class parishes within the city limits. Thus only 10 per cent of the parishioners of San Millán (south of the Puerta del Sol) went to Mass, and only 40 per cent bothered with a priest when they were dying. In Madrid, as in cities other than in the Basque provinces and Navarre, the Church had lost the overwhelming majority of the proletariat.

Behind that loss were the centuries of tensions between Church and State which in the eighteenth and nineteenth centuries had broken out from time to time into open warfare. In that struggle the Church, whose bishops and priests were in the majority of humble origin, had come to ally itself with one of the two aristocratic factions which were fighting for power among themselves. Traditionally, and as successors to the Spanish Jesuit and Dominican philosophers of the seventeenth century in particular, they should have been on the side of the oppressed. The obsession of one of the two factions to destroy religion had driven the Church into the camp of the other, which was the greater oppressor of the poor. Thus the Church in Spain and in particular in Madrid was now identified not merely with the wealthy but with its conservative faction. True enough, in Madrid as elsewhere in Spain, the Church ran numerous institutions for the needy – primary and technical schools, hospitals, orphanages and asylums for old people; but what the proletariat did not see the clergy doing, and only a few individual clergymen did, was preach to the wealthy on the iniquity of their oppression of the poor and their denial of just wages and human dignity to their employees.

The latifundists and the financial and industrial magnates were not the only guilty men. There were only a very few large enterprises even in Madrid. The owners of the many small factories and workshops and retail businesses were no less guilty. Latifundists, industrialists and shop-keepers made much of their membership of pious societies and of

Calle de Alcalá. On the left of the picture can be seen the Gardens of the Ministry of War. Top right of the picture is the Cibeles Fountain.

The Toledo Bridge leading to Toledo Gate.

their friendship with the clergy, and the clergy were not averse to be identified as friends of the Duke of wherever or the owner of the shop round the corner; so a great number of white-collar workers no less than workmen and labourers had concluded that Christianity was hypocrisy.

The King, too, made much of his Catholicism in public. He would get out of his carriage and kneel on the road whenever he heard the bell of a priest taking the Eucharist to a dying man. Each Maundy Thursday he washed the feet of twelve beggars. In the year 1919, at a mound sixteen kilometres south of the Puerta del Sol called the Cerro de los Angeles, calculated as the exact geographical centre of Spain, Alfonso XIII and his Prime Minister, Antonio Maura, had inaugurated a colossal monument to the Sacred Heart. It had been erected as an act of reparation for the anti-Catholic policies of the assassinated Prime Minister Canalejas. The King's attendance was interpreted as a symbol of the union of Altar and Throne. Altar and Throne, power and the Church, wealth and the clergy, religion and the perpetuation of gross social injustice were thus equated in the popular mind, although in fact only about 25 per cent of the middle and upper classes responsible for that injustice were practising Catholics.

It was within the aristocratic caste now concentrated in Madrid, and within the upper-middle class that there existed, as it had for two centuries, a minority with a pathological hatred of the Church. It was a minority which included writers and propagandists of ability. Within living memory, till his death in 1920, the most able, though not the most violent, had been the novelist and playwright Pérez Galdós. His successor was now another novelist-playwright Pérez de Ayala, whose obscene novelettish lampoon against the Jesuits, *A.M.D.G.*, was staged in Madrid in November 1931. Ayala, however, was only one of

17

a whole school of imitators, which in 1931 could be numbered in hundreds and which, by 1936, had 146 daily newspapers to print their daily message of hatred.

Madrid was therefore no stronghold of the Church, but it was of the army. It was not only GHQ of the Spanish Peninsular and Spanish African Armies, but also GHQ of one of the *Capitanías* or military regions into which Spain was divided, GHQ of one of the two infantry divisions and the cavalry division of that Capitanía, and HQ of three brigades. Of the Peninsular Army's 20 500 officers on the active and 'first reserve' list about 4000 were stationed or lived in Madrid and its immediate surroundings. Around a hundred retired generals and possibly as many as 2000 other retired officers also lived there. The officers and NCOs were professionals, unlike the other ranks who were almost all conscripts. The Spanish army had, on paper, sixteen infantry and one cavalry divisions and ten independent infantry brigades. It should have had close on 300 000 men under arms. In fact in 1931 there were only 110 000 other ranks because it was easy, especially for the middle and upper class, to avoid call-up, to obtain exemption either as unfit or on compassionate grounds, or to buy oneself out after only a few months of service. Of those 110 000 there were upwards of 20000 in Madrid and its immediate surroundings.[2]

Madrid was also the national headquarters of the paramilitary Civil Guard and *Carabineros* whose officers were seconded army officers and whose other ranks were ex-army sergeants and privates. Of the 15 000 officers and men in the Carabineros there were only a couple of companies and those on administrative duties at headquarters, for their task was the prevention of contraband; but of the Civil Guard's 29 000 there were 3000 in Madrid and district. They were better armed and trained, and far more efficient a force for the maintenance of order in town and country than the army. They were also better paid. The conscript's pay was 0·25 pesetas a day whereas the Civil Guard of the lowest rank received 245 pesetas a month.

There was much therefore to divide the people of Madrid and create antagonisms: class, wealth, education, occupation, religion. At the beginning of 1931, however, what most divided Madrileños and the rest of Spain was the political question of whether Spain should remain a monarchy or become a republic for the second time in history. Government was currently in the hands of a general, the kindly and elderly Dámaso Berenguer, whom the King had called upon twelve months earlier to take over from the Dictator Primo de Rivera and put in motion whatever was necessary to restore constitutional government suspended in 1923. Berenguer had moved too slowly during 1930 for some army officers, chief among them General Queipo de Llano, and for a group of politicians, who, after a number of meetings in the Madrid house of a once prominent monarchist, Miguel Maura, and a further meeting in San Sebastian, had formed themselves into a Revolutionary Committee and fixed December 15 1930 for the establishment of a Republic by *coup d'état*.

The plan had been for risings of army units throughout the country, to back up action in Madrid. The socialist labour organization *Unión General de Trabajadores* (UGT), was to declare a general strike there. Queipo de Llano was to take over command of the military units on the outskirts of Madrid with the help of a Republican Military Association

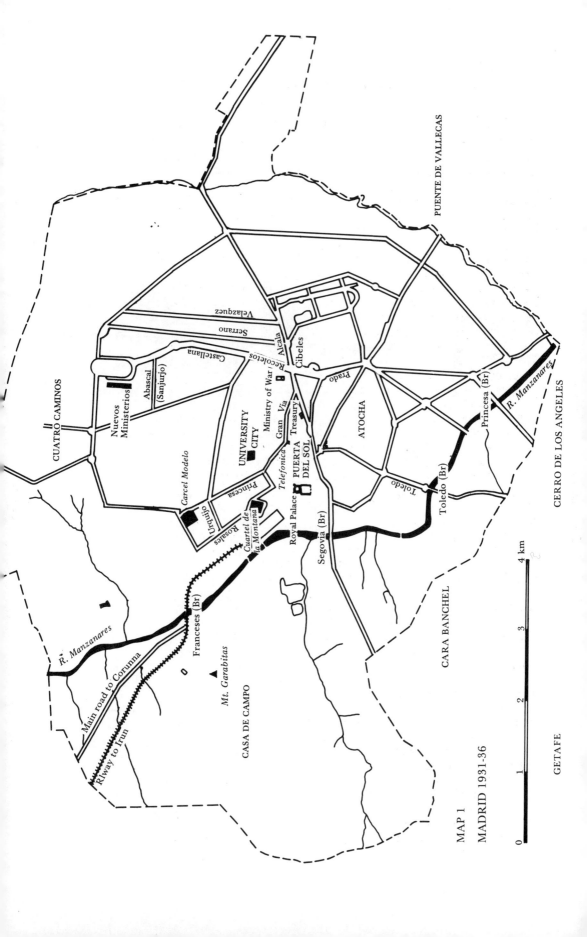

MAP 1
MADRID 1931-36

PUENTE DE VALLECAS

CUATRO CAMINOS

Nuevos
Ministerios

Abascal
(Sanjurjo)

Castellana

Velazquez

Serrano

Recoletos

Alcala

Cibeles

Ministry of War

Gran Via

Telefonica

PUERTA
DEL SOL

Treasury

Prado

ATOCHA

Princesa (Br)

R. Manzanares

CERRO DE LOS ANGELES

Carcel Modelo

UNIVERSITY
CITY

Princesa

Urquijo

Cuartel de
la Montaña

Rosales

Royal Palace

Segovia (Br)

Toledo

Toledo (Br)

Franceses (Br)

R. Manzanares

Main road to Corunna

Rlway to Irun

Mt. Garabitas

CASA DE CAMPO

CARA BANCHEL

GETAFE

0   1   2   3   4 km

(AMR) of which he was the head. Major Ramón Franco, younger brother of the general, was to bomb the Royal Palace. With that, King and Government were expected to surrender. However, on December 12 a Captain Fermín Galán had prematurely declared the Republic in the remote town of Jaca, and advanced on Zaragoza at the head of a column of 800 men. A superior force loyal to the Crown had gone out to meet him, and after a few shots he had surrendered. The result discouraged the other plotters in the provinces. Nevertheless, Ramón Franco had taken off on the appointed day from Cuatro Vientos, the airfield outside Madrid. Seeing children playing in the square before the Palace he had dropped leaflets but returned with his bomb load. Queipo, on his way to raise the military, had seen that the workers were not on strike. The UGT's call had been ignored. So had Queipo's to the army. Loyal troops had advanced on the airfield and Ramón Franco had fled to Portugal. So had Queipo. Some members of the Revolutionary Committee fled to France. Most had been arrested and taken to the Model Prison.

A view of the Puerta de Alcalá.

Now, after the failure of the rebellion, argument was even fiercer as to whether Spain should or should not remain a monarchy. The answer was to come in April 1931 in a way not foreseen by either the plotters or their opponents.

2   Steps to Civil War 1931–33

General Berenguer now fixed March 1 as the date for elections to a constituent assembly. The Republicans made it known that they would have no part in them even when told that they could stand under any label whatever. Berenguer resigned. The King asked the Conservative ex-Prime Minister Sánchez Guerra, civilian head of a military rising against Primo de Rivera in 1929, to form a new government. Sánchez Guerra went to the Model Prison with offers of Cabinet posts for some of the arrested Republicans. The offers were refused. An aged admiral, Aznar, was the King's next choice. The Republicans now declared their willingness to contest *municipal elections* to try out the validity of the electoral roll and efficiency of the election machinery set up by Berenguer. No one expected more from the elections – least of all the republicans and socialists who had just failed to act coherently. April 12 was fixed as the date. Full liberty of the spoken and written word and of assembly was permitted during the campaign. Candidates presented themselves as republicans, socialists and monarchists.

The Government assembled at the Ministry of the Interior, the principal building in the Puerta del Sol, on the afternoon of the election day. By late evening they were aware that more republican and socialist candidates than monarchists had been elected in Madrid and most of the provincial capitals. The final count, with small towns and villages included, would confirm the hope of the Government that more monarchists had been elected than anti-monarchists, but that was irrelevant*. As Madrid was the centre of communications for whole of Spain, so each provincial capital was the centre for that province. Monarchist small towns and villages could not be supported by, nor support the monarchy in a Madrid which was overwhelmingly republican.

The first to realize this was General Berenguer, now Minister for the Army. At 0015 hours on April 13 he sent a telegram to the captains general, that is, the GOCs of the eight military districts into which Spain was divided. They were 'to observe strict neutrality' whatever 'the sovereign will of the people should prove to be'. Next, at 1400 hours, the Revolutionary Committee told the Government that they now took the view that the municipal elections had been 'a plebiscite', and that 'in the name of the majority' they intended 'to implant the Republic'. At 1500 hours the Director-General of the Civil Guard, General Sanjurjo, informed the Government that he could no longer guarantee the loyalty of the men under his command. The wheel had

* The figures now generally accepted as the official were: monarchists 41921; republicans 34368; socialists 4183 – monarchist majority 3370.

turned full circle. General Fernando Primo de Rivera, uncle of the Dictator, had brought the First Republic to an end with a similar statement in 1874. At 2100 hours the General sent a telegram to each of the twenty-nine Civil Guard *tercio* (battalion) commanders: 'issue the necessary orders to the units under your command in no way to oppose demonstrations which the republican triumph might rightfully inspire in army or people'. At 1100 hours on the 14th Sanjurjo presented himself at the house of Miguel Maura, saluted him, offered his sword and put the Civil Guard at the disposal of the Revolutionary Committee. Power had slipped away from the King and his government.

That morning of April 14 the King was telling his Ministers of his decision to leave the country. The old liberal politician Count Romanones met the Revolutionary Committee at the consulting rooms of the King's surgeon, Gregorio Marañon, in the Calle Serrano. They reached agreement. Government would be handed over to the Committee that afternoon. The Committee would not hinder the departure out of the country of the King or his family if they began their journey before nightfall.

At 1530, that is during the protracted dinner time of the Madrileños, the three-coloured flag of Republican Spain replaced the red and gold of Bourbon Spain above the General Post Office. Dinner over, the Revolutionary Committee moved to the Ministry of the Interior at the Puerta del Sol. Crowds waving republican flags and shouting 'long live the Republic' made their way in over-laden trucks and trams or on foot to the Puerta del Sol. By around 1800 hours the plaza was packed. At 2030 the Revolutionary Committee, now the Provisional Government of the Spanish Republic, came out on the balcony to acknowledge the cheers of wildly enthusiastic crowds. A quarter of an hour later, half a kilometre away, the King left the Royal Palace quietly and almost unperceived.

Republican politicians had won the Battle for Madrid of 1931, and with it the whole of Spain: but only with the consent of Generals Berenguer and Sanjurjo, and through them of the army and paramilitary forces as a whole. Without the army there would have been no republic. They had sworn an oath of allegiance to the King, but in the Spanish tradition Country took precedence over King. The Republic, with or without an oath to it, could expect the same loyalty – neither more nor less.

April 15 was declared a national holiday. The day's issue of the official *Gaceta de Madrid* appeared with a drawing of a somewhat buxom woman in place of the royal shield. Some Madrileños spent the day destroying the statues of Spanish kings in Retiro Park and all the royal symbols on public buildings. A few days later the name-plates of the Calle de Alfonso XII, behind the Prado, were replaced with others bearing the name of the new Head of State and Provisional Prime Minister Alcalá-Zamora. New insignia and buttons were ordered for service uniforms. Military bands had to learn a new national anthem, a tune written by a Frenchman in Napoleonic times with words by one of the followers of the early nineteenth-century rebel Major del Riego.

For most of the inhabitants of Madrid the pattern of life changed very little between April 1931 and February 1934. The residents of such areas as that to the right of the Castellana, that is the absentee landowners, financiers, politicians, top civil servants, engineers

General Franco seen
talking to Minister of War
Azaña during military
exercises in the Balearic
Islands.

(a particularly select *élite*), lawyers, doctors, in short the wealthy
10 per cent, lived as they had always lived – with a multitude of servants, in a luxury not always comfortable, and with a long summer
break away from Madrid. They went as before to the exclusive *Ateneo*
or *casinos*, cafes and theatres; and most, even those of them who professed to be radicals or socialists, paid their employees in fields, offices,
factories or home the minimum they could get away with; and that
minimum even after three years of republican government was exceed-
ingly low. The left republican element in the governments of the period
April 1931 to November 1933 had to consider the interests of their
principal supporters, the small entrepreneurs, collectively employers
of 60 per cent of the labour force. The socialists were in a dilemma:
improve the lot of the workers too much and it would be impossible to
rouse them to revolution, the true marxist way to destroy capitalism;
too little and they would turn to anarchism, away from the socialist
labour organization, the UGT, towards the anarcho-syndicalist *Con-
federación Nacional del Trabajo*, CNT. There were some small im-
provements in wages and factory conditions, and some 390 titled
families, most of whom had residences in Madrid, did lose their lands
to impoverished peasants, but it all amounted to next to nothing.

No sooner was the Republic established than the left republican and
socialist Press engaged in rabidly anti-Catholic propaganda. Orators
in the Puerta del Sol called for 'action' against the clergy and Church
property. As priests went about their business on May 1 they were
insulted, and in some instances beaten by mobs. On May 9 Maura, now
Minister of the Interior, was informed of plans to set fire to churches in
Madrid and other cities. Since the city police forces were not equipped
to deal with militant crowds, Maura asked Manuel Azaña, the Minister of War, to protect the threatened buildings with Civil Guard
detachments. The President, Alcalá-Zamora, backed Maura's request,
but eight of the ten other members of the Cabinet were militant opponents of religion. Azaña had himself a hatred of religion which
merits the epithet pathological. They seconded his verdict that he

would rather 'all the churches in Spain should burn than that harm should come to a single republican finger nail'. On May 11, first the Jesuit Church and residence in the Calle de la Flor off the Gran Vía, then in turn a convent, a non-fee paying school for 500 boys, one for 300 girls, an orphanage and Madrid's best equipped technical school, and another five churches were set on fire, as police watched impassively. When the buildings were alight firemen played their hoses only on adjoining buildings.

The subsequent inclusion in the Constitution of the Spanish Workers' Republic and in its Statute Book of the total prohibition of public subsidies to churches or religious institutions for any purpose whatsoever, the ban on religious congregations to engage in any agricultural, industrial, commercial or teaching activity, and the 'dissolution' of the Jesuit order in Spain as 'a danger to the security of the State' had a considerable effect in Madrid. As many as 45 000 of Madrid's 136 000 children would have been deprived of schooling had private individuals not found ways to circumvent to some extent the application of the law. Hospitals would have been denuded of competent nursing staff had the State itself enforced the law fully, for the Spanish middle class had clung to the view that nursing was no fit occupation for ladies. In 1933, however, the sisters were threatened with severe penalties if they tried to smuggle a priest into a hospital even at some dying patient's request.

The closure of the schools run by the religious orders alienated others beside the parents of the children affected, for not all who had rebelled like Azaña against the precepts of the Church shared his belief

The Jesuit church and residence in the Calle de la Flor (off the Gran Viá) set on fire during May, 1931.

that in the precepts lay the roots of the problems of Spanish society. Again, it was not only the regular Mass-goers whose sentiments were affected by the exclusion of priests from hospital bedsides. Though only 10 per cent of the working-class parishioners of San Millán went to Mass on Sundays, 40 per cent called on the priests for the Last Sacraments.

Other acts of government drove into equally opposite camps those who were indifferent to religion. It was in the midst of the debates on the anti-Catholic legislation that Azaña put before the *Cortes* or Parliament, a Law for the Defence of the Republic. The philosopher Ortega y Gasset cried in anguish '*no es esto, no es esto*' – meaning that the Law was a total contradiction of the dream of many intellectuals that the Republic would be Spain's first truly democratic regime. It made it legal for the Government to supress at will all democratic liberties, and to act even more arbitrarily than Primo de Rivera. The Spanish Socialist Party had never made a secret of its intention to support parliamentary democracy only for as long as it was tactically desirable; but the left republicans to which Azaña belonged had professed genuine belief in democracy. This left proved to be as vindictive against those who had supported previous regimes, as ready to order the use of firearms against demonstrators, and to imprison opponents under cover of the new law as any government which later generations labelled Fascist.

Manuel Azaña, Minister of War, later President of the Republic.

Azaña's view, as Minister of War, that there were too many officers in the Spanish army and that it needed complete reorganization, was militarily thoroughly justified. The youngest general in the army, Francisco Franco, and one of the more forward-looking brigadiers, Emilio Mola, shared that view with many others. Azaña's first move, the offer of retirement on full pay to all officers, did not meet with widespread disapproval. Nearly 50 per cent of those on the active and 'first reserve' lists took advantage of it, and were thereafter free to supplement their salaries with income from other employment. His reduction in May 1931 of the number of infantry divisions from sixteen to eight made next to no difference to the number of remaining serving officers or men. Since the end of the war in Africa, the Peninsular Army had never had men under arms enough for more than eight divisions and a handful of independent brigades. The lieutenants-general with the courtesy title of captains-general, and a small number of officers in the Ministry, passed into the 'unemployed' list. On the other hand, the number of NCOs was increased with the introduction of new sub-officer grades (equivalent to the British army's staff sergeant and warrant officer ranks).

It was not the principle of reform but the way that the reforms were carried out which created widespread discontent in the army. The structure of the surviving eight divisions was left virtually untouched, and the real professionals knew that it was wholly out of date and contrary to the principles of concentration and economy of force. They remained badly equipped, especially in artillery. Again and again Azaña presented the reforms as being the 'trituration', the grinding into powder of the army and in other more offensive terms.

Most important of all he followed his reforms with dismissals and appointments which appeared to be based not on merit or ability but either on hearsay evidence about the political beliefs of the individual concerned or merely on his personal likes and dislikes. An episode which would long be remembered and was illustrative of this was his reaction to the arrest of a very republican lieutenant-colonel, Julio Mangada, for an act of gross disrespect to his brigadier, divisional commander and the chief of staff, General Goded, at Carabanchel – just outside the city limits of Madrid. Out of hand Azaña reinstated the lieutenant-colonel and dismissed from their command the brigadier and divisional commander. Goded, already in contact with discontented officers, resigned, and became a conspirator against the Republic. There was another change, which affected all ranks and not just the officers. Never aware of the binding force of symbols and traditions Azaña abolished the territorial and other distinguishing names of infantry regiments.

The army then was neither more nor less prominent in Madrid than it had been before the Republic; but the Madrileños did see with increasing regularity a new uniform, the blue of the Republic's own paramilitary force, the *Cuerpo de Seguridad y Asaltos* (known popularly simply as the Asaltos). This force of 5000 men in 1931, who armed with pistols and truncheons, were best suited for their first task, the breaking up of a riot of infuriated vegetable stall-holders in the Cebada market, expanded in 1932/3 to 10 000. Of these 2000 were quartered in Madrid, and were specially trained in the use of automatic weapons and armoured vehicles in built-up areas.

Government from April 15 to July 14 1931 was by decree and without popular sanction. Ministers were accountable to no one, and each did much as he pleased. Some did nothing. Others issued decrees which should have had careful study and analysis of realities behind them and which were consequently unenforceable. Thus, for example, the Minister of Education's creation by the stroke of a pen of 7000 new teachers and 27 000 new 'schools' which in fact never came to exist. It is noteworthy that the attack on the Church and the 'trituration' of the army were both initiated in this period, even though subsequently endorsed by a Cortes. This Cortes was a Constituent Assembly, elected by male suffrage on June 3 according to a system devised by the self-appointed government to favour the more radical and revolutionary parties. It was a Cortes therefore which should have been dissolved when it had completed its task of making a new constitution, but which Azaña kept for another two years out of the well-justified fear that in spite of the election system adopted, he and the left would not be returned to power. Nor were they, when at last in November 1933 they allowed the electorate to judge them.

The Constitution half promised that the Republic would develop into a democracy. The calm of the November 1933 elections gave some grounds for hope that reality could eventually match the promise. Nevertheless, there were also many signs that democracy was doomed. Nowhere was this clearer than in Madrid where the elections had to be run twice. On the first occasion 60 candidates stood, and not one received the minimum votes required for election. For the second the fringe parties (and that included Azaña's) were excluded, and the line-up was socialist against anti-marxist. The socialists triumphed, but only just. Julian Besteiro, the Socialist Party's theorist and top scorer, gained 177 647 votes while the top scorer among the anti-marxists got 171 496 in a 75 per cent poll. Admittedly Madrid was not Spain, nor could it be claimed that Madrid with 900 000 inhabitants was representative of the whole country of 24 millions. Indeed, in the country as a whole the left had been very severely defeated; but Madrid was, and had long been, indicative of what the provinces (other than the Basque and Catalan which were cases apart) would do on the morrow. Madrid already was, and the rest of the country would become over the next three years, divided almost equally three ways into militant marxists prepared to bring about revolution by force of arms, militant anti-marxists equally prepared to forestall by force of arms such an event, and a final third caught between the militants.

3 The Political Battle 1934–36

The leaders of the Socialist Party and UGT met in Madrid in January 1934 to consider policy. They had won the November elections in Madrid: Julian Besteiro's 6000 majority had entitled them under the peculiar system in force to 9 of the 12 Madrid seats in the Cortes. Nationally, however, they had suffered a resounding defeat. There were only 55 socialist deputies in the new House of 470 members. The several left republican parties had together won a mere 63. The radicals under the one-time revolutionary Alejandro Lerroux had won more seats than any other single party by presenting themselves as right of centre. The Catholic Party, *Acción Popular*, non-existent in 1931, had polled almost as many votes as the Socialist with its fifty years of experience. The Confederation of Autonomous Parties of the Right (CEDA), of which Acción Popular was a member, had the largest number of seats. Lerroux was now Prime Minister by choice of President Alcalá-Zamora, and with the support of centre and right-wing members whose landowning or middle-class interests he promised not to harm, and of the CEDA to whose leader, Gil Robles, he had promised the mitigation or abrogation of the anti-Catholic legislation of the 1931–33 period. The socialists could forgive Lerroux much, but not that. He and his radicals had voted for that legislation.

Largo Caballero, leader of the socialist UGT, argued that since there was no immediate hope of any further progress towards socialism through constitutional means, the Socialist Party and UGT should dedicate themselves to the creation of 'a revolutionary situation', through strikes, civil disobedience and acts of violence, while the leaders should plan the revolution itself. Julian Besteiro insisted that it was the duty of socialists to let the democratically elected Government govern, and limit their opposition to action in the Cortes. Prieto, Secretary General of the Party, sided with Besteiro but transferred his allegiance to Largo in February.

Revolution, as Largo saw it, could succeed only if the anarchists could be persuaded to forget their differences with the socialists, only if the UGT and CNT worked together. He toured the country with the slogan – UHP (*Ooh, Ache, Peh*) – Proletarian Brothers Unite! For some time the Spanish communists (there were only a few thousand) had been calling the socialists 'socio-fascists'. To instil hatred, the socialists now called the CEDA 'fascists' – which in Spanish sounded very much like *facciosos* – seditious evildoers.

From April onwards strikes and acts of violence became frequent. The CNT and UGT acted independently of each other, but the object was the same, the Marx–Engels concept of a 'revolutionary situation'. In Madrid there were not only strikes but gun battles between Socialist

29

Largo Caballero, leader of the socialist UGT.

Youth and the nascent, more truly fascist Falange. Most of them were rather like those in film Westerns, with dozens of rounds fired and no one hurt, but there were some deaths. University students went to lectures armed. They created a climate of fear and disorder.

Madrid had seen nothing of the various anarchist risings which had taken place since the advent of the Republic. It had had a glimpse of the anti-republican revolt of August 1933 led by General Sanjurjo whose loyalty to the Government had been undermined by his demotion from the post of Director General of the Civil Guard. Socialist deputies had demanded it after Civil Guards had killed six socialists in the course of restoring the Government's authority over a village near Badajoz where a detachment of Civil Guard had been killed. In August 1933 a cavalry squadron under the command of a friend of Sanjurjo had approached the Ministry to capture it. Loyal troops had fired on it as it approached the Cibeles fountain, killing twenty troopers, and that had been the end of the revolt.

Asturias and Catalonia were to be the main centres of the Largo-Prieto attempt at revolution, but the UGT and CNT in Madrid were also supposed to play an important part in it. The signal was to be any reshuffle of the Cabinet to include CEDA members: for this, they said, would mean the beginning of fascist rule in Spain, and that made revolution a thoroughly justifiable act. Gil Robles had made the socialist propaganda credible by allowing the Acción Popular Youth movement to organize rallies superficially reminiscent of fascist rallies in other countries. From mid-September onwards there was talk of the imminent entry of the CEDA into the Cabinet. Socialists were told to stand by for action. On October 4 Alcalá-Zamora allowed Lerroux to give three minor ministries to CEDA deputies.

The socialists planned the conquest of the State by revolution on classic theoretic marxist lines, that is a general strike to paralyse the country, the issue of arms to workers and the 'spontaneous' rise of a 'People's Army' of which militia, already trained by sympathetic army officers, were to be the shock troops. The People's Army was supposed to grow and grow as rank and file, inspired by the bravery of workers and militia men, turned on their officers. That was, after all, what the left-wing booklets most popular in Madrid at the time said had happened in Russia in 1917.

It did not work out that way even in Asturias where the revolution had its moment of success. In Madrid the people found no transport working early morning October 5; socialist militia discharged weapons into the air to give the impression that a major battle had broken out; but when no more than a score of the soldiers and Asaltos joined them, the strike collapsed. Two infantry platoons marched round the city, and Asaltos picked off snipers. What the revolution had proved was that the prevailing discontent in the army was not of men against their officers, and that where officers led men still followed.

After the failure of the revolution, socialists continued to speak disparagingly of the army, but at the same time they sought to win more officers to marxism. They established two societies late in 1934, which fused in 1935 into the single *Unión Militar Republicana Antifascista* (UMRA). Sometime in 1933 when Azaña's appointments and dismissals had left many with a sense of insecurity, some officers of field rank and of right-wing tendencies had established an *Unión Militar Española* (UME) to protect the interests of the army and its officers in both the active list and retirement, and it had attracted some left-wing as well as right-wing members. The UME now became almost exclusively an anti-revolutionary body.

Right-wing leader Antonio Primo de Rivera who was later murdered in prison in Alicante.

Gil Robles became Minister of War after another Cabinet reshuffle in May 1935. During his seven months in office he tried to repair the damage done to the army. He sought to restore to officers and men 'job satisfaction' and *esprit de corps*, and to bring its organization and equipment up to date. He chose General Francisco Franco as his chief of staff. The sum required for the fulfilment of the plans was too large to meet with Cabinet approval. The time he was in office (it included the summer holiday) was too short. In terms of re-organization almost all that survived was a new independent or 'mixed' brigade originally intended as Spain's contribution to the League of Nations force which had been talked about as necessary to stop Mussolini in Abyssinia; in terms of re-equipment, increased production of ammunition in the Spanish arms factories, a few 155 mm Schneider guns made in France, and steel helmets for the I Infantry Division whose GHQ was in Madrid. They wore them proudly for the first time for the parade down the Castellana on the fifth anniversary of the Republic, April 14 1936.

The two officers in the Ministry next in importance to Franco were the repentant republican Goded and an ultra monarchist, General Fanjul. In consequence, the removal of a number of officers from command as guilty of irregularities (General Miaja, for example, had helped himself to army property) was interpreted as a move to oust left-wingers; and thus the separation was strengthened of left and right within the army. By the end of 1935 officers could be classed under three general headings: 25 per cent left republican, 25 per cent anti-left, but still 50 per cent neither.[1]

In spite of all that has been written to the contrary, the Spanish army officer of the 1930s was more likely to be faithful than not to the tradition of the previous century. The majority of the army's many interventions in politics during that century had been on the 'progressive' or 'liberal' side. Even Primo de Rivera had had ideas which had won him the support of the socialists. Officers were almost exclusively either middle class or risen from the ranks. In the course of their training they were given to understand, as we have said, that their primary loyalty was to the *patria*, the Motherland. Regimes were transient, the *patria* was eternal. It was not the job of the army to act as arbiter between rival politicians or policies, so long as they did not threaten the safety or the very existence of the State – and in the opinion of 50–60 per cent, in December 1935, no government of the Republic had threatened the State and no political group, with the exception of the anarchist minority and the ever smaller communist minority, intended to do it. In the opinion of about one in five of the officers of 1935, however, the left republican-socialist governments of April 1931–November 1933 *had* damaged the motherland severely, with their failure to control the anarchists, their persecution of the Catholic Church, the 'trituration' of the army, and the excision of Catalonia from the main body of Spain.

About one in ten (including Generals Goded, Fanjul and Mola) were now convinced that if the left got back to power one of two disasters would occur: Spain would either become an area of anarchic communes run on 'libertarian communist' principles free for the taking by a foreign power, or alternatively fall either straight away or after an intermediary period of socialism into the hands of communists who took orders from Moscow. They knew of no way to avoid in December 1935 such possibilities except to get the republican centre or right to declare the country in danger (under the terms of the Law for the Defence of the Republic), and to suppress the extreme left. Leaders of the centre and right were not prepared so to act, and when the prime movers asked the views of their fellow generals whether they would support such a move, they found that the majority would not. Convinced, as many civilians also were, that the elections scheduled for February 1936 would result either in a victory of the left or in a rising of the left following their defeat in the elections, they now prepared to meet either contingency with armed revolt.

Of the twenty-four major-generals on the active list in December 1935 when Gil Robles left the Ministry, twelve were committed left. They included Alcalá-Zamora's son-in-law, General Queipo de Llano. The percentage diminished with descent in rank. Overall about one in five officers, roughly, were of left republican or socialist tendencies. They did not believe that the return to power of the left would lead to the establishment of either a communist state, or a land of 'libertarian communist' anarchy. There were a few communist and anarchist officers (Ramón Franco at the time was one of the latter), but not enough, in the opinion of the non-communist left, to constitute a real danger.

Over the next six months, to the end of June 1936, there were to be many shifts of position, keeping the left and anti-left roughly equal but reducing the number of the uncommitted. Behind those changes were the political events of the period, a tangle of intrigue and counter-intrigue of which even the main threads are twisted.

The left republican, socialist, communist and trotskyist parties, with anarchists in support contested the February 1936 elections as a body under the title Popular Front, and with a joint manifesto calculated to appeal to solid bourgeois ideals and emotions. The twenty-eight non-left parties combined at local but not national level. The Popular Front was particularly astute on the election day itself, Sunday February 16. In Madrid, within three hours of the closure at 1600 hours of the polling booths, a vast crowd assembled round the fountain Cibeles at the junction of Calle Alcalá and the Castellana. With clenched fists, and shouting 'Viva Rusia!' they insisted that the Popular Front had won. Francisco Franco, still Chief of Staff and in the Ministry of War opposite Cibeles, telephoned General Pozas, Director-General of the Civil Guard. Pozas, a crypto-communist, pooh-poohed Franco's fears that the crowd might take over. During the afternoon news reached the Ministry of similar scenes in provincial cities: the left was not waiting for the official results to claim victory. Franco prevailed on his Minister to press for the declaration of a state of full emergency. The President would not have it.

Certainly, the Popular Front had won in Madrid, but the vote seemed very low in the better-class districts. The militancy of the crowds grew during the 17th. Franco approached the Prime Minister, Portela, direct. Portela said he was too old to do anything – let the army act if they felt like it. Franco, with Fanjul and Goded, telephoned the divisional commanders. The majority were still not prepared to act. The commanders of the Civil Guard and Asaltos then pledged themselves to the Popular Front. The 18th was another day of mass demonstrations. On the 19th, even though it was still not certain who had won the elections, the President handed over the premiership to Azaña, as head of the Popular Front.

Azaña supervised arrangements for new elections where those of February 16 had been inconclusive, or where the left claimed that irregularities had invalidated them. The conduct of the last election, in Cuenca, convinced the non-left that democracy was now a thing of the past.

The Popular Front thus came to have in the Cortes a comfortable majority. Azaña concentrated on the re-application of the anti-religious laws and the dismissal of non-left officers from important commands. It soon became evident, however, that the Popular Front was not united. It was, as Salvador de Madariaga put it, 'a revolutionary hydra with an anarcho-syndicatist head, another anarchist, two communist and three socialist heads, and yet another bourgeois head, all biting each other'[2]. Anarchists began to establish 'libertarian' communes which did not recognize the Government. The communists (stalinist but not trotskyist) were prepared to back Largo Caballero whom the Comintern had called the Spanish Lenin, but not Azaña, nor the official Socialist Party leader Prieto. Largo socialists held one parade after another to demand the immediate establishment of the dictatorship of the proletariat. Called upon by Azaña to stop the parades Largo attributed the violence which characterized them to falangists.

The Falange leaders were imprisoned in the Cárcel Modelo at Madrid. The socialist demonstrations and the gun fights between falangists and socialists continued. So did strikes in furtherance of 'socialism now' and rival strikes by the anarchist CNT for 'libertarian communism'. The CNT and UGT had frequent clashes in the streets.

A thousand socialist militiamen took part in the May Day parade. Largo demanded the dissolution of the army and Civil Guard. He engineered the dismissal of Alcalá-Zamora as President. Azaña took over. In his turn Azaña handed over the premiership to his intimate friend Casares Quiroga whose first acts were to close all church schools 'for their own protection' and to expel the remaining nuns and lay brothers in hospitals and other charitable institutions. Senior army officers were moved around to give partisans of the Popular Front the more attractive posts. Franco was sent away from Madrid to be GOC Canary Islands.

4 Madrid July 11–20 1936

After June 16 the incidence of violence in Spain became such that foreigners were advised not to visit the country. The Prime Minister, Casares Quiroga, was one of the few Spaniards who did not fear the worst – armed revolution or counter-revolution. On Saturday July 11 the Director General of Security informed him that a counter-revolutionary army revolt was imminent. Casares replied, 'let them rise: I'm going to bed'.[1] There had been similar reports since February and in his opinion there was nothing special about the latest.

On Sunday July 12 four falangist gunmen killed a lieutenant of the Asaltos, José del Castillo. Castillo, a Marxist, had earlier killed a falangist at the funeral of an officer of the Civil Guard, of known anti-marxist views, whom other marxist Asaltos had killed. In the early hours of the Monday, a Captain Condés, lover of the notoriously revolutionary socialist deputy Margarita Nelken, sent a detachment of Asaltos to Calle Velázquez 34, the house of Gil Robles, while he himself at the head of another detachment went to Calle Velázquez 89, home of Calvo Sotelo, the monarchist politician. Gil Robles was not at home. Calvo was lured out of his house. Condés killed him with a shot in the back of the neck, then dumped the body at the east cemetery as that of an unknown *fiambre* – 'stiff'.

Castillo and Calvo were both buried on the Tuesday – Castillo in the morning, in a coffin draped with a communist flag, with an Asalto guard of honour, and in the presence of a large crowd; Calvo in the afternoon, with members of the Cortes (Gil Robles himself one of them), and a considerable body of civilian middle-class mourners. A Civil Guard detachment protected them from possible attack at the cemetery, but four of the mourners were killed by 'unknown' Asaltos on their way home.

On the Wednesday Gil Robles read to the permanent committee of the Cortes the list of murders, acts of arson, strikes and other disorders of the previous four weeks, and called upon the Government yet again to exert its authority and restore order. On the Thursday Largo Caballero put it to the committee that the only solution was the immediate establishment of the dictatorship of the proletariat. However, Largo's prestige as the leader of the proletariat was momentarily tarnished. Early in June building workers, public works employees, liftmen and others in Madrid, in all 100 000 workers, had gone on strike. Largo had called their action 'mighty ram-blows at the gates of power'. He had hoped that his championship of the strikes would win over to his UGT the now worrying number of workers in the CNT whose headquarters had recently moved to Madrid. However, CNT instructions that in accordance with the principles of 'libertarian communism' strikers should not pay for the food and groceries their families required, had resulted in a swing *towards* the CNT, as well as *petit bourgeois* objections to the strike. Largo had accordingly called on the strikers to return to work. He had not expected the CNT to obey, but what had shaken his prestige was that UGT members would not obey him either. Prieto, the Socialist Party leader who considered unrealistic Largo's demands for 'socialism now', had thereupon approached his Popular Front allies with a view to the reconciliation of the Party with the Front.

On the Thursday and Friday whole families of anti-left sympathizers left Madrid. They included ex-President Alcalá-Zamora and ex-Prime Minister Lerroux. MAOC (Workers' and Peasants' Anti-Fascist Militia) squads had broken into private houses after the murder of Calvo Sotelo in search of 'fascist murderers', and there had been a number of deaths.

Late on July 17, Casares Quiroga received a tiresome report. There appeared to be some trouble at army headquarters in Melilla in North Africa. He located the GOC Spanish African Army, General Gómez Morato, at Larache, at the other end of Morocco, and ordered him to fly to Melilla to find out what was happening. By 2300 hours Casares knew that Melilla, Ceuta and Tetuan were in the hands of rebel officers, and that Gómez Morato was their prisoner. All Madrid knew by then that there was trouble in Morocco. The socialists had known it sooner even than the Government, for the original information had come from a spy in the service of the Melilla socialist party headquarters.

The UGT organized a mass rally and chanted rhythmically *'armas, armas, armas'*. Special editions of Largo's *Claridad* and Prieto's *El Socialista* had banner headlines: *Armas, armas, armas*, arms for the people, that is the MAOC, which was not entirely weaponless. Casares turned a deaf ear to the demand. The rising, he maintained, was purely a local affair. The commanders of the eight infantry and one cavalry divisions were all good left republicans. He ordered the air force to bomb the African cities, and the navy to steam into the Straits of Gibraltar. Then news came of the rising in Zaragoza of the V Infantry Division under its republican General Miguel Cabanellas. His brother Virgilio was immediately dismissed of his command of the Madrid Division. Over the radio the Director General of Carabineros, General Queipo de Llano, was claiming that he had taken over the II Division and had Seville in his power – which was not completely true at the time. In Valladolid the GOC VII Division had been deprived of his command by his brigadiers. The 12 Brigade in Pamplona and its brigadier, Emilio Mola, had risen, but not as yet the other brigadiers in the VI Division with GHQ in Burgos. The GOC Balearics, Goded, was also in revolt. So was the GOC Canaries, Francisco Franco; that was the most serious news of all, for where he led, men as well as officers could be expected to follow.

The army in Madrid seemed quiet, even after the arrest of those officers on the active and retired lists whose views made their loyalty to the Popular Front suspect. The socialist demand for arms grew menacing. Casares resigned. Martínez Barrio, the most moderate of the members of the Popular Front, took over. He telephoned Mola asking him to be his Minister of War in a government of reconciliation. Mola refused.

Largo Caballero declared that he would recognize no government headed by Martínez Barrio, and organized the masses to reinforce his refusal at the Puerta del Sol. UMRA officers had taken over the Ministry of War and army stores and communications centres. MAOC units were in positions ready for action in the event of further delay in the delivery to them of the arms demanded. Martínez Barrio resigned overnight. President Azaña called on the more leftist José Giral to take over. Giral's choice for Minister of War, General Castelló, issued the necessary orders for the delivery of rifles to the MAOC and UGT. On that day 5000 were delivered with newly greased bolts to three lieutenant-colonels and two majors, all marxists, for them to arm five battalions each of 1000 men. Another 50–60 000 were issued without bolts, which, for security reasons, were stored elsewhere – in the Montaña barracks.

There was a heavy concentration in Madrid and district of the regular armed forces of the State. Other ranks in the Asaltos totalled 5000, and there were 3000 in the Civil Guard and Carabineros. There were 20 000 on the nominal rolls of the army units, but in fact many men were on week-end leave and those in barracks were fewer than 8000, possibly even no more than 6500. The Government had nothing to fear from the Civil Guard, especially after Giral had chosen their Director General, Pozas, to be his Minister of the Interior. The Asaltos were largely ex-African Army and Foreign Legionaries with a tradition of blind obedience to officers, and the officers were overwhelmingly left-republican and marxist. Thus, the Asaltos, with twenty-six new armoured cars and other motorized transport, modern automatic weapons and training in street fighting, the Civil Guard with similar small arms and training, and the militiamen whose knowledge of weapons was as good as that of conscripts, constituted a force at the Government's disposal which outnumbered the soldiers in barracks by almost two to one. Whatever the outcome of the fighting now in progress between insurgents and loyal forces in Andalucia, Galicia, the Basque Provinces, Catalonia and Valencia, Madrid was safe enough.

Overnight July 18–19 there had been a gun battle between officers in one of the barracks at Carabanchel on the southern outskirts of Madrid. UMRA officers had attempted to issue arms to militiamen ahead of the Government's decision. There had been no sign of trouble elsewhere. The news now spread of the refusal by Colonel Serra, the officer commanding the infantry regiment* at the Montaña barracks, just across from the Plaza de España, to issue waiting militiamen with the 50 000 rifle bolts stored there. On hearing it, General Fanjul, whom the conspirators had chosen to lead the Madrid garrison to revolt, hurried to the barracks, as did also a number of civilians, mainly falangists, who feared for their lives. Fanjul established there what he called GH QI Division. Another in the conspiracy, the retired engineer General García de la Herrán, hastened to Campamento, the military zone seven kilometres from the Puerta del Sol on the road to Mérida. Scattered about Campamento were the army's infantry weapons and riding schools, the cavalry division's ammunition supply column and horse artillery regiment, an anti-aircraft battery, a battalion of sappers and some signals units.

* At the time there were two brigades in each infantry division, two regiments per brigade, and three or four battalions per regiment.

General García gave orders for the troops in Campamento to prepare to move at dawn on the 20th, with the idea of forming a column
out of that heterogeneous lot. On the 20th the anti-aircraft gunners
would not obey. A captain loyal to the Government persuaded the cavalry school personnel to unsaddle. The horse gunners limbered up,
then received counter-orders and counter-counter orders as their officers argued whether or not to join the rebellion. Aircraft from the airfields at Cuatro Vientos and Getafe, two and six kilometres away,
dropped bombs on them. They repulsed an attack by a MAOC battalion led by Julio Mangada, the lieutenant-colonel whom Azaña had
embraced publicly in 1932 after the incident with his brigadier at
Carabanchel. It was one of the five battalions armed on the 19th. They
then saw advancing towards them a column headed by a field battery
and followed by two battalions of infantry. They threw down their
rifles and surrendered.

Behind the appearance of the column was a similar story of differences of opinion among the officers. The battery (*grupo*) was one of
the two of the field regiment at Getafe. One of the two battery commanders had declared for the insurgents and begun to bombard the
airfield with both batteries when he had been attacked by the regimental commander at the head of a body of riflemen which he had hastily
assembled. The colonel had then sent the commander of the other battery, the then Major Enrique Jurado, against the rebels in Campamento. The other field regiment of the I Division, stationed on the other
side of Madrid at Vicálvaro, had also declared for the insurgents, then
changed its mind without firing a shot.

Inside the Montaña barracks there had also been arguments among
the officers, and those not prepared to follow Fanjul had left. There
were about 1500 officers and men there. They attempted a sally but
were repulsed by a siege force of about 1000 Civil Guards, 1000
Asaltos and a squadron of light tanks. From dawn they were shelled by
two of the 155 mm Schneider guns bought by Gil Robles when Minister of War, and an older 75 mm positioned in the Plaza de España –
virtually point-blank range. Aircraft from Getafe and Cuatro Vientos
bombed them. Later in the morning the besieging forces were joined by
Mangada at the head of his militia battalion. In the background were
several more thousand militiamen waiting for the rifle bolts in the bar-
rack stores.

By 1030 hours Fanjul and Serra lay wounded, and firing from the
barracks had become sporadic. Soldiers obeying loudspeakers calling
upon them to surrender put out white flags. The militia approached
the barracks. Other soldiers, still loyal to their officers, fired machine
guns. Some militiamen were killed. This happened once, possibly twice
more – memories vary. Civil Guards picked off the gunners. At 1100
hours they launched the final assault, and broke into the parade
ground. With firing virtually over the militia hastened to avenge their
fallen comrades. Many of the defenders had their throats cut, some
were shot, some hurled from the highest gallery to the stones below. A
few were taken to the Model Prison by the Civil Guard which also
saved Fanjul and Serra for courtmartial and execution later.

The rebellion was over in Madrid. Such as it had been, it had been
defeated by the loyal Asaltos and Civil Guards, and by loyal army officers at the head of their units. Only one regiment of the Infantry Divi-

sion, only the horse artillery and the ammunition train of the Cavalry Division, and only one battalion of sappers had wavered for more than a moment – in all less than a fifth of all officers and men.[2] On July 21 the Government called on all officers in Madrid, including those on leave, to reaffirm their loyalty. Of the 3500 officers in the armed forces of the State (army, air force and paramilitary forces) in Madrid on July 18 about 100 officers had been killed, some hundreds were in prison, and others had taken refuge in embassies, gone into hiding or escaped to those areas where the rising had been successful; but over 2500 reaffirmed their allegiance.[3]

From the insurgents' point of view, what had gone wrong? In one way, nothing; for they had not expected to win, which as Franco used to say, was the way to lose.

The history of the plot was this.[4] Eight generals, brought together towards the end of December 1935 by the elderly General Emilio Barrera, had invited representatives of the UME to a meeting in January at Barrera's house. There they had agreed that should the February elections result in victory for the Popular Front they would start a *movimiento*, a 'movement', immediately afterwards under Goded's leadership. Goded's posting from the Ministry to the Balearics scotched the plan. They met again, without Goded, on March 8 at the house of the CEDA politician José Delgado. Franco was present. He had just been dismissed from his post as Chief of Staff and appointed to the Canaries. There had been consensus among the conspirators that his commitment to their cause would give it far greater chance of success: he enjoyed greater prestige than any other serving officer, especially among young officers. Franco would not commit himself; but the meeting agreed at Franco's insistence that the 'movement to avoid the ruin and dismemberment of the *patria*' would 'be released only if circumstances should make it absolutely necessary', and that it would be 'for Spain without a label', that is without decision as to whether the new regime would be a republic or a monarchy. Planning was to be left to a committee, a *junta*, of generals resident in Madrid.

Two plans were discussed. One was that the conspirators should seize the Ministry and command of the Madrid divisions, the other that they should concentrate on the acquisition and control of the seven divisions in Spain, whose headquarters were Seville (II), Valencia (III), Barcelona (IV), Zaragoza (V), Burgos (VI), Valladolid (VII), and Corunna (VIII), and from the provinces threaten Madrid. Common to both plans was the expectation that the existing divisional commanders could be persuaded to join the movement, and that their subordinates would follow unquestioningly, whether they were members of the UME or not. Franco was not so sure. As Chief of Staff he had learned firstly that senior officer membership of the UMRA was not insignificant, perhaps as numerous as that of the UME, and secondly that of the conscripts called up in 1935, 25 per cent had been members of the Socialist Youth, UGT, CNT or Communist Party, whose primary loyalty was to their ideology and not the army.

The 'centrifugal' plan, that is Madrid-outwards, had obvious factors in its favour. Madrid was the army's main concentration point, with 25 per cent of all the officers on the active list there and at least that percentage of the retired; and with about 18 per cent of other ranks. It had the major artillery, small arms, remount, transport and ammunition depots and mobilization stores. It was the centre of communications, road, rail and particularly telephones. Burgos could not communicate with Seville except through Madrid: Valencia could with Barcelona, but not as easily as through Madrid. It had, however, one major factor against it. The elections had proved yet again that 35 per cent of the people were of the left, even if those of the right were almost as numerous and the remainder of unstated political affiliation. The Civil Guard might be expected to follow where the army led, but the Asaltos would not, and the Asaltos were better equipped for street fighting than any army unit. Their strength was equal in real numbers to two infantry regiments, and in terms of fighting quality, given the Foreign Legion and Africa service background of so many of them, a probable match for four.

The 'centripetal' plan seemed to have the force of history behind it. Primo de Rivera had issued his *pronunciamiento* in Barcelona: Martínez Campos set out to restore the monarchy in 1874, from Sagunto: Madrid had submitted to Riego's demands of 1820 because Corunna, Barcelona, Zaragoza and Pamplona had followed his lead in Cadiz. Pamplona had been the strategic point for all successful attacks on Madrid by foreign armies.

At subsequent meetings the Junta decided to combine the two plans, that is to try to gain power in both Madrid and the provinces. In March six of the eight infantry divisional commanders were committed leftists. It was therefore decided that conspirators would have to replace them. UME members were to take the place of recalcitrant field and junior officers. General Rodríguez del Barrio, one of the two Inspectors-General of the time, was to lead the movement from Madrid. The date was fixed: April 20. On the 18th Rodríguez cried off.

General Queipo de Llano, Alcalá-Zamora's son-in-law.

Brigadier-General Mola (right) with General Franco.

The Junta now handed over all future planning to Brigadier-General Mola. He had been present at the March meeting. He was in command of the brigade at Pamplona and all his officers were of his mind. He was in touch with the traditionalists (Carlists) and the Falangists, both of whom had been training militias, with numerous politicians of the centre, and with monarchists. He had a methodical mind and enjoyed military prestige second only to Franco. Franco trusted him and so did the exiled General Sanjurjo who was now named as the nominal head of the movement. Mola worked hard over the next ten weeks. He won several hundred officers to the cause, including the colourful General Queipo de Llano. His military plans, in their final version, were the following.

All eight infantry divisions were to be taken over by conspirators on the same day. Success was expected everywhere except possibly in Madrid (I) and Seville (II) divisions. Even assuming success within the army, it was not expected that those divisions would be strong enough to act against the marxists in Madrid or the anarchists in the south. They were therefore to remain on the defensive pending the arrival of help. Divisions V (Zaragoza), VI (Burgos) and VII (Valladolid) were to proceed immediately to Madrid. Division VIII (Corunna) was to go to the aid of the Independent Brigade in Asturias. Division IV (Barcelona) would have enough to do in Catalonia. Half Division III (Valencia) was to help it if required. The other half of III was to advance on Madrid (Map 2). The army in Africa was to be transported by the navy to the peninsula, there to aid Division II, and to advance towards Madrid from the south. Everything was to be over in a matter of days.

On or about July 1 Franco at long last made up his mind that a military rising was really necessary, and that he would take part in it as GOC African Army. He still had his misgivings. He did not share the belief of most conspirators that all would go well everywhere. He advised that the Madrid divisions (infantry and cavalry) should sally out of their barracks immediately and march north to join up with the divisions moving southwards. He did not expect success within days of the start of the movement. He did not believe that all contingencies had been covered.

There were indeed several points of weakness. The political supporters of the rising had not seen eye to eye with each other: the nonleft were still as divided as they had been at the elections. Mola had had to waste valuable days reconciling monarchist objections with republican, Alfonsist monarchist with Carlist, centrist with falangist and so on. Above all, his means of communication with his fellow officers were slow and uncertain. Telegrams were misinterpreted. Young ladies carrying letters did not always reach their destinations in the order in which they had departed. There was in consequence uncertainty over the date of the rising. By no means all those who had promised to help in Madrid knew that Fanjul was supposed to be the leader in the city and García outside it. Fanjul's inactivity on July 18 increased the confusion, and when he did act he did so to no coherent plan. García had no plan either. Mola had done his job at top level and his own local Pamplona level reasonably efficiently, but the majority of his UME collaborators at brigade, regimental and battalion levels had not. It was in the very zones where UME membership had been most numerous that the rising had failed most disastrously.

5 Revolution in Madrid

The crowds which watched the storming of the Montaña barracks, and took part in its final moments, moved in triumph to the Puerta del Sol where many thousands joined them. There was suddenly a sound as of a burst of machine-gun fire. In that square, as in any other, it was impossible to tell its point of origin. Asaltos ordered the excited mob to lie on the ground. They aimed at some figures on a balcony or roof top, and declared the danger over.

The rejoicing went on for hours. Huge portraits of Largo Caballero and Lenin were put up side by side. The victory had been anticipated overnight July 19/20 with the destruction by fire of a score of churches, religious houses and church schools. The Government had thereupon placed guards on those buildings which were considered a part of the 'national heritage', but another dozen were now set on fire.

For most of the men and women who had received rifles on presentation of their UGT or CNT membership cards, or who had subsequently helped themselves to the rifles and ammunition of the dead and captured defenders of the Montaña, and elsewhere, the rifle at this stage was no more than a status symbol. With it slung over a shoulder, they mingled with the crowds in the Puerta del Sol and old city, or demanded drinks and *tapas* (delicacies) in taverns and cafes. For some, however, rifle and ammunition were a spur to action. They commandeered trucks, taxis and private cars. They daubed on them the initials CNT–FAI or JSU, to identify them as either anarchist (*Federación Anarquista Ibérica*) or socialist–communist (*Juventudes Socialistas Unificadas*). They painted a multitude of slogans. The favourite inscriptions were *Viva Rusia* among socialists and communists, and *Libertad* among anarchists, but, above all, the initials UHP, under which anarchists, socialists and communists had come together in 1934 for the abortive October Revolution.

As the daubed vehicles were raced through the main thoroughfares, their passengers chanted rhythmically '$\bar{U} - H\bar{A}CHE - P\bar{E}$.' In beating the air with a clenched fist to the rhythm, inexperienced drivers endangered pedestrians; but the naturally quick reactions of Spaniards, either as drivers or pedestrians, kept down the number of serious accidents. Passers-by were expected to manifest their approval of the touring riflemen. Too obvious disdain could lead to the disembarkation of the riflemen and a rough search of the 'undoubted fascist' for hidden weapons.

Here and there a shot was heard. The immediate assumption was that a 'fascist sniper' was at work. The riflemen took cover, and shot at anything that moved on rooftops and behind windows. Possibly there

Republican Civil Guards seen at a road-block just outside Madrid in July, 1936. The guards are using a confessional from a looted church as a sentry box.

were a few young men of the right with both the pistols and the stupidity to open fire at too long a range to be effective against superior numbers and with little hope of escape. There was more evidence of old ladies paying with their lives for the curiosity that prompted them to windows to see what all the noise was about, than of dead 'fascist snipers'.

By the morning of the 21st there were several hundred bodies to be buried. These were collected from streets and public parks. On Press and radio over the next week there were constant Government and Party appeals to militiamen not to open fire on 'snipers' unless they were certain that there was a sniper; ammunition was being wasted. The killing became more organized. About 200 anarchist, socialist and communist *tchekas** were established in Madrid alone. Their zones of activity were to some extent demarcated to prevent breaches of brotherhood. The tchekas undertook daily round-ups, *paseos*, in search of 'fascists'. The term was applied not only to members of the Falange which a mere 1100 Madrileños had joined since 1933, but the many thousands who had contributed to the February election funds of the opponents of the Popular Front candidates. A lucky 3000 were crowded into the Cárcel Modelo, empty after the release on the 19th not only of those on remand for violence during the prolonged building workers' strike of June–July, but also of common criminals. Many more 'fascists', sentenced to death after a 'trial' which could last for as little as five minutes, were transported after dark to the Casa de

* Term taken from the Soviet 1917 organization which preceded the OGPU.

Campo, the park across the river opposite the once Royal, now National Palace, and there shot in the neck, or to save ammunition, knifed. The municipal authorities collected the corpses each morning, and amongst them were women in night-clothes and children in their pyjamas.

The victims were by no means all upper or middle class, though judges, fashionable doctors, retired army officers and senior civil servants were singled out by the tchekas. Many a workman and clerk figured in the captured lists of contributors to the election funds of the CEDA, and were therefore condemned to death. A worker's reputation as a church-goer was sufficient cause for his execution. Priests came in for special treatment. Those captured by the communist tchekas could expect abominable tortures before death.

The tchekas came to vie with each other as to how many 'fascists' they could kill per night. The most notorious were the 'Dawn Patrol' under the command of the former leader of the communist students at the University, Manuel Tagüeña Lacorte, and the *Brigada de Investigación Social*, whose chief, Agapito Garcia Atadell, was a printer. But the tchekas never enjoyed a monopoly of killing. Anarchist 'judges' in particular did require *some* evidence of the guilt of the accused, and a false witness could find himself on the waggon to the Casa de Campo in place of the man he had calumniated. Therefore those out for personal revenge were wiser who acted on their own initiative. Then there were those anxious to demonstrate their revolutionary fervour and inspire others, like a militiawoman nicknamed *La Pecosa* ('Freckles') who ceremonially and somewhat brutally killed the Bishop of Jaen and his sister in Madrid's most notorious slum, the Pozo del Tío Raimundo, in the presence of around 2000 cheering men and women. He was paying a visit to his family home, for like the overwhelming majority of the clergy, he was of working class origin.

Assassination by the thousand – assessments of how many thousands vary widely – was not the only aspect of revolution in Madrid following the failure of the army rising. The militiamen were not always satisfied with the capture of a wanted man. They wrecked his house. Looting was rare, and forbidden to agents of the tchekas. Destruction was cherished for its own sake, especially by anarchists, but some of the larger houses were requisitioned and saved for the many anarchist, communist and socialist 'committees' which in rivalry with each other interposed themselves between government and people. The major hotels were converted to various uses. There were orphans and old people to be rehoused after the burning of the religious houses.

As the terror started there was a rush of refugees to the consulates and embassies of foreign powers. The Norwegians were outstandingly hospitable, and first thought of acquiring private houses to take the overflow. They came to look after 900 refugees. The overall total of refugees in embassies and consulates, according to the doyen of the diplomatic corps, reached 15 000[1]. Several thousand people fled the city. The militia had established roadblocks on all exits from Madrid, but in the first few days they obeyed their orders literally, to be on the watch for and stop fascist hordes from *entering* Madrid.

Those not of the left who could not get away – and 35 per cent of the Madrileños had voted against the Popular Front – dressed shabbily: good clothes and the wearing of a tie was proof enough of fascism. Any militiaman could feel it his duty to stop a passer-by. The best safe conduct was a UGT or CNT union card, so a flourishing black market in them developed; but the person stopped did well to avoid carefully the utterance of the name of God except in blasphemy. Even *adios* was dangerous: the only aceptable word of farewell was now *salud*.

President Azaña and his Ministers were later to admit that government ceased to exist and that there was widespread murder and pillage in Madrid and almost everywhere else that the insurrection failed. Thus Azaña: 'a proletarian rising occurred, though not directed against the Government. Goods and people were sequestered. Many perished without being taken before a court. Employees were expelled or killed. So were technicians because they were not trusted. Trade unions, cells, libertarian groups and even political parties possessed themselves of buildings, industrial and commercial establishments, newspapers, bank accounts and valuables etc. . . . all of which led to the Government's "impotence and confusion".'[2] When foreign correspondents managed to evade the Government's strict censorship and the news of what was happening began to shock the outside world, socialist and communist apologists took the line that the Government had been left by the rebels 'without an army and without a police force', and the myth was to be perpetuated after the civil war by exiles who hoped that the Western Powers would overthrow Franco after defeating Hitler[3]; but at the time neither the Government nor the extreme left made any such claim, nor did they want such an excuse.

As always on Mondays, the only paper to appear on July 21 was the co-operatively produced *Hoja del Lunes*. On the Tuesday the left republican papers spoke of the defeat of the military rebellion by 'loyal forces' and 'the [regular] armed forces of the Republic'. Even the marxist dailies acknowledged their help however grudgingly. The Government tried to satisfy both moderate and extreme left with the statement that: 'the Civil Guard and Assault Corps, faithful to their courage and tradition, and united with the people [had] managed to defeat the rebellious attacks of soldiers who, deceived by their officers, believed that they were defending the Republic'.[4] The fact is that except for small detachments in the remoter parts of the province, the 3000 Civil Guards in and around Madrid remained steadfastly faithful to the Minister of the Interior, their old Director General Pozas.

If he chose not to use them to restore public order it was either out of sympathy with the revolutionaries (he joined the Communist Party soon afterwards), or under pressure from the socialists to whom the name Civil Guard was obhorrent; but they were there to be used (renamed Guardia Republicana the force was to be welcome, with the same officers, men and organization). The socialists had no objection to the Asaltos. They could certainly have been used. These faithfully obeyed orders to prevent enthusiastic militiamen from attacks on buildings or persons whose safety was of direct interest to the Government, and it was not in defiance of orders that they collaborated with militiamen in the pursuit of 'snipers' and hunts for 'fascists'. As for the army, as we have said, over 2500 officers hastened on July 21 to reaffirm their loyalty to the Government.

With leave cancelled and excluding the members of the units 'suspended' for their brief moment in revolt, the Government had in Madrid alone a force of 16 000 men immediately available. There was,

Republican Presidential Guards in dress uniform.

as we shall see, some confusion among the other ranks of one unit not implicated in the rising as to whether the Government had absolved them from their oath of obedience to officers, but the confusion was short lived.

There was not a single moment of confusion among the regulars who formed the column from Getafe to which the few rebels in Carabanchel had surrendered on the 20th. On the 21st they skirted Madrid and were marched up the Corunna road to occupy the Guadarrama pass known as the Alto del León (the Lion's Peak). The column was composed of two battalions of infantry, two companies of Civil Guards and two of Asaltos, a machine gun battalion and six troops (baterías)* of guns. It was under the command of a Colonel Enrique Castillo. As it advanced groups of militiamen joined it.

A second smaller column of army, Asalto and Civil Guard, went out from Madrid on the 20th to deal with insurgents in the small garrisons of Alcalá and Guadalajara. Troops from Alcalá, and a battalion of militiamen under the Civil Guard Captain Francisco Galán, brother of Fermín who had been shot after the Jaca rising of 1930, set out on the same day to occupy Somosierra, the pass on the road from Burgos. Yet another column, under a Major Burillo, again of army, Asalto, Civil Guard with elements of militia, moved north towards Navacerrada, the pass from Segovia.

The one unit of the army whose other ranks refused to obey the Government, that is, their officers who were acting on orders from the Ministry of War, was a battalion of the I Infantry Regiment. This was on the morning of July 21. Ordered to prepare to march to reinforce the Castillo column, they replied that the Government had absolved

* A *batería* corresponds to the British half-battery or troop, and a *grupo* to a battery.

Republican cavalry.
Cavalry played an
important part on both
sides.

them from the duty of obeying officers. Shots were fired and four men
were wounded. Dolores Ibarruri, the communist Deputy, and a man as
yet little known, Enrique Lister, rushed to the barracks. They harangued the troops: the only officers whom the Government had ordered
the troops to disobey were those who had rebelled; their captain,
Benito Sánchez, was a good marxist, a sympathizer with the October
revolutionaries, and an instructor of the socialist militia. The battalion
marched under him, but with Lister as 'political adviser'. Lister, who
was to rise to high military rank on the republican side, had spent three
years in Moscow, the first in the Lenin Academy, the second as a metro
maintenance worker, and the third in the Frunze military academy.

What in fact were relative positions of each side after the week-end July 18–21? Looked at from the point of view of the insurgents, this was the situation:
- Madrid, Valencia, Barcelona total failure;
- Burgos, Corunna, Seville, Zaragoza partial success;
- Valladolid the only complete success.

The original plan therefore was outdated.
- Divisions I (Madrid), III (Valencia), IV (Barcelona) lost: therefore III not available for a march on Madrid from the east.
- Division V (Zaragoza) would now have to defend itself against attack from the direction of Catalonia, so only a part if any, could now be used as in the original plan in a march on Madrid together with VI (Burgos) and VII (Valladolid).
- Division VI had an unexpected front – the Basque Provinces and Santander: therefore only a part of it, if any, would be available for that march from the north.

The one unexpected bonus was Queipo's capture of Seville by a daring stroke: but Seville was not the whole south, and the part of II with the insurgents was more than balanced by that part which was not.

Yet the capture of Madrid was essential to the whole enterprise.

There was one ray of hope for the insurgents. The Spanish army in Africa was under their control – 24 000 highly trained men (6000 'Moors', 6000 'Foreign' Legion, 12 000 Spaniards). But it was in Africa, not Spain. Colonel Yagüe, one of the chief conspirators, had established a bridgehead for it with about 800 men at Algeciras and Cadiz before Franco had arrived in Morocco from the Canaries to take over command of the whole army. However, the navy was not going to be available for its transport as originally planned. A large fleet was at anchor in Malaga – one battleship, two cruisers, a destroyer flotilla

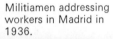

Militiamen addressing workers in Madrid in 1936.

Republican Assault Guards in battledress.

and a submarine flotilla, all faithful to the Republic, even if short of officers after those whom the left could not trust had been eliminated or imprisoned. Franco had nothing bigger than a gunboat to protect any sea convoy he might organize. The Africa Army was therefore only a remotely potential asset.

On the Peninsula the Republicans had three virtually intact divisions whereas the insurgents had only one. They had enough units of battalion and larger size with which to form at least another two. They had 75 per cent of the railway locomotive and rolling stock and about the same percentage of the 200 000 serviceable vehicles in the country, 35 000 of them in Madrid alone; and Madrid was the hub of communications in all directions.

The Government had not been left 'without an army', and it had readily available all the resources necessary, and especially the ability to manoeuvre rapidly, for a plan which would have given them very quick victory:

1 Concentrate navy and air force on the Straits to prevent the transport of the Africa Army to the peninsula.

2 Despatch the Madrid Division by train to the outskirts of Seville, recapture the lightly-held city and destroy the   enemy bridgehead at Algeciras.

3 Despatch the III Division by train to Madrid, then in requisitioned transport, via Guadalajara and round the Guadarramas, threaten

the lines of communication between Burgos and Valladolid, and Burgos and Zaragoza.

4 Support that threat with an attack on Zaragoza by the IV Division from Barcelona.

(1) and (2) would have penned Franco in Africa; (3) would have forced Mola at Burgos, and probably Cabanellas in Zaragoza to fall back on Navarre. The Nationalists in the north were desperately short of ammunition – a factor as we shall see which determined nationalist strategy in August. Cut off in Navarre, Mola would have had to surrender by the end of August or soon after. The war would have been over.

Nothing like that was planned, nor did anyone on the republican side, as far as is known, think of it.

The Republicans were obsessed with the defence of Madrid, not the defeat of the enemy. The Government's very first thought was to order the whole of the Madrid Division to block the Guadarrama passes, and to that end it telegraphed the regiment outlying in Badajoz to entrain for Madrid (the employment of the Castillo and other columns on that job was an afterthought). It called in troops from Murcia to protect the eastern approaches. The rest of the III Division was kept inactive: so also except for small units, the IV. Units of the republican navy patrolled the Straits in a desultory fashion but mostly remained in harbour. The Republicans' 110 serviceable combat aircraft (of the 160 in Spain) were ordered to attack in ones and twos targets here and there and to no definite plan.

Such neglect of the principles of war was to cost them and all Spain very dear.

6 The Battle in the Guadarramas

Mola knew by the morning of July 19 that the rising was not going according to plan even in his own divisional area. He was going to be faced with an unwanted flank to his right. There were not going to be three divisions available for an advance on Madrid from the north, and there was no sign of movement in Madrid. Nevertheless, the capture of the passes over the Guadarramas was still vital. In the original plan they were to have been gateways to Madrid (Map 2). Unless he did something about it they were now going to be gateways to the northern plain of Castille, the one stronghold of the insurgents, or, as they preferred to call themselves, *Nacionales**. Accordingly on that day he despatched south from Pamplona and Valladolid what troops he could spare: two battalions and a troop of field guns under Colonel Gistau to Somosierra; a battalion, a field battery, a cavalry squadron and a Falange militia company all under Colonel Serrador to Alto del León and Navacerrada; and half the Mountain Brigade stationed in Navarre under Colonel García Escámez to Guadalajara, with the double purpose of keeping open the option of approaching Madrid round instead of across the Guadarramas and of outflanking Somosierra.

García moved fast bearing in mind that he had to take the towns of Logroño and Soria on the way. On the 22nd he was at Atienza, seventy kilometres from his objective, when he heard that Guadalajara was now firmly in republican hands, and that the rising in Madrid had failed utterly. Mola orderd him to reinforce Gistau who had got only as far as the foot of the pass that day. At the top a handful of monarchist civilians had been doing battle with the local Civil Guard detachment and local socialist militiamen. They had been reinforced on the 20th by a group of Falangist militiamen who had motored down from Burgos, but on the 21st the Francisco Galán battalion had attacked them. On the 22nd, with Gistau so near, the monarchists and Falangists were overrun. Reinforcements came up behind Galán, including twenty-three artillery pieces, four of them 155 mm, so that when Gistau tried to storm the height on the 23rd he suffered very heavy casualties and had to fall back to Aranda to reform. It was there that García coming across from Atienza joined him that evening. García wasted no time in regrouping his and Gistau's battered troops, and nationalist militia also just arrived (four companies of enthusiastic Carlist *Requetés* and two of Falangists) for a second attempt at recapturing the pass.

Over to the west, at the Alto del León, Castillo with his regulars and what the republican official communiqué called 'uncontrollable mili-

* NB not *Nacionalistas*, a word which would have been acceptable only to the then very small Falange element among them.

tias whose number is unknown',[1] saw Serrador approaching on the
22nd. Republican reports of what happened conflict one with another,
but it would appear that Castillo went down towards Madrid to ask for
help, and that in his absence his troops panicked. Serrador's vanguard
took the height. Militiamen shot Castillo. There was a rush of republican reinforcements: an exclusively communist militia battalion (the
'Thaelmann' under the command of Juan Modesto who was to play an
important role in military operations over the next thirty months),
other militia and Civil Guard, Asalto and regular army battalions, and
artillery. The republican Colonel Morales Carrasco took over command and counter-attacked on the 24th. He might have succeeded but
for the indiscipline of the militia who disobeyed orders.[2]

General Riquelme, GOC Madrid, came up on the 25th, took over,
and attacked again and again on that day and the next, with a force
equal to that of a full brigade. He was supported by light tanks and
nine troops of medium and field artillery. He had a squadron of Bre-
guet bombers and one of Nieuport fighters at call. Serrador too had
received reinforcements; not equal to Riquelme's, but he did now have
five troops of field and one of medium artillery. Occasionally two
nationalist Breguets flew over to help him, but without fighter support
they were ineffectual. Casualties were heavy on both sides, especially
on the 26th. Serrador was wounded in hand-to-hand fighting, and
many of his senior officers killed, but his men held on. Yet more reinforcements arrived for both sides. Attack and counter-attack followed
ceaselessly for another four days. Among the casualties on the republican side was Captain Condés, the assassin of Calvo Sotelo. His body
was given a hero's funeral back in Madrid.

On the 30th Riquelme reported 'the enemy has only one 155 mm
and three or four field guns still firing . . . They must have run out of
fuses. The shells are not exploding.'[3] Still the Nationalists held on. On
the 2nd, following the arrival of a republican regular army battalion
fresh from Valencia, new militia companies from elsewhere and light
tanks and armoured vehicles, Riquelme tried an enveloping movement. The Nationalists countered the move and routed the militiamen,
some of whom went all the way back to Madrid where they spread
alarming rumours. In fact there was no danger whatever. The
Nationalists were far too short of ammunition to risk pursuit, indeed so
short that they were unable to attempt to take the neighbouring pass of
Navacerrada. Further republican attacks during August failed to dislodge the Nationalists who renamed the pass *Alto de los Leónes*.
Colonel Asensio Torrado, a disciplinarian, took over from Riquelme
on August 7, and deciding that further attempts to recapture the pass
would cost more lives and equipment than it was worth, set up a
defence line on the Madrid side. Navacerrada remained in republican
hands.

In the meantime, at Somosierra, García Escámez had carried out an
outflanking movement and forced the Republicans away from the pass
on the 25th. After three days of republican attacks this front was also
stabilized on the Madrid side of the pass. The Republicans built up
their strength there to 2000 before the end of July and 5000 by the end
of August, but made no serious attempt to retake it. Instead they established a continuous line of positions over a wide front, as at the Alto del
León. Patrols and skirmishes gave the 2900 militiamen included in the

force battle experience, and they began to realize the value of discipline in war. One of the militia chiefs was Valentín González, a natural leader of men who called himself *El Campesino* (the farm labourer), though in fact he was by trade a road contractor. His beard, his huge size and monstrous strength, coupled with extraordinary courage under fire, made him a hero. As a guerrilla fighter he would have been brilliant; as a commander in more orthodox warfare his value was mostly his public image, but in orthodox warfare it was always possible to have behind the inspiration of a flamboyant personality the stability of good staff officers – and this he was to have. The Spanish Communist Party, which had taken him for one of theirs, ensured that he would not damage their prestige; and it was in the battles in the Sierra that another communist gained a reputation for military ability, the Moscow-trained Enrique Lister.

Each side had been taking stock of its resources and deciding what to do with them. The events of the week-end July 17–22 had left the Government and Nationalists with the following troops:

	Total	*Government*	*Insurgents*
Army	117 500	55 200	62 300
Airforce	5 500	3 200	2 200
Civil Guard, Asaltos and Carabineros	67 500	40 500	27 000
	190 500	98 900	91 500[4]

The split was all the way from top to bottom, but not an even split. Of the twenty-four major generals only four had joined the rebels – Cabanellas, Queipo, Goded and Franco – and only thirty-one out of sixty-eight brigadiers, whereas the junior officers were divided roughly 65:35 in favour of the insurgents. The Republic retained twenty-four major generals and brigadiers in its service, lost two to the enemy and gained two, imprisoned eight and shot fifteen, including López Ochoa who had served the Republic faithfully, but whom the socialists would not forgive for his direction of the operations in Asturias against the enemies of the Republic in 1934. The Nationalists retained nineteen generals and brigadiers in their service (lost two and gained two), imprisoned ten and shot six.

Of the 15 300 officers of field and junior rank on the active list (army and paramilitary forces) some 7300 found themselves in what proved to be republican zones after the events of the first week-end. One thousand took refuge in embassies and consulates. The rest were gradually vetted by a committee at the back of the Ministry of War building, headed by the founder of the UMRA, Captain Eleuterio Díaz Tendero, who placed the letters *F, I* or *R* against the names on a nominal roll. 1500 *Fs* ('*fascistas*') were thereafter shot in batches. A like number of *Is* (*indiferentes*) were imprisoned in the first place though after a while some were given minor commands. The remainder, 3500 *republicanos*, were retained in military employment.[5]

Of the 7800 officers in the nationalist zones, 500 at least were shot, imprisoned or dismissed; of the remainder 2300 were in the Africa Army. So, the officer strengths of the two sides were 3500 Republican and 5000 Nationalists, a deficiency partly offset in terms of numbers (though exactly by how much it has not been possible to determine) by the greater number of officers in the first reserve who sided with the Republicans: but of course numbers were not everything. In battle the youth of the bulk of the nationalist officers was to give their side an inestimable advantage. In the case of sub-officers and NCOs, the split was about even.

Sixty per cent of the cavalry were with the Nationalists, but the Republicans had virtually all the tanks and armoured cars. Each side had about 600 guns. The Republicans had a slightly greater share of engineers, signals and army service men and equipment, but fewer infantry.

Of course, the Africa Army tipped the balance the other way, that is 24 000 added to 91 500 gave the Nationalists a total of 115 500 against the 99 000 Republicans. However, the numerical difference was not decisive. Even granted that transported to Spain the Africa Army could be a miniature 'manoeuvre force' (being as it was properly organized and equipped and capable of much more flexible deployment than either the 99 000 or 91 500 facing each other in the Peninsula), its number was far from adequate to warrant hope of a quick decision in favour of the Nationalists.

As we have said, immediate action by the Government to a bold strategic plan would probably have given them a quick victory. Three factors militated against the conception of such a plan. One was the Government's obsession with the defence of Madrid which we have noted. A second was the belief that time was on their side, and the third the politico-military theories of the sector of the Popular Front which directed the 'proletarian revolution'.

The belief that time was on the side of the Republicans was based on this important fact: they had in their zone, as the socialist leader Prieto told the insurgents in a broadcast, 'the major cities, the industrial centres, all the gold and silver of the Bank of Spain, enormous reserves of men . . .'. That was no exaggeration. With the exception of a small artillery factory in Seville, all the arms and munition factories, vehicle and aircraft assembly plants, iron and steel works and textile mills were in the areas where the rising had failed; and ironically they had Gil Robles and Franco to thank that those arms factories were better organized and turning out weapons of more modern design than those in the hands of the insurgents. The factory in Toledo, clear of, though near to, the Alcázar, where 1100 Nationalists were holding out, could alone turn out 800 000 rounds of small arms ammunition per day.

The politico-military factor was the belief of socialists that armies, as organized in non-socialist countries, were and could be nothing but instruments of capitalist repression. They agreed that the 99 000 men of the armed services who had remained faithful to the Republic should not be wasted, for they were trained and armed, but in their opinion, the army of the Capitalist Republic had to be dissolved first before a genuine People's Army could rise. The anarchists went further. They were doctrinally opposed to armies, 'people's' or 'capitalist', and to such concepts as 'good order and military discipline'.

General Castelló, appointed Minister of War on July 19, contended that the loyal forces and the militia should be incorporated into a single fighting unit without the dissolution of either. The Guadarrama disasters gave strength to his argument that the Republic had need of all it had or could get. 'Republican' though many officers were proving to be under the meticulous eye of Eleuterio Díaz Tendero, few of them

Republican army and volunteer officers.

were so socialist as to approve of Largo Caballero's demand for the immediate dissolution of the army and re-incorporation of its members into 'people's' militia units. The full satisfaction of the extreme socialist view could therefore result only in a civil war within the civil war, that is, a war of left republican army versus militia. More moderate socialists, like Prieto, agreed, and when the Government called up on July 27 the 1934 and 1935 reservists, moderate socialist mayors in those areas of Spain over which Madrid still had direct control cooperated in the task of ensuring that the reservists reported at the appointed army centres, though in Santander and Catalonia the reservists were drafted into militia units. As a result the republican army not only made good its losses in battle but increased in number by around 30 000. However, a government decree of August 2 to form 'volunteer battalions' out of the militiamen, in effect to convert the militia into army units under proper military discipline, was completely sabotaged by the socialists.

The decree is interesting in the political and military situation of the time. In its preamble it was alleged that it was prompted 'by the desire of the combatants in the militias themselves, to be organized into proper regular fighting units, and made subject to the norms of discipline which would multiply the efficacy of the effort expended and render maximum results at minimum cost'. The units were to have regular army, Civil Guard or Asalto officers and NCOs. The men were to wear a distinctive uniform. Service was to be 'for the duration or a minimum of two months'.[6]

A few non-socialist militiamen answered the decree, and nationally perhaps as many as fourteen battalions came to be formed from militia and other volunteers – but the socialists kept themselves aloof. So did the communists.

The communists did not want the dissolution of the army. What they had been working for quietly was the acquisition, by open or crypto-communists, of a sufficient number of key posts in order to control the army. They wanted control of the militia units as well. From the start they sought to achieve both ends by the force of example. Representatives of communist-led militia units asking for supplies from the Ministry knew exactly what they needed, and asked for the minimum, thus acquiring the respect of army officers irrespective of party affiliations.

Units under communist commanders such as Lister, Modesto or

Enrique Lister with political commissars José Fusimaña and Santiago Alvarez Gómez.

Martín Blázquez (one of the UMRA officers who seized the Ministry), obeyed orders and stood their ground rather better than others. These units belonged in the first place to the fifth of the five 'battalions' formed by the officer recipients of the first 5000 rifles issued on July 19. This 'battalion' not only sent out units immediately as did the other four, to join the army columns heading for the Guadarramas, but uniquely established a headquarters, recruiting centre and training depot in the ample premises of a boys' secondary school – that run pre-war by the Salesian Brothers in Calle Francos Rodríguez.

Here it changed its name from battalion to regiment, and under the direction of the Italian communist Vittorio Vidali and a group of mainly communist regular army field and junior officers, it set out to form and train units of militiamen not only better than average in discipline, handling of weapons and knowledge of elementary infantry tactics, but also in some measure indoctrinated in orthodox marxist-leninism. The product, companies at first and battalions later, was perhaps not as outstanding as communist propaganda inside and outside Spain made it out to be, but as good as that of the army infantry depots of either side; and those 'Fifth Regiment' companies and battalions offered an example and challenge to the other militias. In the 'Fifth Regiment' punishments were brutal and the death penalty far from infrequent, but there was no shortage of volunteers for it. Never as numerous as communists claimed at the time and in retrospect[7], the number of its members did reach 2700 by the end of July, 5800 in August, and at its peak in October 22 250.[8] The best of everything available, especially food, went to it. In the time allotted the political indoctrination could not be more than superficial, and conversion to communism was not made a condition of membership of the trained units, but the people who watched them as they marched out 'to the front' behind Madrid's municipal band in July and August, identified them as communists, admired them, and in consequence many joined either the 'Fifth Regiment' or the Party.

With the success of the call-up of the 1935 and 1934 reservists, and the arrival from France of thirty-two of the latest Potez and Amiot bombers and forty-four Dewoitine fighters (flown in by French pilots – some of whom stayed – or sent crated overland), the Government had even less reason to remain on the defensive in the first week of August. By then also it should have appreciated exactly how weak its opponents were to the north of Madrid, not only as a deduction from the fact that the Nationalists were not prepared to descend from the captured passes, but also from the experience of a column of 6000 militiamen and soldiers under Colonel Mangada. He had roamed at will through the province of Avila and found in a first excursion no one to fight except handfuls of nationalist Civil Guard and armed civilians and in a second only some 800 badly organized nationalist militiamen. These he had routed without difficulty. But still no thought was given to the possibility that the enemy could be defeated through coherent action. Within the Ministry of War and the Cabinet thought was still dissipated on the satisfaction of the demands of individual militia battalions, and on argument as to whether the republican army should be one in which the best use was made of what existed, or one exclusively of militiamen under the control of political parties or political trade unions.

The conviction that time was a factor against the insurgents was particularly strong among socialists and anarchists. The defeat of the enemy was not in their opinion the most pressing problem. The pressing problem was whether anarchism or socialism was to triumph. The UGT and CNT had been 'at war' long before the rising. Their rivalry now took a new form: a scramble for the control of public services and utilities, and of private manufacturing and commercial enterprises. The Government might decree this or that at Cabinet level — but the enforcement of those decrees was now totally subject to the criterion or whim of the local 'committee'.

In the midst of this 'indiscipline, anarchy, disorder, dissipation of time, energy and resources'[9] the Government was indeed 'paralyzed': and that paralysis gave the insurgents a chance they should never have had. It was in vain that the Government put up posters depicting the mingling in death of the blood of a CNT and a UGT militiaman. In life, in battlefield and in city, the most that could be hoped was armed truce. But that was not all. The socialists were divided into supporters of the moderate Prieto and the convinced marxist revolutionary Largo Caballero, and standing in the background ready to manipulate socialists, left Republicans and all others, were the leaders of the still very small Spanish Communist Party.

7 Franco's March towards Madrid

On July 20 Franco held a Council of War in Africa. Given that the navy was not going to be available, how was the Africa Army to be transported to Spain? Three decisions were taken; convoys were to be organized with whatever shipping was available locally; bomber and fighter aircraft would be sought abroad to give them air cover and frighten off enemy warships; in the meantime the five Fokker military and civilian transport aircraft in insurgent hands would airlift to Seville what they could.

On July 30 Franco received nine Savoia bomber-transports from Mussolini. With them and a civilian Junkers 52 which he requisitioned, the airlift became possible of 100–150 men per day. At that rate it was going to take weeks to get across the 5000 men and equipment which Franco considered the barest minimum required to prevent the complete collapse of the insurrection. Madrid was still to be the objective of the Africa Army as in the original Mola plan – but with a difference. Mola's ammunition stock was now near total exhaustion. The immediate objective therefore had to be the establishment of a link through which Mola could be supplied from the substantial reserves in Africa. To that end the troops sent by the then Colonel Yagüe to Algeciras and Cadiz and those air ferried to date were organized into two little columns each of a *tabor* of Moors and a *bandera** of the Legion ('Foreign' only in name, for in fact 90 per cent of its members were Spanish), and a troop of either 70 mm or 75 mm infantry support guns. The first column, under Lieutenant-Colonel Carlos Asensio Cabanillas, left Seville late on August 2, the second under Major Antonio Castejón on August 3. On August 5 Franco embarked 1500 men and sent them across the Straits with his one old gun boat as escort. Six of the Savoias and his whole airforce of eleven fighters provided air cover. The convoy carried guns and heavy equipment, and several million rounds of ammunition for Mola. These troops brought up to strength the 'battalions' already on the march and provided a third column of two 'battalions' and a troop of guns under Major Helí Tella. It left Seville on August 9. The three columns had a combined numerical strength of around 3000 men – a pittance compared with the numbers which Madrid could by then deploy to meet them; but they were convinced that they could sweep into Madrid.

Franco's instructions were to proceed due north to Mérida, establish the junction with Mola in the north, clear Badajoz of enemy so as to establish a link with Portugal (through which supplies from abroad might reach the insurgents), then make for Madrid.

* *tabores* were units of 350 Moroccans when at full strength, and *banderas* battalion-type units of 550 legionaries.

61

The selected route to Madrid was not that which the Republicans expected. General Miaja had collected at Albacete a force of 6000 men from the Valencia region – three infantry battalions and a battery and the rest militiamen – and had taken up defensive positions sixty kilometres to the east of Cordoba on the main Seville–Madrid road. However, the call-up had enabled the garrison at Badajoz to be built up again to regimental strength (it had been depleted of battalions transferred to Madrid), and with local militia it numbered about 8000. As soon as its commander heard of the advance of Asensio towards Mérida he sent out some of his men to meet him.

The first serious clash between the two forces occurred on August 5 just south of Mérida at Almendralejo. Asensio was halted. On the following day his men were subjected to aerial attack. His Moors and Legionaries, inexperienced to attack from the air, suffered heavier casualties than they should have. Asensio was ordered to wait for Castejón. Colonel Yagüe, Franco's trusted lieutenant of the Riff War, assumed overall command, and with the two forward columns assaulted Mérida on the 11th. The Republicans, after desertions and casualties, fell back in two sections, one of 5000 towards Badajoz and the other of 2000 eastwards. Through the gap Franco's men effected the junction with Mola just north of Mérida, and passed over to him the ammunition of which he was now in very serious need. The Tella column caught up with Castejón's and Asensio's. Yagüe left Tella in Mérida to protect him from possible counter-attack by the men on the Madrid road, while he went for Badajoz with Asensio and Castejón. In that frontier town the defenders contested every street. There were about 1000 killed and many more wounded in the battle. The Legionaries lost whole companies but advanced undaunted, and they and the Moors won the day.

The Italian tri-motor Savioa SM 81 bomber/ transport aircraft was one of the first foreign types to be supplied to the Nationalist forces.

After such serious casualties, and a counter-attack on Mérida as expected, a general eastward advance towards Madrid could not be resumed until the 20th, but Tella kept contact with the enemy and forced them back past Trujillo to Navalmoral. On the 22nd Castejón routed a fresh and numerically strong column of militiamen, the 'Phantom' column of anarchist militia, which was moving towards Mérida alongside the Guadalupe Sierra to outflank the Nationalists. Though heavily attacked from the air by the French squadron, and harassed by ground troops, the Yagüe force pressed forward along the valley of the Tagus towards Talavera. At Talavera yet another concentration of between 6000 and 8000 men barred their way. Once again Yagüe, putting into practice plans prepared by Franco whose headquarters was now Cáceres, outmaneouvred the Republicans, attacked and routed them. Talavera, the last town of any importance on the road to Madrid and only 114 kilometres away, fell on September 3.[1]

The news could not be kept a secret from the people of Madrid. It caused all the more consternation because they had not been told of the fall of Badajoz, and the advance on Mérida had been explained as a deliberate stratagem to lure the enemy into a trap.

Much had happened in Madrid during August. Output and supply of food and other essential goods had fallen as the UGT and CNT had proceeded to close down small enterprises on the grounds that the small workshop, factory or commercial establishment was as great an offence against socialism or libertarian communism as the large firm or farm. The committees of control were now doing totally as they pleased. The Communist Party, however, was now playing a subtle, and successful game. Where once they had urged – as before the war – all power to the 'Spanish Lenin' Largo Caballero, and he in gratitude had handed over to them control of his Socialist Youth, they now posed as the defenders of the *petits bourgeois*, small entrepreneurs and smallholders against the UGT and the committees; and with that they were winning over by the thousand the supporters of the left republican politicians. Where Largo spoke of revolution and the establishment of a socialist State (when not speaking to visiting British MPs), they, the Communist Party, championed 'the democratic republic'; and the left republican Ministers became even more frightened and ineffectual.

A republican position on the North East approaches to Madrid.

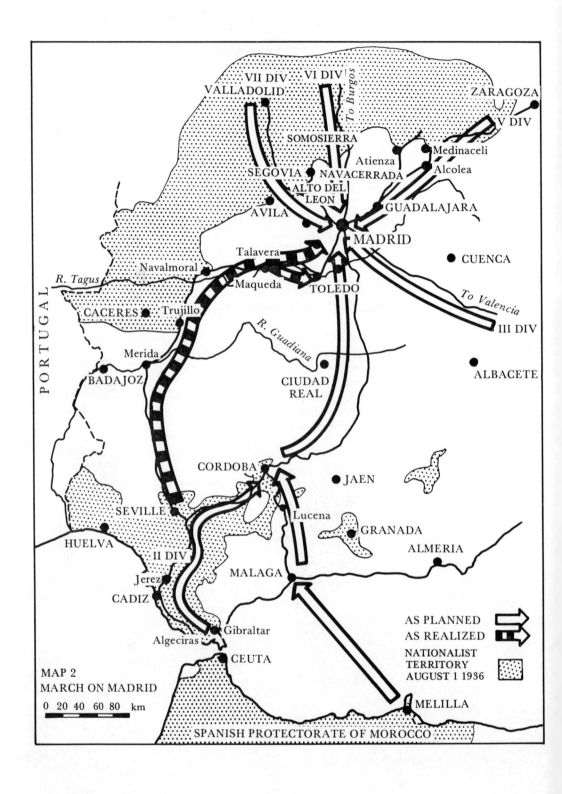

MAP 2
MARCH ON MADRID

0 20 40 60 80 km

AS PLANNED
AS REALIZED
NATIONALIST
TERRITORY
AUGUST 1 1936

General Franco with Lt.-Col. Yague in Seville,
August 1936 at the start of the march to Madrid.

The Prime Minister, Giral, was not ignorant of the facts of the military operations to date: the passes in the Guadarramas had been lost through the incompetence of the militiamen; the triumph awarded Mangada on his return from the incursion into Avila had been unmerited; 3000 professional soldiers had defeated and routed 8000 at Mérida and Badajoz, because the militia elements in the defence forces had refused to do what they were told. The Republic was losing the war. Whatever Lenin may have written to the contrary, it remained a fact that the militia had proved no match for the professionals. With the enemy ever closer a simple command was needed at the front and a single government at its rear to back it. Since so many of the militiamen were UGT and so much of the country was in the hands of the UGT there was only one man to lead the country – the UGT leader, Largo Caballero. The Comintern had called him the Spanish Lenin, and in 1934 he had got the CNT as well as the UGT, behind him. He might do so again.

On September 4, President Azaña announced that he had accepted Giral's resignation and appointed Largo Prime Minister. It was the right moment, but in fact preparations for the change had been in progress since the fall of Badajoz. Largo was going to have to put into effect measures against which he had been preaching since July and long before. To save face with his own UGT, those measures had to be decreed by the outgoing government.

The Republic had need of every man who had had some military training. Therefore, on August 14 all reservists and retired military personel were invited to join the 'Volunteer Force' units. Largo's newspaper *Claridad* was allowed to criticize the decision which implied the expansion of the army whose dissolution he had so often urged. The Communist Party welcomed it – for the non-communists. On August 15 the pay of militiamen who were serving in properly constituted units was raised from one to ten pesetas per day (five times the pay of a farm labourer). When soldiers complained of the unfairness of their pay in comparison (0.25 pesetas per day) *their* pay was raised to the same level – the overall effect therefore being a recognition of the parity of the soldier and the militiaman. It was not just the officers but the army on whom Largo had looked upon with disdain in so many speeches and articles, and not just the army but the paramilitary forces whose part in the battles to date had been considerable. On August 29 the Civil Guard was renamed the Republican National Guard. Thus renamed its members could be increased and make possible the enforcement of government decisions at local levels.

On August 23 a 'reform of the administration of justice' was decreed for Madrid and two days later for the rest of the republican zone. Cases of 'rebellion, sedition and espionage' would in future come before special tribunals presided over by three professional magistrates and two representatives from each of the seven major political organizations in the zone – Socialist Workers Party, UGT, Communist Party, Left Republican Party, Republican Union, CNT and FAI (Iberian Anarchist Federation). The magistrates were to ensure some semblance of judicial procedure. A simple majority in the jury of fourteen would decide the guilt of the accused, but since conviction could not be obtained by any one party on its own there would be an end to the mutual accusations of UGT and CNT tchekas that they had picked off

Members of the Asturian militia in Madrid.

each other's adherents as well as 'fascists'. The tribunals were gradually to deprive the tchekas of their prescriptive right of executing people at will. On August 13 104 priests had been shot – a record number for a single day. On the very day of the decree, a fire had occurred in the Model Prison where 3000 political prisoners were still being held. The militia guards, in circumstances never established, had opened fire on the prisoners, killing forty outright, and then another selected thirty as 'instigators of an attempted revolt'.

The tribunals as such could not put a stop to the *paseos* – the overnight hunts for 'fascists'. At the end of August, however, night-watchmen were deprived of their keys to houses, and porters were instructed to bar the doors to buildings after 2300 hours and summon the police by telephone if militiamen demanded entry. The activities of the tchekas were proving more than an embarrassment to the good name of the Republic in Western Europe and the Americas. The non-intervention agreement had committed France to sending no more aircraft or arms to Spain, but there was still the possibility of using French railways and ports as avenues for material from further afield,[2] and for men coming to fight in Spain, so long as the French government was not forced by public opinion to look too closely into such traffic. American arms manufacturers might likewise find their government demanding proof that the final destination of their products was the one stated on manifests.

Arms from abroad were even more important to the Republic than in July because Germany and Italy had supplied their enemies with aircraft comparable with those received from France. Fiat CR 32 fighters had fought successfully against the Dewoitines. Eleven of twenty Junkers 52s, sent by Hitler and operational in the first week of August, were airlifting troops from Africa, and the other nine were co-operating in the advance on Madrid of Franco's columns.

The Soviet Union presented the best possibility as a source for the arms that Giral's military advisers considered essential: aircraft equal or better than the German or Italian, bombs of heavier weight than the 11 and 15 kilogrammes being produced in Spain on either side, guns,

Junkers aircraft supplied by Hitler played an important role in Nationalist bombing attacks. This Ju 52/3 in Nationalist markings (as opposed to those of the Legion Condor) was one of the last aircraft delivered and belonged to a night bomber squadron.

shells, tanks. The Soviet Union might publicly join the non-intervention agreement but was secretly prepared to help – at a price. The price in the first place was gold and the acceptance of Russian political and military advisers. Accordingly over 70 per cent of the Spanish gold reserves were got ready for shipment and taken to the port of Cartagena, from which eventually (on October 25) they were shipped to Odessa. Vladimir Antonov Ovseenko, commander of the Red Guard which stormed the Winter Palace in Petrograd in 1917, arrived in Barcelona on August 25 with a large staff, and two days later Giral welcomed in Madrid the trusty Stalinist Marcel Rosenberg, as ambassador with an even bigger staff which included General Ian Antonovich Berzin and a group of officers of field rank. They were the precursors of several hundred *amigos* ('friends'), among them Marshals Rokossovsky, Koniev, Nedelin and Malinovsky, and Generals Kulik, Goriev, Pavlov, Voronov and Rodimtsev.[3]

When first approached Largo had made his acceptance of the premiership conditional on the inclusion in his cabinet of communists and anarchists. He did not want the socialists to bear all the blame in the event of disaster. The anarchists were prepared to join Largo in a National Council of Defence – but *government* no, as contrary to the principles of libertarianism. The communists would not enter government without instructions from Moscow. Rosenberg's arrival made rapid consultation possible. Largo had to be content with no anarchist or communist ministers; but the Cabinet did include two men in key positions whose views were indistinguishable from those of the Soviet Union, Alvarez del Vayo (Foreign Affairs) and Juan Negrín (Finance).

After Largo's accession life in Madrid and much of republican Spain began to change. There was mass recruitment for the Republican National Guard, the Asaltos and the Carabineros. Members of the tchekas were offered the choice of entry into the paramilitary forces, membership of a new 'Vigilance Militia' subject to police control, or being declared outlaws. The execution rate declined sharply. *Claridad* began to hint that the workers committees were hindering the work of the Government. It urged them to co-operate; they began to do so and were allowed to remain in existence for the moment. Madrid began to take on the aspects of a fairly orderly existence. To give colour to Largo's assurance to foreign visitors from France and Britain that his government was essentially 'elected by the free will of the people' and accountable to parliament, there was even a meeting of what was left of the Cortes on October 1.

Largo's most pressing problem on taking office was, of course, to stem the advance of Franco's forces. His very first measure was to dismiss General Riquelme as GOC Centre Theatre of Operations (*Teatro de Operaciones del Centro de España* – TOCE) and promote a new man into his place, Asensio Torrado. Asensio was temperamentally a very different man. He believed in attack. He collected twenty-two companies of militia, army and paramilitary forces, and sent them to reinforce those who had fallen back before Talavera, bringing their total up again to around 6000. They were to attack immediately. After an aerial bombardment of Talavera they did so on September 5, and again on the 6th, and for a third time with tanks and an armoured train in support, on the 8th. Yagüe's positions remained undented. His forces, augmented by a cavalry column under the then Colonel Monasterio, set off from Talavera on the following day.

As they advanced they received reinforcements from Africa, and local volunteers were allowed to join the Legion. A fourth infantry column was created under Delgado Serrano, and each column was reorganized to consist of a bandera, two tabores, a troop of guns, signals, sappers, etc. – 1500 men all told. Asensio Torrado's men fought a harassing rearguard action against them. The militiamen were excellent at this, and they held the advance over the next fifty kilometres down to an average of five per day. Maqueda, a townlet on an important road junction, seventy-four kilometres from Madrid, did not fall until the 21st, and three days of counter-attack followed the fall.

Each day that the advance of those seemingly invincible Legionaries and 'Moors' could be delayed was vital to the defenders of Madrid. Recruitment of new men for either militia or army was proving difficult in the city, and Asensio Torrado had to bring units in from Andalucia, Murcia, Valencia and even Barcelona. With them the strength of the Republicans to the west of Madrid increased to 33 000 men. Among them were a couple of companies of Italians, Poles, Hungarians and French communists who happened to be in Spain on July 18. The quality of the troops under Asensio varied from very good to poor. The hitherto amorphous and unruly CNT militia began now to think in terms of working together as military battalions: they had begun to realize the considerably greater effectiveness of the battalions of the 'Fifth Regiment' and the loyal half of the army.

On the Africa Army side a fifth column under Lieutenant-Colonel Barrón now came into existence. Yagüe, who had fallen ill after Franco had rebuked him for the slow rate of the advance from Talavera, had been replaced by the forceful General Varela. The five infantry columns and Monasterio's cavalry, around 8500 men in all, could easily be outflanked by the TOCE. Accordingly Mola now had to adjust his forces to the north of Varela's. They were now to push forward of Avila and east of the Gredos mountains. They began to do so, and Varela was to have only one instead of two flanks to guard.

An episode was now to occur which was to give Madrid a respite.

Right back on July 20, General Moscardó, commandant of the Military Academy at Toledo, had declared for the insurgents, and promptly barricaded himself with over 1000 men – cadets, army, Civil Guard – in the Alcázar there. This action was essentially mediaeval. Cooped up in that quasi-fortress they had not the slightest strategic or tactical value. What he should have done, of course, was to have formed a column and made his way northwards to Mola who could have done with those 1000 men. But the republican reaction had also been mediaeval. The thousand in that fortress had no weapons other than small arms. Their presence had been totally irrelevant since July to the defence of Madrid or the defeat òf the insurrection. Yet since then the Republicans had wasted men and ammunition in its siege.

At Maqueda Franco was at a cross-roads. One road led straight to Madrid; another led to Toledo. Franco had to choose between the relief of his friends whose defence of Toledo was undoubtedly heroic, and the possibility that he might yet frighten Madrid into surrender if the 8000 men under Varela continued to make for the capital as fast as possible. At the time Franco's and the Republicans' propaganda co-incided in stating that Madrid was being attacked by a *grande armée*. He chose to relieve Toledo as 'a matter of honour'. Republican reaction was equally out of its time: they redoubled their efforts to reduce the Alcázar before it could be relieved. Such was their determination that Largo Caballero himself went to exhort his troops. Sixteen thousand men were concentrated on the road to the Alcázar and round it, and much artillery. Such was the republican confidence in success that a 'Fifth Regiment' battalion (the Thaelmann) stood by to have the honour (and propaganda value) of being the first to enter the fallen fortress. Michael Kol'tsov, *Pravda*'s correspondent, and the Soviet author Ilya Ehrenberg, arrived to report the battalion's glory.

Franco gave Varela six days from September 23 to take Toledo. He scattered the forces before him using only three of his five columns, and on the 28th he was embracing the defenders of the Alcázar.

When Talavera had fallen Asensio Torrado had established a line of defence pivoted at Maqueda, and a second pivoted at Navalcarnero. The relief of Toledo gave Franco two converging lines of approach to Madrid: the main through Navalcarnero and the other through Illescas; and yet a third approach was possible – up the valley of the Tagus to Aranjuez, then north. This third line, however, was vulnerable to flank attack.

The troops under Varela had been on the march now and in daily contact with the enemy for sixty days. They had inflicted thousands of casualties while suffering many hundreds themselves. They had captured enormous quantities of war material – 12 000 out of 17 000 rifles sent by Mexico in the capture of Talavera alone[4]. Nevertheless the republican forces had not diminished. On the contrary, on October 7, the day after Varela's troops began to move forward after regrouping, Asensio Torrado had 25 000 men and fifty-one pieces of artillery barring the direct approaches to Madrid, and another 7400 men and ten guns at Aranjuez. There were also some thousands of militia who did not recognize Asensio's authority but were prepared to help in the defence of Madrid.

The last forty-five kilometres to Madrid were not going to be 'a walk over'.

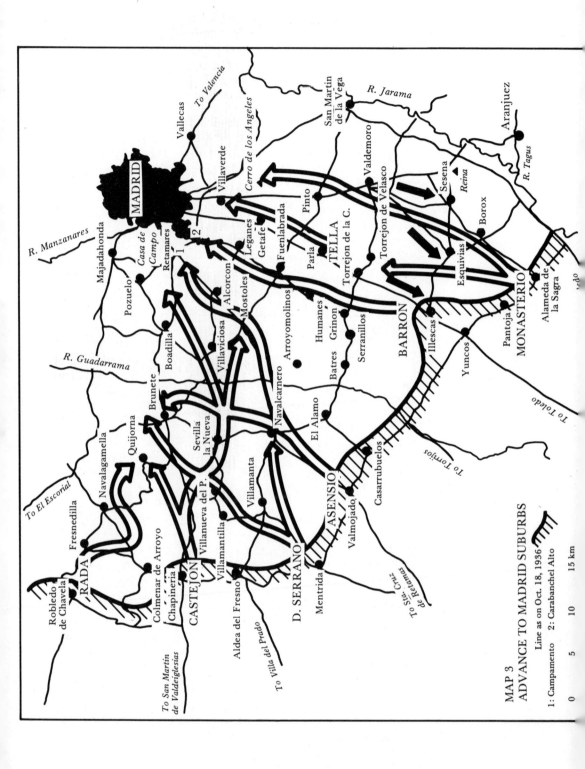

MAP 3
ADVANCE TO MADRID SUBURBS

Line as on Oct. 18, 1936

1: Campamento   2: Carabanchel Alto

0   5   10   15 km

8 The People's Army

The disastrous performance of the militia units whenever they faced Franco's army of professionals and mercenaries finally convinced Largo Caballero that to fight an organized army an organized army was necessary. However different the motivation of regular army conscripts, volunteers, communist militias, socialist militias and anarchist militias, all five would have to be coalesced into one single organism. In the face of a disciplined enemy, there had to be a single chain of command and an acceptance of orders from top to bottom. That was the advice not only of the army officers who had remained loyal to the Popular Front Government, but also of the Soviet ambassador who attended Cabinet meetings and did not want Russian military equipment wasted in the same way as so much of what had been received previously from Mexico and France[1].

On September 28/29 Largo Caballero decreed the 'militarization' of all militia units. They were to be reorganized properly as battalions with officers and NCOs. Militiamen could aspire to the rank of *alferez* (ensign) as militia, or higher as army officers. Subsequently, to smooth the tempers of those socialists who considered this to be deviation from marxist revolutionary theory, the five-pointed star of the militia replaced the republican insignia of the regular and volunteer army units. The clenched fist became the salute of all the armed forces henceforth to be called firstly the '*Ejército del Pueblo*', and later '*Ejército Popular de la República*'. The purpose of this army was stated to be 'politico-social', and therefore ideologically correct and quite different from the 'instrument of capitalist oppression' which it superseded. To make that 'politico-social' purpose clear, to guide the men into 'correct political thinking', to instil in them hatred of the enemy, keep up morale and ensure obedience to orders, every unit was to have a political commissar – just as 'capitalist armies' had their chaplains. The corps of army commissars was headed by a committee of three, a socialist, an anarchist and a communist, presided over by the crypto-communist cabinet minister, Alvarez del Vayo.[2]

Infantry battalions, artillery, etc. were now to be grouped into mixed brigades in preference to divisions. Soviet Army officers then in Spain were subsequently to claim credit for their smaller tactical unit, and it was they who obtained its adoption, in spite of strong opposition from the Spanish republican General Staff[3]. Nevertheless, the composition adopted was one very similar to that of the Mixed Mountain Brigades in existence in the Spanish army under the monarchy and at the outbreak of war.

This was the structure which was laid down for them:
– One cavalry or armoured car squadron;

- Four infantry battalions, each of four rifle companies, one machine-gun company and a mortar platoon;
- Two grupos (batteries) of field, medium and anti-tank guns;
- Signals, engineer, army service, veterinary and medical units.

Their complement, full strength, was 3850 men: in practice some brigades were to have only three battalions and only one artillery *grupo*. The first twenty-one were to be numbered 1–6, XI–XV and 16–25.[4]

Brigades 1–6 were quickly organized with regular, 'volunteer', carabineer and 'Fifth Regiment' battalions by the Spanish regular army Major Segismundo Casado under the direction of 'a Russian general and two Russian colonels'[5]. The full equation of the latter with the 'professional' was not unjustified. A by-product of the policy of the Communist Party to protect the *petits bourgeois* had been the enlistment in their regiment of a higher proportion of men with some education than in the UGT units. The command of three of the first six mixed brigades went to members of the Communist Party.

Major (later Colonel) Segismundo Casado, organiser of the Republican Mixed Brigades.

General Lukacz (the Hungarian Mata Zalka) seen with the Bulgarian Ivan Petrov (the latter is to the right of the picture).

XI Brigade also formed in October was to be the first of five of very special composition. Its three battalions were of Germans, Poles, Hungarians and Yugoslavs despatched from the Soviet Union where as refugees they had long been an embarrassment to Stalin, and of Frenchmen and Belgians recruited by Comintern agents. Its OC was the Hungarian Lazar Stern, alias Kleber, a graduate of the Soviet Frunze Military Academy, who had arrived in Spain in September[6]. Its depot, as that of XII–XV for which recruitment was in progress in Western Europe and North America, was at Albacete, 280 kilometres southeast of Madrid. The commanders of the depot were the French communist leader André Marty and the Italians Luigi Longo and Giuseppe de Vittorio. Gottwald and Ulbricht also had jobs there. Josep Broz ('Marshal Tito') was made responsible for the transport of recruits from Paris to Spain as also, more importantly, of war material from west and central European markets.

To help the welding of the regular, volunteer and militia units into the new People's Army, Prime Minister and Minister of War Largo Caballero added to his posts that of Generalissimo of the Army Forces, and reorganized the General Staff to include representatives of the political parties of the extreme left. Vidali and Kleber were also given posts in it: the foreign element in the army warranted their inclusion. Soviet officers had full access to documents, and played important roles in meetings of the General Staff but were not officially part of it.

Outside the army there were such men as the methodical Togliatti and Erno Gero behind the fiery Dolores Ibarruri, and Arthur Stashevsky in the sybaritic Dr Juan Negrín's Ministry of Finance, charged by Stalin with the task of 'manipulating the political and financial reins of republican Spain'[7]. Such a concentration of men whose names were to resound in international politics during the 1950s was a sign that Moscow saw a future in Spain. It was a very reasonable supposition that Varela's few thousand men could be held by the sheer weight of numbers on the republican side and by the construction of conventional defence works long enough to allow the ultra-modern equipment, then on its way from Odessa, and the new Spanish and International Mixed Brigades to reach Madrid and be thrown into the battle decisively.

Over on the nationalist side there had also been changes in political and military command. With a solid connexion established between Mola's northern forces and Franco's southern there had to be a Generalissimo to plan overall strategy; and with the Nationalists in control of more than half the number of provinces there had to be a Head of Government. On October 1 the senior officers among the insurgents had chosen Franco to be both Generalissimo and Head of Government. To the surprise of the electors the communiqué announcing their decision had named him Head of State as well.

Franco promptly appointed Mola his commander in the field. Mola had been facing since July three very determined enemies – the tough Basques and Asturians, both protected by the mountains of their lands, and Catalan anarchists who had brilliant guerrilla leaders. He had made some progress in adjusting his eastern front to be the better able to ward off the hit-and-run raids of the Catalan anarchists, but it was still 600 kilometres long. He had captured virtually all Guipuzcoa, albeit till mid-August he had been, as we have said, short of ammunition. Currently he had troops committed to two major operations, the conquest of Vizcaya, and the relief of Oviedo.

Oviedo was another Toledo. There a force under Colonel Aranda had been besieged since July, and their relief had become as much a matter of honour as the relief of the men in the Alcázar; but it was incomparably more difficult. The whole of the Cantabrian region was ideal for defence: a section of riflemen well placed on a mountain could make the advance of a whole company costly. The relief of Oviedo depended on driving a wedge through just such terrain, and the attempt was proving expensive in men and materials of war.

Franco told Mola that the capture of Madrid was to have top priority but not to the prejudice of the rescue of Aranda. Mola therefore had to thin out his eastern front to danger point, and to postpone his plans for Vizcaya in order to provide Varela with the support he needed in these final stages of the drive to Madrid. What Varela needed most was stronger protection on his left flank. Accordingly Mola sent into the Gredos mountains a force of 5000 army and Requete and Falangist militia in five columns, under the overall command of his fellow brigadier, Valdés Cabanillas.

Thus, as on October 6, the total nationalist force deployed on 'objective Madrid' was of a mere 13 500 men, with 40 field and infantry support guns. Face to face with them on the republican side there were then 25 500 men with 51 guns, and ready to pounce on the nationalist right flank from across the Tagus another 7650 men with 10 guns more.[8] The proportions were therefore the very inverse of what they should have been in attack and defence. Yet fifteen days later, that is, dawn October 22, the Republicans had been forced back along the whole of the 100 kilometre front between the Tagus and the Gredos mountains.

Valdés Cabanillas's columns had difficult ground to traverse – mountain and defile – and fog and rain made quagmires of the roads, but they accomplished their task of clearing the enemy from the Gredos mountains and of denying the Republicans any possibility of outflanking Varela in the northern sector. Simultaneously Varela used his five infantry and one cavalry columns in a series of thrusts and outflanking movements (see Map 3). With Valdés securing his left flank, Varela switched the cavalry to his right flank along the Tagus. In that manner he reached Navalcarnero.

Navalcarnero, twenty-six kilometres from the outskirts of Madrid, was protected by a double line of trenches, each with a double barrier of barbed wire, and effective even if rapidly constructed concrete defence works. Varela ordered Barrón to attack up the Toledo–Madrid road. Illescas, half-way between Toledo and Madrid, fell to him on October 18, and the Republicans were seemingly deceived into thinking that this would be the main thrust. They brought up their forces in that sector till they outnumbered Barrón 5:1 in both infantry and artillery. They were in a sense right to think as they did, for had the Nationalists had at that moment a reserve to throw in behind Barrón then they might have swept up the southern routes to the capital with a rapidity disconcerting to the enemy.

Navalcarnero remained the key objective. Time was now the vital factor. Disturbing intelligence had reached Franco by round-about routes from republican-held Cartagena, Albacete and Barcelona. On October 19 he sent Mola a signal intended both to urge greater speed and to exhort to action: 'the international situation, the policies of the Red Government, the low morale of its troops and militias, *the imminent arrival of important reinforcements* make advisable the concentration of maximum force on the Madrid front to speed up the fall of the capital'[9]. If time was now so important it could not be wasted in a switch of the main effort over to the right. The Navalcarnero defences and all the other defences behind them would have to be breached. The outlook was none too good. There was the River Guadarrama to cross. There were reports, which proved to be true, of a belt of defence works in depth along an arc running from Brunete due west of Madrid, through Móstoles and across the Toledo–Madrid road to the *Cerro de los Angeles* due south of the city: and behind that arc, yet a third system was developed along the line Casa de Campo–Campamento–Carabanchel and right round the southern perimeter to Vallecas.

Oviedo had been relieved on the 16th after bitter fighting: but those troops were exhausted. Mola still did not have very much available to concentrate on Madrid. He brought up Varela's forces depleted by casualties up to strength again, and he cajoled the senior among sixteen Italian officers who had arrived at the end of September with eight Fiat-Ansaldo tankettes, sixteen infantry support guns and four anti-tank guns, to allow his men to man guns and tanks for which trained Spaniards were not yet available. This equipment, with their mixed Italian and Spanish crews, Mola sent to Varela.

Varela delegated to Yagüe the co-ordination of the Delgado Serrano and Asensio columns. Two shortages from which the Nationalists had suffered from the beginning were now proving serious disadvantages –

a lack of enough signals equipment and personnel, and of ordnance survey maps. Madrid had the stock and the plates. Nationalist units were using small-scale motoring maps.

Yagüe hammered away at Navalcarnero and used the Italo–Spanish contingent on the 21st. The Fiat–Ansaldos were really little more than machine gun carriers, but good enough to trample the barbed wire under tracks, and the anti-tank guns could cope with the republican armoured cars and even Renault tanks. The Republicans launched a fierce three-day counter attack on Barrón at Illescas, but Barrón held on, and then launched a new attack which took him to Torrejón de la Calzada eight kilometres beyond Illescas and twenty from the outskirts of Madrid. Varela ordered Yagüe to keep up the pressure beyond Navalcarnero, but for the moment he could make little progress.

Where Mola had the advantage over the Republicans during October was in the air. He allocated about sixty aircraft of miscellaneous types to the Madrid operation: three Savoia 81 bombers, fifteen of the Junkers Ju 52s now in bomber form, sixteen Heinkel He 46 army co-operation aircraft, a dozen Heinkel He 51s and nine of the 21 Fiat CR 32s received in August and September – the others had been shot down or crashed. When raiders caught the republican aircraft on the ground at Getafe and Cuatro Vientos, the Nationalists achieved local air superiority, and in consequence it became the turn of the Republicans to complain of lack of air support.

The Fiat CR 32 bi-plane fighter was supplied by Mussolini to the Nationalist forces in considerable numbers.

Each side accused the other in violent terms of 'the bombing of civilians', and it may be that individual pilots did deliberately drop bombs on towns: but it was certainly not the policy of either side to do so at this stage in the war. Aircraft and bombs were too scarce. What each side was slow to learn – and what the nations which provided those aircraft and many of their pilots were to notice – was that the bomb sights of the time were too primitive to ensure direct hits on small targets, such as a bridge, a gun position or a headquarters, and that hits were 'lucky shots'. A few bombs had been dropped in August and September on Madrid, aimed at military targets like the Ministry of War, the centre of telephone communications for the whole army, and major barracks – but as frequently as not they had landed wide of their mark. Neither side had ground-to-air communication beyond the most elementary and in a battle a 'friendly' aircraft could be as dangerous as an 'enemy'. In August even the legionaries had been frightened of attack from the air, and attributed too much importance to aircraft. This was true of all men-at-arms anywhere, because they had been conditioned by imaginative writers into a state of fear. Aircraft had their value certainly, but at the time what they could do, given the small numbers involved, was only to supplement artillery and machine guns somewhat expensively.

People in cities were no different from the men in the battle fronts. They too had been conditioned into fear by science-fiction in film and cheap paper-back, by sensational journalism and political propaganda. In October raids became more frequent, by as many as three aircraft at a time. By then, however, most Madrileños had become inured to them. Some people went quietly to the shelters; most continued with their business unperturbed. The Madrileños were then much more concerned with the ever closer sound of artillery fire which they had first noticed on October 13. The proximity of the rebel Fascists could no longer be concealed from the public.

The Government had appealed to the CNT to allow the building workers to help with the construction of the defence works from the Casa de Campo outwards as far as Navalcarnero, and every day since the first week in October, that is, since it had been realized that the main thrust would not be along the Toledo–Madrid road, they had been going out in trucks very early each morning. There were complaints of scarcity of picks and shovels in the city, but that was because they were all needed on the approaches. The traffic was intense with trucks passing through Madrid taking cement and metal reinforcement; and observers, prone to underestimate how much material even one pill box required, began to imagine that the construction was in progress of an impenetrable Maginot line. This was not to everyone's liking, civilian or military. There were still a few romantics who considered trenches, let alone concrete emplacements, unworthy of real men in battle, an attitude which cost many lives – mostly Requetés on the one side and anarchists on the other.

The less romantic but more imaginative became ever more apprehensive (or elated if of the 40 per cent who were not for the Republicans) as it began to appear that the phantom concrete wall did not seem to be holding. Madrid's double-decker buses were now being used to take reinforcements to the front. Deserters exaggerated the strength of the forces of the Nationalists and their power. Indeed, even official

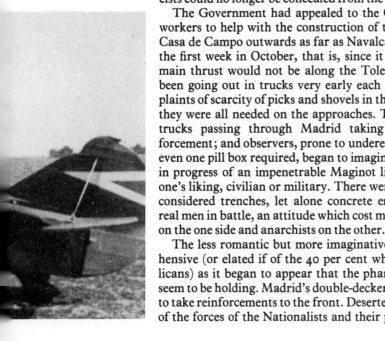

communiqués did. Thus the one admitting the loss of Navalcarnero[10] spoke of twenty-six tanks in action when all there had been were six tankettes, and of 5000 'fascists' in the attack when the number had been 1500 and of 'many of our companions being squashed by the tanks' which is difficult to believe seeing the size of the Fiat-Ansaldo, and of 'the field of battle sown with the corpses of our troops'.

The republican authorities now launched a campaign to terrify the people of Madrid into resistance. The Press carried the most lurid stories of 'the massacre at Badajoz of all people of the left' in a bull ring packed with 'pious women . . . virtuous friars and white-whimpled nuns of humble look'. At the sound of trumpets 'all liberals, republicans, socialists, communists and anarchists, old men and children alike, male and female' were said to have been driven into the ring and to have been mown down by machine guns to the laughter and clapping of the Badajoz upper class. Readers were assured that Yagüe had promised a bigger show at Madrid's bull ring, that he had in mind the shooting there of 100 000 Madrileños[11]. (One of the men supposed to have been shot at Badajoz was Colonel Puigdendolas, who in fact was currently at the head of 7000 men facing Barrón, having returned to republican territory via Portugal and France. He was more truthfully reported 'assassinated by an anarchist' on October 29.) The Moors, of course, had raped all the women of the left between Seville and Navalmoral, before putting them to death in barbaric ways.

The only known result of this propaganda was a fresh outbreak of assassinations of real or imagined 'fascists'.

Civilians in Madrid construct defence lines under military supervision.

Refugees streamed into
and through Madrid,
homeless and poverty-
stricken, in vast numbers.

Madrileños sheltering
overnight in the Metro.

As the sound of battle grew yet nearer columns of peasants carrying what they could on tumbrils, bicycles and donkeys began to pass through Madrid on their way eastwards. Next came refugees from the outer suburbs. President Azaña had given the capital for lost on October 19 and fled to Barcelona without word to his government. When his absence began to be noticed, the government announced that he had gone on 'an extended tour of the front'. Less eminent citizens of Madrid followed his example. The exodus from Madrid reached substantial proportions. Emigrants outnumbered immigrants, but the middle-class emigrant, irrespective of his political belief, carefully bolted his living quarters against the immigrant. There was widespread homelessness and misery.

On October 28 Varela's five columns were poised for the next attack. The immediate objectives were points as near as five kilometres from the gates of Madrid.

9 Thrust and Parry

On October 28 the Varela 'army' of five infantry and one cavalry columns, each of approximately 1500 men, was spread out over a front still fifty kilometres wide. Monasterio with his cavalry was on the right flank, covering the sector down to the River Jarama. To his left was Tella astride the Toledo–Madrid road; next Barrón covering a minor road; Asensio forward of Navalcarnero on the main road from Badajoz; and lastly Delgado Serrano and Castejón south-west and west of Brunete.

On the evening of that day the republican Prime Minister, Largo Caballero, broadcast an address to his 20 000 men deployed over the same front:

'The fascist hordes have spent their energy, have dissipated their strength in their long march to Madrid. The time has come to deal them their death-blow. While the traitors have been bleeding and losing their power to fight, our ranks have been gaining cohesion and number. Their power of attack has multiplied.

Tanks and aircraft are important in the weakening of an enemy. But those arms, comrades, are in themselves not enough for a victorious counter-offensive. They demand the support of your revolutionary will to fight. The fire of aircraft and tanks must have behind it the thrust of infantry. What the fire of tanks and aircraft smashes must pass into your hands in a victorious infantry attack, and must never be let go. Infantry must utterly destroy whatever is left of the rebel columns and seize their arms.

Listen to me, comrades! Tomorrow, October 29, at dawn our artillery and our armoured trains will open fire against the enemy. Our aircraft will immediately appear, hurl bombs at the enemy, and unleash the fire of their machine-guns. At the very moment of the aerial attack our tanks will hurl themselves over the enemy at their most vulnerable point and sow panic in their ranks. That will be the hour for all combatants, as soon as they receive the order from their commanders to hurl themselves violently against the enemy, attacking him until he is annihilated.

Our wives, our sisters and our children, who were going to be immolated, will be saved by the thrust of your arms. We have tanks now. We have aircraft. Forward! Comrades at the front, heroic sons of the worker-people! Victory is yours!'[1]

At dawn the following day nationalist airfields were bombed by twin-engined Tupolev SB-2s which were too fast to be intercepted by Fiat CR 32s. Meanwhile, Tella's column came under heavy bombardment from two armoured trains on the Madrid–Illescas railway line, and from more artillery than had ever been experienced by his troops. Polikarpov I-15 single-engined aircraft machine-gunned his position. Over to the right Monasterio's cavalry column was also subjected to

the same treatment. They then heard, next saw fifteen tanks of a size hitherto unknown, with cannon in revolving turrets as well as machine-guns – T-26s, fast and thickly armoured.

It was all material landed from a fleet of Soviet cargo vessels in Cartagena and other Mediterranean ports in mid-October. Tanks and aircraft were manned by Soviet army and air-force personnel, the tanks under the field command of a Major Paul Arman ('Greisser'), the aircraft under General Yacob Shmouskievich, alias 'Douglas'*; the artillery was under the overall direction of General Nikita Voronov. According to the then Colonel Krivoshein[2], Arman's senior officer, it had been intended that the tank crews should be mixed Russian and Spanish, but there had not been time to train any Spaniards.

The tanks advanced down the Aranjuez road and reached the villages of Seseña, Esquivias and Borox. There the cavalry engaged them in an obviously unequal battle. Right behind the tanks came Lister with the new 1 Mixed Brigade (three of its battalions 'Fifth Regiment', the fourth 'Volunteer Army', and its artillery, new Russian 105 mm Howitzers and 45 mm anti-tank), and also an *ad hoc* column mostly of 'Fifth Regiment' battalions under Juan Modesto and Mena.

The discrepancies in the account of what happened thereafter suggest that there was some confusion among the Republicans as to what their other troops were supposed to do. The objective appears to

Spanish Republican troops and Russian T-26 tanks at an assembly area in the Aravaca sector of Madrid.

* Soviet personnel likely to fall into enemy hands had pseudonyms and false passports of any nationality but Russian.

84

have been to break through to Illescas. Various republican units, with a total of upwards of 15 000 men, were in the area. The 13 000 under Uribarri and Burillo were certainly supposed to take part, according to Voronov – some of those under Colonel Puigdendolas as well, according to Spanish republican accounts. Be that as it may, Lister's battalions seem to have given up the advance at the twin villages of Torrejón de la Calzada and Torrejón de Velasco, six kilometres behind the tanks. At Seseña one of the tanks broke down. On the return of the others, the nationalist cavalry captured two by throwing on them what came to be known in World War II as 'Molotov cocktails'*.

The attack had failed. Over the next few days Varela not only regained the lost ground on his right flank, but advanced the whole 'front' forward of the minor road connecting the villages of Brunete, Villaviciosa, Móstoles, Fuenlabrada and Pinto. He was now fifteen kilometres from Madrid at the nearest point. He was through all but the last of the defence rings.

In connexion with these operations there was what the Republicans called 'heavy' bombing in Madrid, though in fact it was carried out by between six and nine aircraft at a time making two sorties a day, and on these dates directed at military targets, principally the airfields at Getafe and Cuatro Vientos, in an attempt to weaken the Russian squadrons. Nevertheless, on one of the raids of the 30th on Getafe bombs fell on a nearby school killing sixty children.

The raids on the airfields were indeed far from successful. On that very day in Burgos Franco agreed to accept from Germany a force of forty-eight bombers and a similar number of fighters totally under German control. This was to be the famous Condor Legion. However, they would not be operational till mid-November, too late to play a part in the next and crucial stage of the Battle for Madrid.

Publicly Franco and Mola expressed full confidence in the immediate future. Mola assured journalists that Madrid would fall because in the last stage the opponents of the 'Reds' in the capital would rise in support.* Privately they were extremely doubtful about the possibility of taking Madrid[3]. Mola's 'restricted' instructions of the 31st to his senior officers in the field re-echoed Franco's to him of the 9th: 'The international political situation and the attitude which the enemy has adopted these last few days' – a reference here to the attack of the 29th, the first sign of a serious determination to fight – 'together with the probability of immediate help on *a grand scale*' – that is much more than so far witnessed – 'obliges us to speed up the advance on Madrid.

---

* The original nationalist mixture was petrol and tar with a handgrenade tied to the bottle. To cooped-up crews the noise of the explosion could sound like a direct hit from a shell and the burning tar and petrol make it appear that the tank was on fire. If the crew jumped out, the tank was captured. These 9-ton T-26s and the later 12-ton TB-5s were Russian developments of the Vickers 'Cardens' and American 'Christies'. Neither the baby Fiat-Ansaldos nor the Maybach and Krupp PzWs Mks I and II which the Nationalists had just received were a match for the 45 mm (5-pounder) gun of the Russian and accordingly, towards equality of forces, the Nationalists had to acquire them from the Republicans in working order.

* Noel Monks in the *Daily Express* reported Mola as saying that he was advancing with *four* columns, and that he had a secret 'fifth column', the secret supporters of the Nationalists in the city. However, Mola had *eleven* columns: the five in the northern sector, and the six under Varela.

You will realize that the paralyzation of our operations, or even a delay could seriously prejudice our cause. . . .'[4]

He wanted daily intelligence reports at his headquarters in Avila on losses suffered during the previous twenty-four hours. The sooner he knew the sooner he could arrange for replacements. The pressure had to be kept up whatever the cost, and in the week that followed the strength of the six Varela columns was to drop at times to 6000 men.

The Republicans now had over 250 000 men under arms[5]: the Nationalists fewer than 180 000; the TOCE, after the mobilization of the 1934, 1933 and 1932 'classes', had something in the region of 80 000, of which 30–35 000 were deployed on the Madrid front, and another 5500 were quickly available reserves. Nevertheless it would appear to have been the view of General Pozas, who had replaced Asensio Torrado as GOC TOCE, of Asensio, whom Largo had retained on his staff in spite of communist opposition, and of Largo Caballero himself before the attack of October 29, that there should be a withdrawal from Madrid – this to enable the new Mixed Brigades, Spanish and International, to be fully trained in the use of the weapons received from the Soviet Union and elsewhere, and in the tactics required to make full use of the tank force to maximum effect, that is suddenly, and in full strength. The fifteen used in the battle were only one-quarter of the sixty which had already been landed, and none of the twenty armoured cars which had also reached the Soviet base at Archena in southeast Spain could be got ready for battle in the time available. What had happened here was reminiscent of Cambrai in World War I. The few tanks used had not demoralized the enemy. When next used they were no demoralizing surprise.

Largo's idea to withdraw from Madrid made good military sense. Madrid had ceased to have any strategic value for the Republicans. It was no longer the centre of their communications. Road, rail and telegraphic communication with Barcelona or the southern cities still in their hands was possible only via Valencia. That with Asturias, Santander and Vizcaya was possible only via Valencia and then either Barcelona and France or by sea. Valencia, therefore, was the centre for that part of Spain not lost to Franco, and the right place for government and for the conduct of the war.

The surrender of Madrid made good military sense in other ways. Madrid no longer meant anything in terms of the principle of mobility in the conduct of war. Holding on to it implied a dissipation of force. To the east there was a line of defence to satisfy the principle of economy of force – the River Tagus, already in part the dividing line between the two halves of Spain at war with each other. Beyond the river, due east of Madrid, was the rising ground of the Serranía de Cuenca; and in those days when aerial reconnaissance was still adolescent, the possession of the higher ground was important both in defence, and as the starting point of an offensive. A withdrawal to that line would have made possible the release of thousands of men from which a trained strike force could have been formed, a strike force without which the Republicans could not hope to regain the initiative and defeat their enemy.

Madrid would have been a Grecian gift. Had the Republicans handed Madrid to the enemy, they would have burdened the Nationalists to breaking point. Its administration alone would have absorbed manpower the Nationalists could ill afford at the time. They would have had to pour soldiers and security forces into it to control a population of which 40 per cent were hostile. It would have been they, and not the Republicans who would have been unable to keep men back for training and the formation of that substantial 'army of manoeuvre' with which they were eventually to win.

There were, however, not only military but political considerations, and the Government and its advisers had to consider the probable political consequences, internal and international, of the surrender of the capital.

Germany and Italy had made it known that they would recognize Franco as the ruler of Spain the moment that he took Madrid. But what effect would that have had on the war? It is a temptation to think that other nations of central and western Europe and Latin America would also have recognized Franco. That is doubtful. Certainly, to newspaper readers anywhere, the surrender of Madrid would have seemed a major victory for the Nationalists and the beginning of the end if not the end for the Republicans, but hardly so to the British Foreign Office or the Quai d'Orsay. Memories of the War of the Spanish Succession and the Peninsular War would have deterred France and Britain from the conclusion that the loss of Madrid meant the loss of the country. They would have required other evidence that the republican cause was irretrievably lost; and what France and Britain did in the 1930s carried much weight with the rest of the non-communist world, and at that time even in Moscow.]

What was the reaction which could have been expected within Spain? The areas in republican hands were Vizcaya, Asturias, Santander Province, Valencia, Murcia, eastern Andalucia and a part of New Castile. Their peoples were providing the greater part of the manpower of the republican army and were to do so in an increasing degree thereafter. To those not of Castile, Madrid meant little where it did not mean hateful overlordship. True enough, it was not only to falangists that 'the unity of Spain' was sacrosanct. It had been the ultra-monarchist Calvo Sotelo who had cried out against the process of granting autonomy to Catalonia; 'better a Red than a broken-up Spain'. The nineteenth-century history of *liberalismo* (a concept radically different from the usual lexicographic English equivalent 'liberalism') had been one of centralization of power in, and exaltation of, Madrid. One factor in the failure of socialism in Catalonia and among the true Basques (as opposed to the immigrant workers of Bilbao), had been the similar centralist attitude of the Socialist Party and UGT leaders until the late 1920s. Their support of the Catalan Statute in the Cortes had been purely tactical. Middle-class non-Catalan left-republican and moderate socialist leaders would certainly have felt deeply the loss of Madrid — very deeply; but they were intelligent men, unlikely to have considered the surrender of Madrid even the beginning of the end.

Largo was in fact to be given no choice. The Communist Party was determined on the defence of Madrid, influenced perhaps by such episodes in the history of the Russian Revolution as the sieges of Petrograd and Tsaritzyn. They popularized through loudspeakers in the streets of Madrid, a new rhythmic incantation, *nò pàsàràn* — they shall not pass, a slogan which was neither new nor communist in origin. The policy had the approval also of the anarchists who were now prepared to join Largo in government contrary to their principles though that was. On October 23 *Claridad*, the Madrid organ of the CNT, had announced the decision of the anarchist leaders that to join the Government was no surrender of principles: 'in order to win the war and save our people and the world [anarchism was] ready to collaborate with anyone in an instrument of leadership, whether that instrument calls itself a council or government'.

Such a concession had called for one from Largo. Back in September he had offered the anarchists one seat in the Cabinet. He now offered them four. They asked for five, but settled on the four, Justice, Commerce, Health and Industry, in a Cabinet expanded from thirteen to eighteen to accommodate the newcomers and a Basque Nationalist. The Cabinet, however, continued to be dominated as before by the advice given it by the open and crypto-communists in it, whose work was made even simpler by the expansion of the Cabinet, for whereas before they had had to work on the antagonisms between its socialist members they could now set these and the anarchists against each other. The composition of the new Cabinet was announced on November 4, the day after a second unsuccessful attempt by the republican forces and the Russian tank squadrons to break up Varela's columns.

An order signed by Pozas on November 2 gave as the objective of the new counter offensive 'the destruction of the enemy in the zone Pinto–Parla–Fuenlabrada–Arroyomolinos–Griñón–Torrejón'.[6] The Burillo columns (10 000) with Uribarri's (1800) were to proceed from across the River Jarama in the direction Valdemoro–Torrejón and cut the Madrid–Toledo road at Torrejón – a fifteen-kilometre penetration. Lister and his brigade and a column led by Buero (2250) were to advance down the Aranjuez road from the Cerro Rojo (the Red Hill, as the Cerro de los Angeles, the Hill of the Angels was now called) to Pinto, then turn westwards and aim for the Toledo Road. Tella's column would thus be surrounded. This time forty-eight Soviet tanks and nine armoured cars would be employed in the attack.

The tanks were organized as four squadrons, one under Paul Arman to support Lister, the other three directly under Krivoshein to spearhead the Burillo attack. Krivoshein kept one squadron in reserve and despatched one of the others to Valdemoro and Pinto, and the other, under a Spanish Captain Faurié Barrera, straight for Torrejón. He used the armoured cars to protect the left flank of the tanks. They took the road to Seseña.

Once again the infantry's movements were not co-ordinated with the tanks.* Some troops did reach Torrejón de Velasco but were driven back by a nationalist counter-attack. Two tanks were lost, victims of the new weapon prepared by Monasterio's cavalry. As Faurié's squadron passed through Valdemoro on their way back to base, Nationalists on the balconies of the houses again showered 'Molotov cocktails' on them.

The failure of this second attack further demoralized the republican forces. Over November 5 and 6 they fell back in a not very orderly

---

* Liddell-Hart's idea of concentrating armour and using it for long range strategic thrusts was quite unknown at the time to Krivoshein, or Krivoshein's superior officer, General Pavlov.

Nationalist cavalry in an unidentified village on the Madrid front, November 1936.

fashion. Castejón (Column 4) occupied Retamares, Asensio (Column 1) Cuatro Vientos and Campamento, Barrón (Column 2) Carabanchel Alto, and Tella (Column 5) Villaverde – the very outskirts of Madrid. The most forward troops were now a mere seven kilometres from the Puerta del Sol. Monasterio was in possession of the Cerro de los Angeles covering the right flank, and behind him there was a new 'Column 8'. Behind Barrón and Tella there was another new 'Column 6'. Behind Asensio, there was Delgado Serrano, and guarding the left flank at Brunete a third new column, number 7, under Bartomeu.

Varela had in all twenty-eight units 'of battalion type', twenty-four troops of guns (field, medium and anti-tank), fifteen armoured cars and about thirty tankettes and Pz W I and IIs[7]. The total strength of it all came to just over 12 000 men – one division: still hardly the army to take a city of a million inhabitants. To defend that city there were

Republican army Lt.-Col. Ricardo Burillo with communist militia leader Enrique Lister and staff officers.

(upper) General Varela
and (lower) Lt. Col. Yague
during the advance on
Madrid.

now 13 700 men on the west side of the River Manzanares, another
10 000 immediately behind the formations up front, and by the
Jarama possibly another 10 000 men, figures which in comparison
with earlier official returns suggest that there were heavy casualties in
the attacks of October 29 and November 3 and substantial desertions
thereafter. The Russian armoured cars, tanks and artillery were still in
the area, and at Vallecas, the XI International Brigade, under 'General Kleber', was ready for action.

At 1000 hours, November 6, General Varela issued his orders for the
following day. Operations on the morrow were to intended 'to occupy a
platform for the attack and assault on Madrid: to occupy and hold a
line to protect the left flank'.[8]

At 1500 hours Largo Caballero explained to Generals Pozas and
Miaja as GOCs TOCE and Madrid Front that government could no
longer be conducted from Madrid; he and his Cabinet were leaving
that evening for Valencia. He handed each an envelope not to be
opened till 0600 hours the following day.

They did not wait, and then discovered that the Prime Minister's
orders to them were in the wrong envelopes. Pozas was to set up
TOCE headquarters in Tarancón, eighty kilometres southeast of
Madrid, across the Tagus. It could be that a withdrawal from Madrid
might become necessary, in which case he would be informed of what
the new line should be. Miaja was to remain in Madrid and conduct its
defence with a junta of representatives of all the Popular Front parties.

Miaja chose as his chief of staff Lieutenant-Colonel Vicente Rojo,
ex-Chief Instructor in infantry tactics at the Infantry Academy, a man
much respected by army officers on both sides in the war, an intellectual, an organizer, a tireless worker, a man who by example and
work could galvanize even the indifferent and depressed. Miaja could
have chosen no better man; but Miaja had to accept also the presence
on his staff, advice and perhaps veto of the Soviet General Vladimir
Yefimovich Goriev[9].

Rojo believed in attack, Goriev in trenches and concrete. Miaja's
own record in the Riff was of cautious and stolid competence. He was
temperamentally the antithesis of his opponent Varela who had been
twice decorated with Spain's highest honour for valour in the face of
the enemy. Miaja's chief weakness was his vanity. The Communist
Party decided to turn him into a hero figure, although in Malinovsky's
opinion he was 'the very model of military atrophy'.[10]

The task before Miaja, Rojo and Goriev on the evening of November
6 was far less difficult than the communist-inspired propaganda on
'fascist hordes' suggested. Their forces outnumbered the attackers by
three to one, and they had plenty of reserves available within half a
day's march away. The attackers had ahead of them undulating
ground to traverse down to the Manzanares, land with shrubs and
trees better suited to defence than to attackers in a hurry. The Manzanares might be 'a mere apprentice of a river', but it was an obstacle,
and the ground rose sharply from it on the Madrid side. Mere handfuls
of troops had always been able to hold up companies and even battalions in street fighting. Twelve thousand men, of whom not more
than half could be committed simultaneously to an assault without
grave risk of disaster, were no formidable mass. There were no
'hordes': there was not even an army. In the words of the then Major

Barroso whom Franco was about to appoint Chief of Operations at his GHQ, *'ibamos en dedo de guante'* – loosely 'we were a mere finger of an army'. Madrid was being attacked because Franco had decided on it. He had so decided because the supporters of the insurgents were mostly Castilians to whom Madrid did mean Spain, Navarrese who dreamt not only of the restoration to their kingdom of its ancient liberties, but also of the installation of the Carlist pretender to the throne of Spain, and others who still attributed to Madrid the strategic importance it had had in July, but had since lost.

Barroso remonstrated with Franco: 'it can't be done. We haven't the strength. It's a hopeless task.' Franco replied: 'Let Varela try it. He's always been "lucky". The capture of Madrid is psychologically important.'[11]

⌐The object of war is more properly defined as 'the destruction of the enemy's will to fight' than as 'the destruction of the enemy'. In this way was Franco right to attempt to take Madrid, and the communists to insist on its defence: the capture of Madrid would have raised the morale of the Nationalists to the point at which mathematical calculations are largely meaningless. To the one side, therefore, the capture, to the other, the successful defence, was important – though to neither vital.⌐

10 The Assault

Varela planned 'to secure a line to protect the left flank', and 'to occupy a platform for the attack and assault on Madrid' in this manner (Map 4):

Barrón (Column 2) was to move from Carabanchel Alto to Carabanchel Bajo, and forward in the direction of the Segovia Bridge.

Tella (Column 5) was to advance up the Toledo road towards the Toledo Bridge and secure the right flank.

Columns 2 and 5 were to give the enemy the impression that they were the spearhead of the attack.

Castejón (Column 4) was to proceed NNE from Retamares into the Casa de Campo, past its high point Garabitas; cross the Manzanares by the Franceses Bridge; and establish itself astride the river, with HQ at Km 3 on the Madrid–Irún railway. Its object: protection of the left flank.

Asensio (Column 1) was to come up behind Castejón, cross the river and occupy the 500 × 500 metres area of streets and buildings bound by the Calles de Moret, la Princesa, Urquijo and the Paseo Rosales.

Delgado Serrano (Column 3), advancing behind Asensio was to go forward of Asensio, and occupy the streets and houses bound by Urquijo, Princesa, Plaza de España and Rosales and the mound of the Montaña Barracks.

Miaja's orders (through Rojo) to his troops were: 'to hold the present positions at all costs, to contain and break the enemy'. He instructed the International Brigade under Kleber to stand by at Vallecas for a possible attack on the enemy's left flank and the reoccupation of the 'Red Hill' (Cerro de los Angeles). Lister's Mixed Brigade and the Presidential Guard were to stand by at the Toledo Bridge, but the 3 Mixed Brigade under José Galán was to move over to Pozuelo, to strengthen the republican right flank.[1]

Rojo had obviously prepared for the three possibilities: that the Nationalists might attack frontally across the Segovia and Toledo Bridges: that they might have in mind the easier approach through Aravaca right round the northern perimeter and across to the Corunna roadbridge, and then come down from north of the University City: or thirdly, go right round the southern perimeter, cross the Manzanares by Villaverde, and come up to Madrid by Vallecas and Vicálvaro. If the Toledo and Segovia bridges proved, as seemed most likely to Rojo, to be the main objectives, then he would launch the Mixed and International Brigades on the flanks and seek to envelop the attackers.

All three possibilities had indeed been studied by the Nationalists. Varela had favoured the northern approach[2], and Yagüe, who was directly in command over Castejón and Asensio, had favoured the

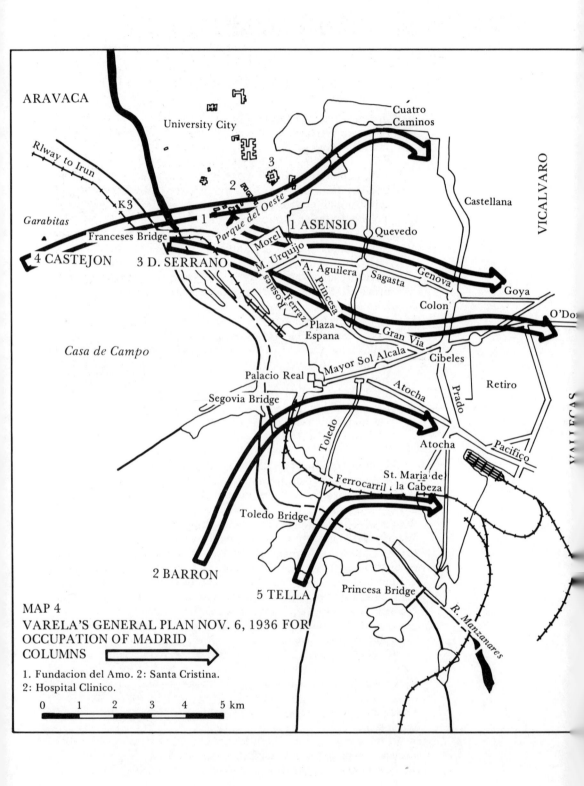

ARAVACA

University City

Cuatro
Caminos

VICALVARO

Rlway to Irun

Castellana

K 3

Garabitas

Parque del Oeste

3

2

1

1 ASENSIO

Quevedo

Franceses Bridge

Morel

4 CASTEJON

3 D. SERRANO

M. Urquijo

A. Aguilera

Sagasta

Genova

Goya

Rosales

Ferraz

Princesa

Colon

O'Do

Casa de Campo

Plaza
Espana

Gran Via

Cibeles

Retiro

Mayor Sol Alcala

Palacio Real

Atocha

VALLECAS

Segovia Bridge

Prado

Pacifico

Toledo

Atocha

St. Maria de
la Cabeza

Ferrocarril

Toledo Bridge

2 BARRON

5 TELLA

Princesa Bridge

R. Manzanares

MAP 4
VARELA'S GENERAL PLAN NOV. 6, 1936 FOR
OCCUPATION OF MADRID
COLUMNS

1. Fundacion del Amo. 2: Santa Cristina.
2: Hospital Clinico.

0   1   2   3   4   5 km

Troops of one of the International Brigades; in the foreground are Soviet-made machine guns.

southern. Franco had ruled out both on the grounds that in either case if anything went wrong the assault force could find itself surrounded. The Vallecas approach had the added disadvantage that Vallecas was such a crowded working-class district. Yagüe and Varela both opposed the approach through the Casa de Campo because of its physical characteristics: there was a wall all round it; the lie of the ground with its irregularities and its shrub and stunted vegetation provided excellent cover for troops in defence and were a hindrance in attack.

As Castejón approached the Casa de Campo the 3 Mixed Brigade, headed by part of the Soviet tank force, bore down behind him from Pozuelo. Column 5 had to turn to repel the threat. Castejón was wounded and Bartomeu took over command. He halted the republican brigade and the tanks, but the day ended with Column 5 almost as far from the river as it had been at dawn. Columns 1 and 3 therefore could not be brought into the battle as intended.

Barrón and Tella each moved forward as planned, but they had to cut through a trench and pill-box system, and as they got into the built-up and cemetery areas on the west bank of the Manzanares, they met the most steadfast resistance they had ever encountered: 'ferocious struggles in which the principal arms were the bayonet and handgrenade: street by street, house by house, room by room, not always sure whether enemy or friend was being killed'[3] – and at nightfall neither Barrón nor Tella were anywhere near either the Segovia or Toledo bridges.

Nowhere, therefore, had the Nationalists got as far as they had hoped, and their casualties were such that Bartomeu's original command, Column 7, had to be disbanded to provide replacements for the casualties suffered by the others.

The five forward columns, Castejón (hereafter Bartomeu), Asensio, Delgado Serrano, Barrón and Tella, were to renew the attack on November 8, but a substantial surprise awaited the attackers. The Republicans had found a copy of Varela's plan of attack on the body of a tankette officer killed on the northern front[4]. They therefore knew the direction of the main thrust, and accordingly the International Brigade was instructed to move from Vicálvaro right across the city to its northern end, then cross the river to form part of a large concentration of miscellaneous units under the Spaniards Enciso and Clairac. Their task was the protection of the Franceses and railway bridges, which, according to the captured plan, Varela's men were due to cross. José Galán's 3 Mixed Brigade took up positions further west, and still further west so did Barceló's large column with the Soviet tank squadron under Paul Arman.

With other new troops including the newly arrived half of the 4 Mixed Brigade, Rojo reinforced the troops already in the Casa de

A republican artillery observation post in the Guadarramas.

Campo. The International Brigade was put under the command of Miaja, but support from 'Douglas's' air force and from Krivoshein's tank force had to be asked for, if required, through the Russians at his headquarters, the senior among them at that moment being General 'Grigorovich' Stern, more properly Grygorij Mikhailovich Shtern.

The Soviet airforce dropped leaflets calling on the population to resist the 'fascist hordes' who were 'going to slaughter half the population'. Radio Madrid broadcast the same message constantly, and called on the inhabitants to build barricades, which, had they been built, would have been as much a hindrance to the defenders as the attackers. The whole population was declared 'mobilized' and thereafter 120 000 rations were drawn daily for 'the defenders', though there is little evidence that more than 40 000 had any real claim to them. Loudspeakers in the streets diffused endless impassioned harangues by Dolores Ibarruri. She called upon the women to send their menfolk 'to the front', and themselves to prepare boiling oil to pour upon the attackers. A 'battalion' of militiawomen took up positions at the Segovia bridge.

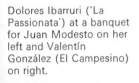

Dolores Ibarruri ('La Passionata') at a banquet for Juan Modesto on her left and Valentín González (El Campesino) on right.

The people of Madrid were not only 'to fight to the end' but 'to search out and destroy the enemy in their midst'[5]; and the Communist–Socialist Youth did so mercilessly. The Russian Chief Commissar, 'Miguel Martinez', fearing that the good name of the Spanish

Soldiers of the XIV International Brigade in the Madrid sierras.

Republic might once again be tarnished, sent out the political prisoners in the Cárcel Modelo in the direction of Alcalá de Henares. They did not get very far. Their guards killed them a short distance outside Madrid. Some tens of thousands left the city by the same route (which today leads to the airport of Barajas) but the bulk of the population freely, or because they had no real choice, remained.

Those who were of the left were heartened at the sight of the Soviet aircraft flying overhead; but what really raised their morale was the excellent bearing of the well trained and equipped XI International Brigade, as it marched splendidly through the Calle de Alcalá and the Gran Viá that evening. As it did so the crowds cheered *'vivan los rusos!'* – which, of course, they were not: but it made a change from the constant *'no pasarán!'*

At dawn November 8 Barrón and Tella renewed their drive towards the Toledo and Segovia bridges. They again came up against a determined defence in the southern outer suburbs. In this hand-to-hand fighting in narrow streets and houses the superior understanding of infantry tactics among the legionaries counted for little. Conscript, militiaman and legionary were equally brave and determined. As Bartomeu moved forward over on the left with Delgado Serrano behind, the genuiness of the captured plan was proved, and accordingly Rojo ordered Barceló to work his way towards the rear of the Nationalists and Clairac and Galán to support Barceló; some members of the International Brigade appear to have accompanied Clairac and Galán. Delgado put Barceló's forward troops to flight. Bartomeu's vanguard got as far as the railway line, but then came under heavy fire from the Internationals and from other battalions rushed to the area. Once again Yagüe's net gains were negligible.

On the 9th the battle developed to a similar pattern, but with a detachment of Nationalists skirting the Casa de Campo and reaching the Franceses bridge which they could not hold, and the guns of Arman's tanks providing support for the Republican flank attack of the day.

The battle continued into the 10th when, according to Kleber, it was his Internationals who forced the nationalist columns back. Certainly Yagüe tried to battle his way northwards instead of westwards, but it was Galán's Mixed Brigade and the troops under Enciso which held him at bay. Bartomeu and Delgado Serrano went back to their points of departure.

On the 11th Yagüe used his three columns, Bartomeu, Asensio, Delgado Serrano in parallel instead of sequence. They cleared much of the Casa de Campo on that and the following days; nevertheless the 11th and 12th were primarily days of artillery duels, and of both sides reforming after the heavy casualties of the previous days. Miaja's forward troops had diminished to 22 500 men; the International Brigade was down from 2500 to 1600. Varela's five columns were down to 6000.

From November 8 it had become clearer each day that the Republicans were acquiring both artillery and air superiority. Under the direction of the Soviet Colonel Voronov the forty-four heavy, medium and field pieces at their disposal, though positioned scattered in Madrid (Cuatro Caminos, Atocha, Retiro), had been linked to a single observation and overall command post – the top of Madrid's one skyscraper, the Telephone Exchange (*La Telefónica*). The whole battlefield could be observed with ease from it, and it was to become the target for both nationalist guns and aircraft, but too small a target and too strong a building for the accuracy of either at that time, and in

International Brigadiers assembling prior to an attack.

Republican soldiers
resting during a march.

consequence travel along the Gran Via became dangerous. Yet civilians continued to use it. The cafes remained open.

At the end of October Mola's allotment to the Madrid front of the aircraft at his disposal had been: twelve Ju 52s crewed by Spaniards, and six crewed by Germans; six SM 81s with mixed Italian and Spanish crews; ten RO 37 army co-operation and eighteen Fiat CR 32 fighters piloted by Spaniards or Italians. On November 3 a squadron of Russian-piloted Polikarpov I-16 monoplanes with retractable undercarriages made its appearance, and shooting down five nationalist aircraft without loss to themselves in a brief encounter acquired a well merited reputation as being technically far superior to anything on the nationalist side. That success was followed by others daily. On November 8 Mola despatched another nine Fiats and twelve Heinkel He 51s to the front – the Heinkels for want of anything else, for they were even less capable of matching the I-16s than the I-15s encountered earlier. The idea appears to have been that though one to one even the Fiats were inferior to the Russians in quantity the nationalist fighters could provide some cover for the bombing missions for which Varela made constant demands in support of his ground operations. On the 11th the Italian Colonel Bonomi instructed his fighter pilots that they were not to sortie other than in formations with a minimum of fifteen aircraft.

Notwithstanding the increasing artillery and air superiority, and the arrival of yet more fresh troops which enabled the Republicans to rest some of the men who had been in action daily for so many days, Miaja prepared on November 11 a contingency plan should the Nationalists break through into the city. He divided it into nine districts and allocated units to each for its defence 'street by street and house by house'. Varela, for his part, had issued orders on November 6 with the same contingency in mind, detailing the routes that his forward columns were to take through Madrid. Neither was the one an act of pessimism nor the other of optimism, but both of good generalship. Varela hoped for, but could not expect, success: Miaja had

The Polikarpov I-16 'Mosca' fighter supplied to the Republicans by Russia proved a formidable opponent for the older and slower Nationalist biplanes.

rightly to be prepared for the possibility, however remote, that in spite of his superiority in men and weapons, the enemy might break through. Rightly there was hope on both sides, but there was also realism. The fact that Mola, back at Avila, also had six teams for Courts Martial ready for the trial and execution of *los responsables*, which both sides in the war thought necessary and just, and that he also had supplies of food and clothing of which he thought the population would be in need loaded on trucks, caught the attention of reporters, but it would have been remiss of Mola not to be prepared.

Varela made up a new Column 6 from what remained of the old sixth and the seventh after he had reinforced his depleted front five. He put the new column under the command of Siro Alonso. Miaja was reinforced by the rest of the 4 Mixed Brigade and other Spanish units, and by an incomplete International Brigade (the XII, with German, Italian and French–Belgian battalions) under the Hungarian Mata Zalka. Buenaventura Durruti, the legendary anarchist fighter, also arrived from Catalonia with 2000 men who acknowledged his leadership.

Rojo persuaded Miaja to attempt a counter offensive on November 13. Barceló was to cut south well to the rear of the nationalist front. José Galán, Kleber and Enciso were to head for Cuatro Vientos and Campamento on the Badajoz road. Durruti was to crash through the Casa de Campo also towards Campamento, flanked by Francisco Galán's column. The troops facing Alonso, Barrón and Tella were to stand their ground, but Lister's and the XII International Brigade were to take Cerro de los Angeles and cut the Toledo road. Arman was to support the right flank of the attack. Two squadrons under Krivoshein were to enter into the battle on the left. TOCE troops under General Pozas were then to join in surrounding the whole of Varela's army.

It was an ambitious plan involving 50 000 and perhaps more[6]. In concept it was an adumbration of the Soviet encirclement of von

Paulus at Stalingrad. Largo Caballero came up to Pozas' TOCE GHQ from Valencia to watch the battle.

As planned, there was intense bombardment from land and air beginning at 0800 hours. It was followed by aerial machine-gunning. The ground attack was timed for 0900 hours. At that very time Bartomeu, Asensio, and Delgado Serrano were also on the move forward. To their left the line held against the republican attack. The Nationalists took Mount Garabitas and reached the bank of the Manzanares along a 400-metre front. On the republican left a company of Krivoshein's tanks headed for the Cerro de los Angeles together with the XII International Brigade. Though, according to Krivoshein, his tanks 'surrounded it and fired on it'[7], and though it was only lightly held by Monasterio's cavalry column, yet the brigade failed to take it. Koltsov, *Pravda*'s correspondent, wrote in his diary: 'their nerve failed when they came under fire from the enemy, and they stuck to the wrinkles of the ground'[8]. Encomiasts of the brigade excuse its lamentable performance by alleging that they had just marched fourteen kilometres before the battle. That was not so; they had spent at least one night a mere two to six kilometres away from their objective, though it may well be that owing to inefficient organization they had passed it cold and hungry. General Batov, Soviet adviser to Lister, refers to 'defects in our improvised organization'[9]. At the other end of the line the XI had done little better. By nightfall it was back to its point of departure.

November 13 which was to have been the dawn of victory for the Republicans thus proved to be, as Koltsov said, 'a day of disillusion and bitterness'. It would be wrong to attribute the failure of this offensive to the poor performance of the foreigners. They constituted no more than 15 per cent of the total numbers involved on the republican side. It would be equally absurd to attribute the nationalist success to 'Moors, Germans and Italians'. In this particular stage of the battle for Madrid the Moroccans in Franco's forces were down to below 20 per cent of those taking part. There were at most twenty Italian pilots, and no part of the German Condor Legion, just landed in Spain, was operational till two days later, when they received the rude shock that their fighter aircraft were not good enough.

The plan was sound. The Republicans had air and artillery superiority and vastly superior numbers. They were better equipped than their opponents. With the exception of Lister, their brigade and column commanders were, like their enemy, professional Spanish army officers. The men had all had conscript service. A few had been legionaries in their time. The nationalist legionaries and mercenaries (for that is what the Moroccans were in the pre-war Spanish African Army, as the Gurkhas in the British Indian Army) had had no more, and indeed many much less, experience of war than most of the members of the International Brigades. The factors which gave victory and defeat must therefore be looked for elsewhere, and perhaps they were these: firstly, on this day the Nationalists did have more professional officers at the levels that count in battle once it has been joined, that is, at company and platoon level; and, secondly, the spirit of revolutionary indiscipline acquired in the halcyon militia days by so many in the republican Peoples' Army had not as yet been totally eradicated, even in those battalions which the 'Fifth Regiment' claimed as its own: but the Republicans were learning fast.

Both sides rested on November 14. For the 15th Miaja planned a new attack on Varela's left flank, with Durruti, the XI International Brigade and all the other troops which had taken part in the unsuccessful counter-offensive in that Franceses bridge sector. This attack was timed to begin at 1230 hours. For that day Varela decided on a last desperate attempt at crossing the Manzanares by that very bridge (Map 5). He pulled out Barrón from the centre. He needed him as reserve behind Asensio and Delgado Serrano who were to lead the approach. He gave each column five or six PzW Mk Is and a 65 mm battery. Even so, the total strength of the force was no more than 3000. Varela asked Mola for as much air support as possible. If they got across the river Asensio's men were to occupy given buildings in the University City while Delgado Serrano's were to take the Cárcel Modelo and adjoining infantry barracks. The attack was timed to begin at first light (0800 hours), and thus outdated Miaja's attack before ever it began.

For the initial stage all the nationalist tanks were concentrated forward, and the infantry followed closely behind. The advance to the edge of the Casa de Campo was difficult against the number and fire power of the defenders. Two breaches were made in the scrubland's perimeter wall for the tanks and infantry to go through. There remained now little more than a hundred metres to the river bank and bridge; but it was a channel without cover, extremely well protected by troops on both banks, and deployed in the university buildings on the further bank where the ground rises sixty metres very steeply from the river. Three times nationalist infantry tried to reach the parapet of the bridge, and each time they were mown down. The tanks got bogged down on the banks. At noon the bridge was blown up by the defenders.

A less determined man than Varela might thereupon have allowed Asensio to stay put. Asensio himself wanted to go on: at 1600 hours, with barely an hour of good light left, he ordered what was left of one of his tabores to rush *en masse* to the river bank and wade across. The anarchists on the east bank fled. The Moroccans pursued them up the steep bank. By nightfall Asensio had a tenuous hold of the University playing fields and School of Architecture. Overnight he transported the rest of his column across by making use of a rapidly constructed pontoon bridge. Miaja ordered an immediate counter-attack. Six thousand men including Durruti's and the XI International Brigade were to drive back or destroy the 800 Nationalists in the University City on the 16th. At the end of the day Asensio's men had occupied two more buildings, one of them the Casa de Velázquez where a company of the Polish Battalion of the International Brigade resisted heroically to the last man. The same units were ordered to try again on the 17th, but it was on the 17th that Delgado Serrano and Barrón got across the river.

With all three columns in the University City, the Nationalists did their best to widen the area in their possession. There was a flash of hope on the 17th, that the little corner of Madrid which they had taken would prove to be the 'platform for the capture of Madrid' of which Varela had written in his orders for the assault on the 15th. Some anarchists in the Parque del Oeste were put to flight by a couple of tanks and infantry. The tanks went in pursuit down the Paseo de Rosales and Calle de la Princesa towards the Plaza de España with thirty infantrymen running behind. The infantry were halted by a company of the 4 Mixed Brigade and a unit of Asaltos, and the tanks had to retreat rapidly.

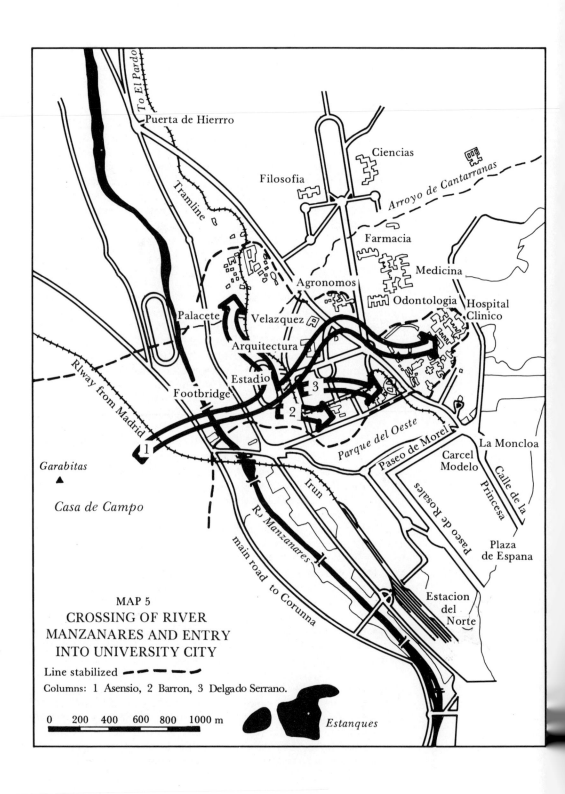

To El Pardo

Puerta de Hierrro

Tramline

Filosofia

Ciencias

Arroyo de Cantarranas

Farmacia

Agronomos

Medicina

Odontologia

Hospital Clinico

Palacete

Velazquez

Arquitectura

Estadio

Footbridge

Rlway from Madrid

3

2

1

Parque del Oeste

Paseo de Morel

La Moncloa

Carcel Modelo

Paseo de Rosales

Calle de la Princesa

Garabitas

▲

Casa de Campo

Irun

R) Manzanares

main road to Corunna

Plaza de Espana

Estacion del Norte

MAP 5
CROSSING OF RIVER
MANZANARES AND ENTRY
INTO UNIVERSITY CITY

Line stabilized   – – – –

Columns: 1 Asensio, 2 Barron, 3 Delgado Serrano.

0   200   400   600   800   1000 m

Estanques

The University City Front during the winter of 1936-7. This photograph shows the view from the Republican positions in the Faculty of Medicine.

The combined strength of the three columns was now under 2000 men. There were 11 800 Republicans and allies in the immediate vicinity of the one square kilometre of Madrid in Nationalist hands. After two days of hard fighting Asensio's men captured the little Palace of Moncloa and after three the large Hospital Clínico. Barrón and Delgado Serrano made an attempt on the 22nd to cross the Parque del Oeste in order to capture the Model Prison and adjoining infantry barracks: but they lacked the strength to do it.

There were similarly republican attacks on the 18th, 19th and 20th but they failed to dislodge the Nationalists from their little bridgehead. Durruti was killed on the 19th in circumstances which suggest that one of his own men assassinated him. On the 21st an attempt to cut the links between the bridgehead and the forces on the other side also failed. It was obvious that stalemate had been reached.

Every day since the 7th the aircraft of each side had bombed the other's positions. From the 15th onwards they both tried to pinpoint the buildings in the University City occupied by their enemies. No one can say whether the republican bombs fell always on nationalist-occupied buildings, or vice versa, but only that all the great buildings which had been the pride of Alfonso XIII were very severely damaged, and what destruction aircraft bombardment did not complete, artillery fire did.

Republican artillery superiority increased even more from November 15 as extra guns arrived, but it was otherwise in the air. The

German Condor Legion entered the Madrid theatre. Up to then bombing had been limited to essentially military targets in Madrid, and the raids had been carried out by between one and eight raiders. There now followed, at the demand of the Germans, but with the consent of Franco[10], a series of air raids with up to three squadrons of Junkers 52s and one of SM81s – that is up to thirty-six aircraft – accompanied by every fighter available (forty-eight He 51s and twenty-seven CR 32s). The object was the demoralization of the civilian population. When the air raids proved somewhat costly in terms of aircraft, especially He 51s, the Condor Legion turned to night attacks with incendiaries.

During the days and nights of the period November 14–23 244 civilians were killed and 875 injured, and 303 buildings were damaged[11]. Enthusiastic or too credulous journalists at the time gave much higher figures and thereby perhaps encouraged the Germans into the belief

A house in the Moncloa district of Madrid on the University City front damaged by artillery fire.

The Plaza de la Moncloa on the University City Front during the winter of 1936-7.

Houses overlooking the Casa de Campo in November 1936.

Madrid front, Cuesta de la Perdices. The buildings on the left were in the possession of the Republicans and the 'Casa Camorra' restaurant on the right was in Nationalist hands. This photograph was taken from a Republican pillbox.

that wars could be won by the bombardment of cities. In fact the one thing that those air raids did not do was achieve their purpose: the population was not demoralized. Quite the contrary. Many a person unmoved by all the republican and communist propaganda on what the Nationalists would do if ever they captured Madrid began to wonder whether there was not some truth, after all, in that propaganda.

On November 23, Franco met his Generals Mola and Varela at Leganés, from which up to one month previously they could have taken a tram all the way to the Puerta del Sol. Franco decided that there were to be no further attempts at the capture of Madrid by frontal assault. He gave three reasons:

1 the lack of adequate means;
2 the presence of 'foreign perfectly organized units';
3 the Nationalists' poor tactical situation[12].

The gamble which Franco had taken had not succeeded. General Varela had not been as 'lucky' as Franco, who had known him in Africa, had hoped he might be.

A Heinkel He 51 of the Legion Condor photographed in November, 1936, shortly after the German forces had commenced operations over Spain.

11 The Siege

The assault had failed.

According to the Comintern-inspired propaganda of the time, their International Brigades had saved Madrid. According to republican propaganda, the capital had been saved by 'the people of Madrid' showing heroism and steadfastness against an enemy vastly superior in numbers and equipment.

As we have seen, the International Brigades had played an important but not a decisive role. In both quantity and quality the weapons available to the defence had been superior to those of the attackers. Though 85 per cent of the defenders had been Spaniards only 25 per cent were of the city or province of Madrid.

The facts were well known to Miaja's Chief of Staff, Colonel Rojo, as documents which he drafted and signed at the time reveal, though in his memoirs he was to tell a different story[1]. He was too professional a military man to be satisfied with the fact that it had taken 40 000 to hold 10 000. On that basis the Republicans were doomed to defeat. If they suffered no further loss of territory, they could now be reckoned to have no greater sources of manpower than the Nationalists. However, while 4:1 had been the overall ratio of defenders to attackers, wherever the new Mixed Brigades, Spanish or International, had faced Varela's columns, the ratio for successful defence had been 2:1 and even 1:1.

There had been complaints of shortage of ammunition, yet overall there was ammunition in plenty. The Republicans were now armed with rifles and machine guns of four, and artillery of nine, different calibres*. That would have been problem enough to any army, but here it was aggravated manifold by a heritage from the early days when militiamen had grabbed whatever weapons they had seized or prevailed upon the Ministry to give them. All four small arms calibres could be found within a company and even platoon and as many as three in a troop of four guns. The solution was obvious. Weapons would have to be standardized at battalion if not higher level.

Serious mistakes had arisen in the economic deployment by GHQ of forces. The root cause was the surviving variety in the organization of units and commands. *Agrupación* and *columna* could mean anything. The infantry element of a columna alone varied from 600 ('columna Fernandez Cavada') to 4500 ('columna Barceló'). The various decrees on the organization of the Peoples' Army into mixed brigades had still to be fully implemented, and in Rojo's opinion their full implementation was urgently necessary.

* small arms: 7.00, 7.62, 7.92, 8.03 mm
  guns: 20, 37, 70, 75, 77, 105, 114, 125 and 155 mm

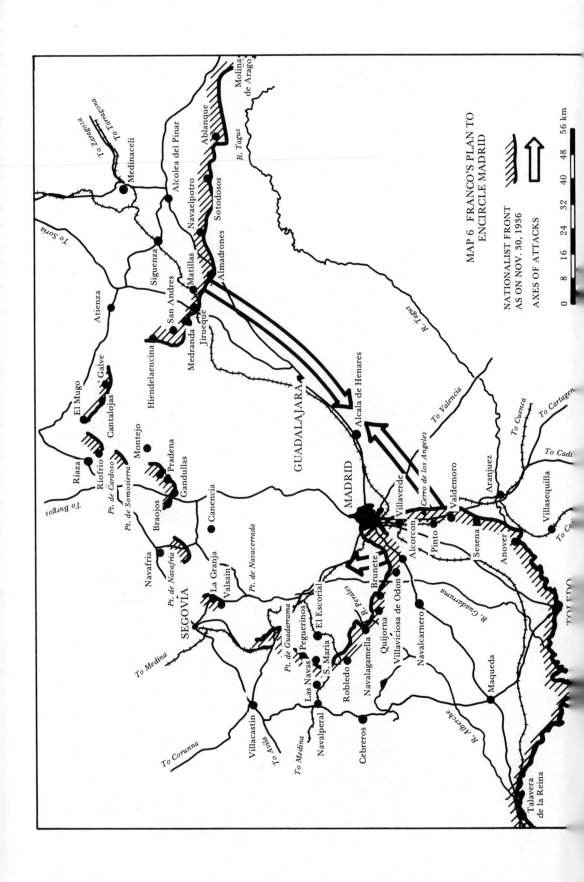

MAP 6 FRANCO'S PLAN TO
ENCIRCLE MADRID

NATIONALIST FRONT
AS ON NOV. 30, 1936

AXES OF ATTACKS

0   8   16   24   32   40   48   56 km

On November 26 Rojo submitted to Miaja, and on November 27 Miaja and 'friend' Goriev accepted a plan to reorganize the various columns into standard mixed brigades, and to divide the whole of the sinuous Madrid front into four sectors only, each under the command of a single man. Kleber was given the biggest and most important – the north side of the University City and the line westwards from there to the mountains. Kleber accordingly handed over command of his brigade to the German Hans Kahle. The two middle westward-looking sectors went to the professional Spanish army Colonels Alvarez Coque and Mena, and the southern to Lister. The assumption of commands took place straight away. The conversion of 'columns' into brigades took some weeks, and so did the rationalization of their weapons; but it was done.

Over the previous three months the Nationalists had also been building up their new army, much more traditional than the new republican in organization and discipline, but no different in its human material – that is to say, a few thousand Moroccan mercenaries apart, it was of Spaniards, conscript, volunteer and militia. The political militia on the nationalist side had been much less numerous than on the republican at the outbreak of the war, and Franco, once chosen Generalissimo, had been ruthless with both Falange and Requete. He had given them no choice but to accept full military discipline, and incorporation in formations mostly no larger than companies, into proper army battalions. Franco had had to be convinced of their fighting qualities, and was still loth to have Falange companies in important operational positions. Indeed, the only men in whose fighting quality he had had full trust till now, were those of his old regiment the Legion and the ageing Moroccan veterans of the Riff War: but the supply of those was nigh exhausted.

For his new strategy Franco was going to require very much larger forces than those he had used in the attempt to take Madrid by storm, though he would still choose the ex-Africa battalions for his *fuerza de maniobra* (strike force) in preference to others. Since his early days in the army he had had doubts gained from experience in Africa about the efficacy in battle of men with no other training than the superficial one given them during their service as conscripts. The time was approaching for the deployment of all his forces, on the major war pattern of divisions, and not as up till now the colonial war system of 'columns'. To co-ordinate what he had in mind for the Madrid front he carried out a reorganization of his higher commands. All troops on that front and its rear areas were grouped under the title of a division and placed under the command of General Orgaz. The division was subdivided into three brigades, with Varela as commander of the 1 Brigade operating in the immediate vicinity of Madrid. Brigades were still to operate divided into 'columns', but only as a short-term measure.

Franco's new strategy for the capture of Madrid was its encirclement; but before anything so ambitious could be attempted, before even the troops could be concentrated for it, there was one pressing need. Not just the units in the University across the river but all those in the Casa de Campo were in a precarious position. A straightening of the front was desirable to include at least Pozuelo and Humera (Map 7A). Varela prepared two infantry columns under Bar-

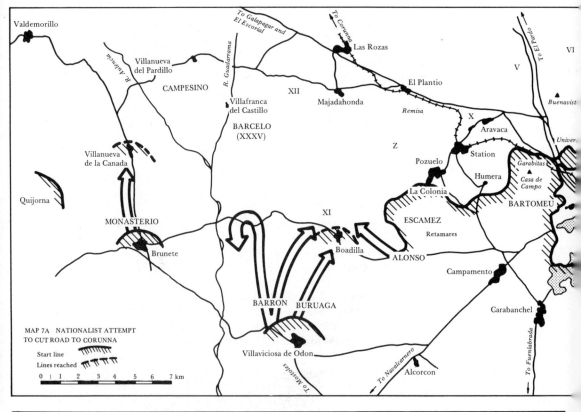

MAP 7A NATIONALIST ATTEMPT
TO CUT ROAD TO CORUNNA

Start line
Lines reached

0 1 2 3 4 5 6 7 km

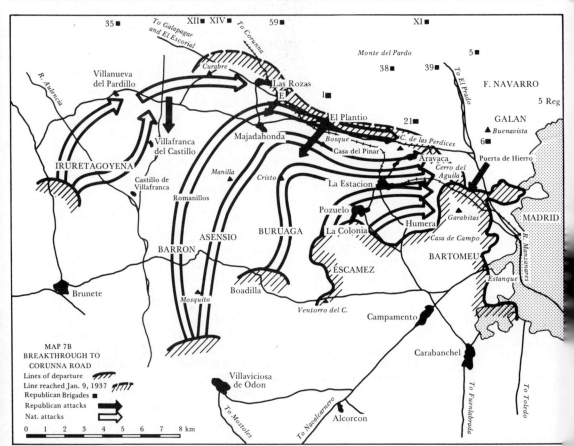

MAP 7B
BREAKTHROUGH TO
CORUNNA ROAD
Lines of departure
Line reached Jan. 9, 1937
Republican Brigades ■
Republican attacks
Nat. attacks

0 1 2 3 4 5 6 7 8 km

tomeu and Siro Alonso, and a third of cavalry under Gavilán, 7000 men in all, and launched them northwards from points southwest of the Casa de Campo. That was on November 29, the very day Miaja had ordered Kleber to attack the Nationalists in the scrubland. After six days of intensive fighting with such casualties that the republican 3 Mixed Brigade had to be withdrawn, both sides had to stop. The nationalist line was only slightly improved, and Pozuelo–Humera still in republican hands: further proof that in brigades the Republicans in defence could better match the Nationalists in attack. The manpower ratio had been only 2:1 in favour of the Republicans.

On December 7 Franco ordered a more ambitious project. Varela was to surge forward 'in a sudden and surprise attack' along the whole of the northern sector of the Madrid front. The main thrust was to come from Brunete (Map 7B). The final objective was the advance of the front to points running east–west from Buenavista, a height (665 m) three kilometres north of the University to the mountains. Such a line, north of the Corunna road, would deny the enemy a dangerous access route to the rear of the Nationalists.

The operation was timed for December 13. The explosion on the 11th of a mine right under the Hospital Clínico causing the death of thirty-nine Moroccans in the building was a warning that time was not on the side of the Nationalists. Early in the war 800 Asturians had rushed to the defence of Madrid, and they were professionals in underground workings. December 13, however, proved to be a day of thick fog. A start was made on the afternoon of the next day when the fog lifted slightly, but visibility was again zero on the 15th. On the 16th 10 000 Nationalists attacked about the same number of Republicans. Those starting at Villaviciosa reached Boadilla by nightfall though Kleber threw into the battle his reserves, which included the XI and XII International Brigades, and asked for Soviet tank support. It was a bloody battle. Fog stopped its renewal until the 19th, by which time the Nationalists had lost totally the element of surprise, and were again outnumbered two to one. Varela withdrew keeping, however, Boadilla and Villaviciosa. He intended to renew the attack after Christmas, but was wounded on that day.[2]

Just as the Nationalists had looked for a weak spot near but not at Madrid, so Pozas now planned an offensive aimed at Sigüenza to start from his positions twenty kilometres beyond Brihuega and fifty from Guadalajara (Map 10A). The Nationalists had been inching their way down towards Guadalajara over the previous three months. Pozas reckoned rightly that a mere 3500 Nationalists were holding thirty-five kilometres of front either side of Brihuega. On January 1 he launched 7000 Republicans against them, including three battalions from the International Brigades, with Soviet tanks in support. The results were unrewarding. A two-to-one ratio of republican attackers to nationalist defenders was still not good enough. Seven days later the Internationals and tanks were switched back to the Madrid front where their presence was urgently required.

Under orders from Franco, given on December 19, Orgaz had renewed the offensive on the Corunna road on January 3, with 12 000 men in three infantry and one cavalry columns. The Republicans had 20 300 men in the area[3]. The nationalist columns differed from those of the earlier attempt not only in numbers, but also in the greater ratio

within them of ex-Africa infantry units (Legion and Moroccan) to Spanish, and of tanks (about forty) and artillery to infantry. Now whereas in the earlier attempt the Nationalists had hoped to surprise the enemy and fog had lost them that element of success, in this they had no such hope. Nevertheless the Republicans were caught at an awkward moment, and there was no reaction to the attack until the following day, when one of the infantry columns, under Barrón, advanced to within two kilometres of the Corunna road just east of Las Rozas, and the cavalry column, under Iruretagoyena, broke through the republican lines to the west (Map 7).

Behind the republican inaction there was confusion. Kleber was just being replaced in the command of that very sector; for some time there had been serious friction between him and Rojo, not least because of Kleber's propensity to provide Miaja's headquarters with totally erroneous claims of successes. A Spanish Colonel Cuevas de la Peña was taking over. One of the three Spanish Brigades, the 35, was Barceló's 'column' under a new name and management; Barceló had been wounded in the face by one of his men three days earlier, and an Italian, Nino Nanetti, had just taken over.

In heavy fog on the 5th the three infantry columns (Barrón, Asensio and Buruaga) prepared to change direction eastwards, towards Aravaca, so as to surround the Pozuelo–Humera area. A counter-attack overnight failed. On the 6th, a day of intense fighting and severe casualties on both sides, Barrón with Asensio on his right reached the road west of Las Rozas which was being held by the German and Polish battalions of the XI Brigade. Buruaga skirted Pozuelo. On the 7th García

Escámez, waiting on his right for just that moment, overran Pozuelo, and threatened to trap the French battalion of the XI, a squadron at least of Soviet tanks, and three Spanish battalions now under enfilade fire along the western wall of the Casa de Campo. A diversionary republican attack on Garabitas by the 6 Mixed Brigade had no effect. However, the tanks – all but one – got away. The republican infantry was decimated. By the evening of the 9th Barrón, Asensio, Buruaga and García Escámez were in Aravaca, and firmly in possession of ten kilometres of the Corunna road. The objectives of the operation as defined by Franco in his December 19 orders had been reached.

How firmly they could be held was now to be put to the test. The XI International Brigade had been withdrawn because of the heavy casualties it had suffered, but the XIV had been rushed to take its place. The XII was back from Guadalajara–Brihuega, and three tank squadrons were ready for action. On the 11th those formations, together with the 35 Brigade and another six fresh battalions, attacked down the River Guadarrama west of Las Rozas. There was little to hold them, and the tanks could have gone deep into enemy territory, but as before they would go no further than the infantry could march, and fog stopped progress on the 12th. When it lifted on the 16th Iruretagoyena's cavalry and Asensio's infantry column drove the infiltrators back across the Corunna road.

Since the Republicans had suffered about 6000 casualties in battle and 4000 through illness, the Nationalists had lost 1500, and the weather was hampering both sides, there were no operations over the next three weeks, except for minor unsuccessful republican attacks on the University and the Cerro de los Angeles.

Madrid had been zoned by the Junta for its defence into 'forward' and 'rear' areas, the 'forward' just a few blocks near the University, the river and southern perimeter. There, naturally enough, cafes, taverns and shops were mostly boarded up: but not all the civilian inhabitants had left or were prepared to leave. Some foolhardy souls continued to inhabit damaged houses from the windows of which the trenches across the river could be seen clearly. Some of the homeless lived in the metro stations.

Air raids had become rare and limited almost entirely to single aircraft. An ME 109 and an He 112 were seen fleetingly on December 4 – pre-production aircraft sent by the makers to test their capabilities and for the Germans to decide which of the two was to be the Luftwaffe's standard fighter in the World War to come. The Condor Legion was extremely loth to operate on this front. the I-16 was too good a fighter.

There was more danger to civilians from ill-aimed shells. The Royal Palace received a few hits on its northern and western façades. Government propaganda had it that 'Italian and German artillery [had] cowardly destroyed the magnificent façades of the Palace' which had been 'spontaneously converted, by the united desire of the people and government into a museum of history and tradition'[4]; but in fact the damage to it even after another year of battle was astoundingly superficial bearing in mind that it was a building which was in the direct flight path of shells aimed at the Telefónica fired from guns in the Casa de Campo. With the Telefónica still being used as the main artillery observation post, the Gran Vía was notoriously a dangerous road in which to loiter, but not so dangerous that it was ever deserted. Cafes and shops along it were still open. Soviet and International Brigade officers lodged in several of its hotels.

Marshal Malinovsky was to recall later the contrast between the 'forward' and the 'rear' areas:

> 'the atmosphere [in the rear areas] was entirely different. Shops did a roaring trade. Cafes, cinemas, the Zarzuela, which had a review *Women of Fire*, were crowded out, especially with soldiers. What if a shell pierced the roof and revealed the twinkling stars of southern skies? It improved the ventilation. . . .'[5]

The trams and metro were running. Life was almost normal – up to 2100 hours. Beyond that hour those not in uniform were liable to be stopped repeatedly by police patrols. No one was now setting fire to churches, for they were in regular, sometimes daily use for 'pep' talks and political meetings at which several speakers would in turn deliver cliché-infested speeches each one as long as the pre-war sermons of priests who had fancied themselves great orators. One or two churches remained open to satisfy the curiosity of foreigners who questioned the official government propaganda line that there was freedom of religion. Mass was said much more widely behind closed doors in private houses, with someone on the look-out during its celebration, and much circumspection by those attending as they arrived and left: for religious belief remained a mark of secret 'fascism'. However, the importance of keeping the Basques on the side of the Republic made it expedient that their religious susceptibilities should not be offended, so the Basques in Madrid enjoyed special privileges[6].

There was a new class structure. The man in uniform, the man or woman in militia dress had the freedom of the city. Few civilians dared to give them offence. The civilian prominent in politics left-republican, anarchist, socialist or communist, particularly the last, could get anything, especially food. There was a shortage of food, not because Madrid was besieged, for that it never was, but because the provision of supplies from the agriculturally over-wealthy Valencian region was badly organized and subject to political interference *en route*, as anarchist, socialist and communist patrols each challenged the validity of 'permits' not issued by themselves. When food did arrive in Madrid money helped: there was a flourishing 'black market'; but it was even better to be *enchufado*, 'plugged in', to a political organization or political boss, especially though not exclusively, a communist. Men of principle, not of great wealth, and ideologically opposed to marxism in any form were the people who went most hungry[7].

An incident on December 23 led to a number of important changes in the life of the city. Pablo Yagüe, 'food supply counsellor' in the Defence Junta and prominent member of the UGT, narrowly escaped death at the hands of 'unidentified' men in militia uniform. They were believed to be CNT. On the following day the Junta decreed that only the military had authority in the 'forward' areas, and that in the 'rear' zones, any police work to be done would be reserved exclusively for the Asaltos. It ordered the complete disarming of all 'rear areas militiamen'. The 'Fifth Regiment' closed down its Salesian school depot. Men in militia dress not on leave were sent to front line units. With battle casualties even heavier in December than in November, there were plenty of vacancies. Illness had also been more prevalent than in November among the troops at the front: such a large proportion of the men under arms came from the south and east of Spain, and were not used to the harshness of a bad Madrid winter.

With the 'rear area' militiamen disarmed, the last of the tchekas and unofficial 'people's courts' which had survived the numerous decrees for their suppression, suspended their activities. The Junta, which *de facto* exercised a substantial degree of autonomy from the Government in Valencia, approved an order of that Government creating a new *Cuerpo de Seguridad*, a fusion into a single body of the Security, Assault and Republican National (ex-Civil) Guards. The new *Cuerpo* had two departments, one of uniformed and the other of secret police. Men with tcheka or other rear area militia background were encouraged to join it, subject to a security check. Trotskyists and anarchists were carefully excluded, and the new police force came to be feared by the 'deviationist' marxists as much as the tchekas had been feared previously by non-marxists. Behind the communists in the new force many saw the spectre of the Soviet NKVD: its senior official, Alexander Orlov, had arrived in Spain in September or October[8] with the task of watching over Russian and Comintern personnel; his organization had expanded and *Pravda* had made it no secret in mid-December that the elimination of Spanish 'trotskyists and anarchists' had begun in Catalonia[9]. It was not unreasonable to expect that their elimination in Madrid would follow.

As in the Government, so also in the Junta, the Communist Party now had a preponderant influence, but the minutes of its meetings reveal that the non-communist members would not and did not accept communist proposals without challenge, even when experience taught them it was futile. Almost every vacancy was filled by a communist; thus Yagüe's successor was of the Party. Michael Koltsov, of course, continued to enjoy a special place in the Junta, as adviser extraordinary.

The replacement of Kleber was a minor reverse to communist aspirations to obtain complete control of the People's Army, a reverse, however, to their prestige rather than power. Kleber had been built up in propaganda within and outside Spain as a latter-day Napoleon; a command was to be found for him later elsewhere. In the meantime he went to live in Valencia. However, Voronov continued as Commander Artillery Madrid, Vladimir Goriev as 'friend' to Miaja. Pavlov had replaced Krivoshein towards the end of December as 'adviser' on tank warfare. From the third week in January Pavlov could offer a whole tank brigade of forty armoured cars and one hundred and twenty tanks, and his 'advice' now carried a correspondingly greater weight than Krivoshein's before. Voronov had had all the guns calibrated, and worked out tables so that their fire could be concentrated and co-ordinated as required. He had earned the respect of the Spanish artillery men. Soviet officers began to make their appearance at brigade and even battalion level. At the latter and lower levels the commissar gained a new importance. Their orders now were 'to watch and supervise the political, social and military conduct of those who are in the army, without meddling in questions of discipline or authority which correspond to the military commander': a 'definition' which in fact blurred the limits of their power. As in the Defence Junta, so also in the political commissar structure, members of the Communist Party filled vacancies as they occurred.

At the end of December Miaja had had 80 000 men under his command as his losses had been made good. On Kleber's departure the front had been redivided into five sectors, each defended by a 'division' of 10 000 men. Each division was composed of three Mixed Brigades (with five, instead of four battalions). Miaja's substantial immediate reserves included the XII and XIV International Brigades.

The size of the nationalist forces facing him had also been increased in obedience to Franco's orders of December 19 that Madrid should be totally encircled as soon as possible. The Corunna road operation had then been foreseen as only one prong of a pincer. The other, now to be attempted, was to break the republican front before the River Jarama, cross the river, cut the Madrid–Valencia road, and meet up at Alcalá de Henares with nationalist troops which would advance down the Barcelona road from their positions north of Brihuega. On January 10 Mola gave Orgaz the orders to complete the Franco plan. Orgaz had 57 800 men under his command: 35 200 in defensive positions, 18 600 men organized into five brigades ready to strike, and a reserve of 4000[10].

The failure of the Varela's original Corunna road offensive had made it patently clear to Pozas that the Republicans should be thinking again in terms of offensive as well as defensive action: their troops were now of a military standard incomparably better than in November. Both Spanish and Soviet advisers recommended moving into the offensive with an attack down the Guadarrama (where the nationalist defence had been broken in the January 11 counter-attack) or further west, down to Brunete, and on to the Badajoz road at Navalcarnero or Móstoles, coupled with a drive from the Jarama to the same place, thus encircling completely the nationalist army before Madrid (the 'Stalingrad' idea again). It was agreed that Miaja should provide the strike force for the attack from the north, and Pozas the force for the southern.

Orgaz planned his offensive to begin on January 24 (Map 8A). The first stage ahead was over rolling steppe land and some difficult peaks before the descent down to the River Jarama. This river, which in summer diminishes to a trickle of water, in winter, and especially in heavy rain, swells into a raging unfordable torrent. On January 24 and for the next ten days it poured with rain. As the Nationalists attempted to advance the ground turned to mud. Orgaz ordered them back to their assembly areas.

Pozas and Miaja were planning *their* offensive for February 5. Largo Caballero was invited to Madrid to witness its beginning. Valuable time was then lost with arguments mainly on the *political* implications of the appointment of this or that man as commander-in-chief of the offensive.[11] The nub of the argument was whether it should be Pozas, in which case Largo Caballero could claim the credit, or Miaja whom the Communist Party had taken for their own and exalted in their propaganda into a hero and military genius. Largo wanted the main thrust to come from the south under Pozas. Miaja, with Rojo in support, maintained that it should be from the north: Brunete was the strategic point; the approach to it was far easier from the north; furthermore (a curious argument for military leaders to use) the main thrust should be on the side where the enemy had the greater number of troops: the north. In the end there was compromise. Miaja had his forces increased to twenty-three Spanish Mixed Brigades, of which seven were to be the strike force. Substantial arrivals from France and the Soviet Union in December and January had provided the weapons for new formations[12]. The Pozas strike force was limited to six Spanish and three International Brigades. Pavlov's Tank Brigade was split — sixty with Pozas, thirty with Miaja and the rest in reserve.

When the weather improved on February 4 each side learned from aerial and other reconnaissance that the other was poised for attack. Rojo and Miaja got cold feet. The Nationalists had switched the major part of their troops to the south. Orgaz's reaction to the fact that his left was threatened was to decide that the sooner he attacked on the enemy's left the greater the chance of success (Map 8B). He allowed a day for the ground to dry up sufficiently. His strike force was grouped into three brigades under Varela (recovered from his wound) and two under García Escámez. Between them they had forty-five Pz Ws I and II, whose performance was to be watched carefully by the German then Colonel Ritter von Thoma, one hundred and one guns and fifteen cavalry squadrons. The artillery included a battery of the German 88 mm gun which in World War II with reason came to be looked upon as one of the finest artillery pieces of its day. The Republicans had planned to have a hundred and five guns in the area, but seemingly had managed to assemble only seventy-one[13]. Only in artillery were the Nationalists better off than the Republicans.

Cavalry, tanks and infantry advanced over the bare sandy steppe fanning out from an original fifteen-kilometre front. Varela's forward brigade, under Rada, headed towards La Marañosa, a village dominated by a 697-metre peak. It happened to be where Miaja's responsibility ended and Pozas' began, and the two republican commands had not co-operated in effecting a good junction between them. Rada exploited the situation to the full and reached the village. García Escámez's right wing made for the small town of Ciempozuelos. It was stoutly defended by the 18 Brigade which suffered 1300 dead before they withdrew. By evening the Nationalists were five to ten kilometres from their starting points. On the following day Rada met stiff resistance from the heights of Coberteras, and Barrón coming up behind him had unexpectedly to come into action in support. Together they reached the confluence of the Jarama and Manzanares on the 8th. All the way to Ciempozuelos twenty kilometres to the south the Nationalists advanced to the line of the Jarama canal, above the river.

By the 5th, neither Pozas nor Miaja had been in any doubt at all that the Nationalists were going to launch an attack to the south of Madrid; but they wrongly interpreted their enemy's intentions. They were sure he would make straight for Vallecas, along the very perimeter of the city, and Miaja had redeployed his troops accordingly. It was only on the 8th and with bad grace that Miaja, persisting in his belief that the eastward direction of the attack was a feint, sent Pozas Lister's communist ex-Fifth Regiment brigade which had just been rearmed with new Russian weapons. Lister was instructed to retake the Coberteras heights. On the 9th he drove the Nationalists away from the confluence of the river, but his claim that he had recaptured the heights was untrue, and might have seriously misled Rojo had he

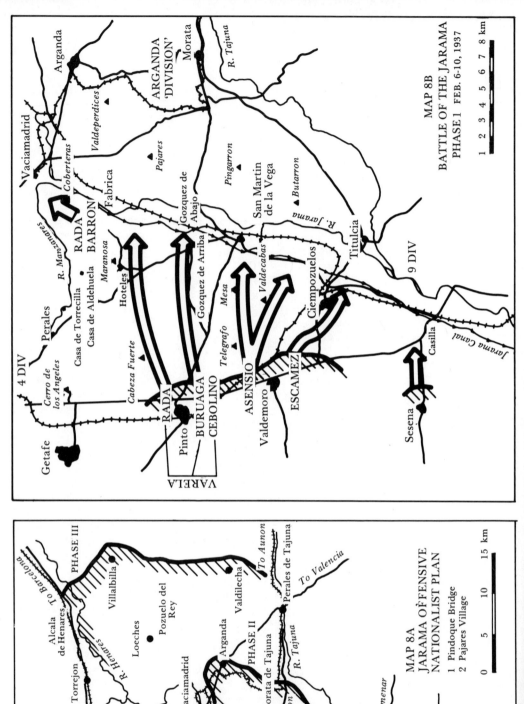

MAP 8A
JARAMA OFFENSIVE
NATIONALIST PLAN

1 Pindoque Bridge
2 Pajares Village

0   5   10   15 km

MADRID

Villaverde
Leganes
Getafe
Pinto
Valdemoro
Sesena
Vallecas
Cerro de los Angeles
R. Manzanares
R. Jarama
Torrejon
Alcala de Henares
To Barcelona
R. Henares
Loeches
Pozuelo del Rey
Villalbilla
PHASE III
Vaciamadrid
Arganda
Valdilecha
PHASE II
Morata de Tajuna
La Maranosa
San Martin de la Vega
Ciempozuelos
Titulcia
PHASE I
START LINE
Pingarron
R. Tajuna
Perales de Tajuna
To Aunon
To Valencia
To Colmenar
R. Tagus
Aranjuez
To Cuenca
To Cadiz
To Andalucia
Canal

MAP 8B
BATTLE OF THE JARAMA
PHASE 1   FEB. 6-10, 1937

1 2 3 4 5 6 7 8 km

Getafe
Cerro de los Angeles
4 DIV
Perales
R. Manzanares
Casa de Torrecilla
Casa de Aldehuela
Cabeza Fuerte
Maranosa
Hoteles
Pinto
RADA
BURUAGA
CEBOLINO
ASENSIO
VALDEMORO
ESCAMEZ
VARELA
Gozquez de Arriba
Telegrafo
Mesa
Valdecabas
Ciempozuelos
Valdemoro
Fabrica
RADA
BARRON
Cobarteras
Vaciamadrid
Valdeperdices
Pajares
Gozquez de Abajo
Pingarron
San Martin de la Vega
Butarron
R. Jarama
Titulcia
Casilla
Jarama Canal
Sesena
9 DIV
ARGANDA 'DIVISION'
Arganda
Morata
R. Tajuna

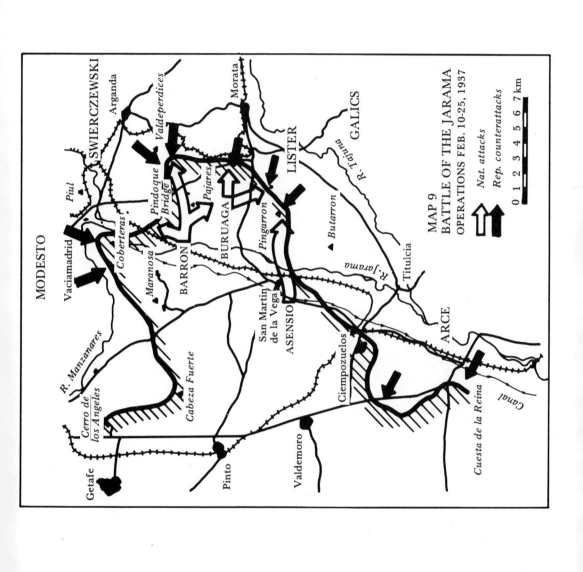

MODESTO
SWIERCZEWSKI
Getafe
R. Manzanares
Cerro de los Angeles
Cabeza Fuerte
Pinto
Valdemoro
Piul
Arganda
Vaciamadrid
Coberteras
Maranosa
BARRON
Pindoque Bridge
Valdeperdices
Pajares
BURUAGA
Morata
San Martin de la Vega
ASENSIO
Pingarron
LISTER
Butarron
R. Jarama
Ciempozuelos
R. Tajuna
GALICS
Titulcia
ARCE
Cuesta de la Reina
Canal

MAP 9
BATTLE OF THE JARAMA
OPERATIONS FEB. 10-25, 1937

Nat. attacks
Rep. counterattacks

0 1 2 3 4 5 6 7 km

not learned from experience that Lister's information reports were not fully to be trusted.

Pozas wanted more help and insisted that the correct tactic now was to let the enemy wear themselves out in the south; Miaja and Rojo maintained that now was the very moment to launch the republican attack directed at Brunete; this was no moment in their opinion to start switching troops about and an attack on Brunete would be bound to make the enemy call off their offensive.

Largo Caballero agreed with Pozas.

On the 10th Varela himself reconnoitred the situation from the heights above the river, and sent cavalry to reconnoitre the banks and test the defences of the one possible bridge, the Pindoque railway bridge. The cavalry reported that the bridge was defended and the river unfordable.

Overnight a platoon of Moroccans and a company of sappers made their way down the steep slopes to the bridge. At 0300 hours they fell upon a company of the André Marty Battalion (XII International Brigade). After throwing handgrenades they charged with bayonets fixed. Of the ninety defenders eighty-six were killed. The sappers then disarmed, as they thought, all the explosive charges. One, in fact, remained unperceived, but did little damage when it was exploded. The bridge was of the most primitive construction: main girders with cross members on which the rails were laid directly; it was therefore impassable to cavalry and difficult for infantry, so planks had to be found and laid across the cross members. Barrón and his brigade got across as fast as they could, but dawn came before they had all crossed. Heavily shelled and attacked by Soviet fighter aircraft they suffered

Propaganda picture of a Political Commissar addressing troops during a rest period from the platform of a T-26.

substantial casualties. Some T-26 tanks were observed. The brigade's 37 mm Italian anti-tank guns were rushed across and nationalist artillery on the slopes of Marañosa were asked to help. The tanks turned after two had been put out of action and others damaged. The cavalry then charged up the heights above the eastern banks while the infantry fanned out and dug in: a few olive trees was all the shelter there was. They had to beat off a second attack by twenty-five tanks that afternoon. In the evening a second brigade, Buruaga's, crossed by the Pindoque bridge. The Nationalists were across in force sufficient to hold their gains.

Meanwhile to the south the brigade under Asensio crossed the canal at dawn, and overran the village of San Martín de la Vega. Beyond it lay the one road bridge in the whole area. As they neared it they heard explosions. Tanks went ahead to reconnoitre. They found it just slightly damaged but well defended, and Asensio decided to capture it overnight in a manner similar to the one used at Pindoque. At dawn the following day his men made for the heights of Pingarrón beyond the river. There they met very stubborn resistance, principally from the British battalion of the XV International Brigade, 225 of whose 600 members were killed or wounded before the survivors withdrew. A tank counter-attack on the slopes failed, and another T-26 fell into nationalist hands.

To the north Barrón faced the XI and XII International Brigades. Buruaga came up on his right. He pressed eastwards while Barrón headed northwards. Rada was now under attack from the 19 Mixed Brigade which was on the Coberteras slopes and the bend of the Manzanares opposite Vaciamadrid. More republican Spanish brigades were thrown into the battle. On the 13th Barrón took Valdeperdices, but the resistance was growing stiffer and the attack was losing momentum. Pavlov's tank brigade was now distributed all along the front, and joining in the battle hull-down.

There were only minor nationalist gains during the morning of the 14th. Orgaz informed Varela that the reserves were exhausted. In the afternoon Varela saw concentrations of tanks and infantry among the olive groves ahead of Buruaga. He asked for an air strike, but the Russian fighters had obtained air supremacy for the Republicans as early as February 11. So on this as on earlier occasions, the German and Italian aircraft were intercepted by the Russians, and failed Varela. The republican tanks and infantry attacked. Buruaga lost ground, then in counter-attack recovered it, but could get little further on that day or the next, or the two days after that. Nor could Barrón or Asensio, as all the nationalist brigades met with ever heavier fire and more determined resistance.

The nationalist offensive was over, as Mola saw for himself on February 16. It had failed, for the Valencia road, though under fire, was still uncut. It remained to be seen whether Pozas had been right in his appreciation that once the force of the offensive was spent then the Republicans would be able to drive the Nationalists back not only to their line of departure but to Navalcarnero. Against the nationalist remnants of forty battalions and fifteen cavalry squadrons in the Jarama salient, the Republicans now had seventy-four battalions and the whole of the Pavlov tank brigade.

A factor in the nationalist breakthrough and the ineffectiveness of

the republican countermeasures had undoubtedly been the division of
responsibility Miaja–Pozas and the rivalries between the two generals.
Miaja's command was now renamed II Army and extended over the
whole front down to Aranjuez. Miaja persisted in his doubts about the
possibility of success at Jarama and still insisted that Rojo's plan for a
drive on Brunete was more promising. His pessimism was shared by
'friend', later Marshal Meretskov[14]. Burillo was appointed operational
commander of all the front, which was redivided into four 'divisions'
(Map 9). Their commanders were Karol Swierczewski (a veteran of
the Russian Revolution and ex-professor of the Moscow Military
school), Janos Galics, alias Joseph Ivanovich Gal (a Russian citizen of
Hungarian birth), Lister, and the Spanish Lieutenant-Colonel Juan
Arce Mayora, a founder member of UMRA. To the right of those four
divisions, each in the hands of a trusted communist, there were
five brigades grouped under the equally fervent Communist Juan
Modesto.

Modesto was instructed to recover Marañosa, Swierczewski to drive
the enemy from the slopes above Arganda (Valdeperdices), Lister to do
the same from the outskirts of Morata, 'Gal' to make for San Martín
de la Vega, and Arce to attack the enemy right down in the Seseña
area. They tried to carry out their orders between February 18 and 27
in daily fierce combats in which both sides lost thousands in dead and
wounded. There were anxious moments for the Nationalists. The
Condor Legion withdrew its support as it had lost too many He 51s.
The Italian pilots in the Fiat CR 32 squadrons, which could put up
some sort of a fight against the Polikarpov I-15s, and even the more
modern I-16s, refused to fly, so Spanish pilots took over the machines,
and shamed some of the Italians into joining them. On the ground the
Nationalists had to yield a few kilometres before Arganda and Morata.
The climax was reached on the 23rd and 24th with a determined
attack on Pingarrón by several brigades including the XV International, and with Pavlov in support. The nationalist line held; and
thereafter the republican offensive petered out.

The battle had ended in a draw. The result pleased neither side. For
the Republicans it was unsatisfactory that the enemy should still be on
the east bank of the Jarama. For Franco it was even more unsatisfactory that the Valencia–Madrid road was uncut. He had lost 6000
men to no real purpose: the Republic 10 000[15].

Franco's ace had been trumped: but he still had a picture card in his
hand.

12   The Last Offensive

Franco's severest armchair critics were Hitler's ambassador to Franco, Wilhelm von Faupel, and Mussolini's Foreign Minister Count Ciano. The sixty-three-year-old von Faupel, an unsuccessful corps commander in World War I and ex-Inspector General of the Peruvian Army, had been instructed by Hitler not to meddle in military affairs, but even within days of his arrival in Spain he was writing home that one German Army division together with one Italian could win the war with the greatest ease and rapidity. The Condor Legion was essentially a group to test the efficacy of German equipment in battle conditions and to try out various theories on the tactical use of air power in war. To the Germans the Spanish Civil War was a training school for Luftwaffe pilots. The Legion could not win the war for Franco, or even capture Madrid. The German High Command dismissed Faupel's suggestion. Not only was it militarily absurd, but the High Command had no intention of being instrumental in the premature closure of their testing ground and school.

Mussolini, on the other hand, had no doubts about the superiority of Italian arms and men. He liked the idea of sending an expeditionary force. He accepted Ciano's view of the Civil War as a heaven-sent opportunity to show the world the might of the New Roman Empire. The major powers had belittled its Abyssinian victory: in Spain the enemy would be Russian, Polish, German, French, British as well as Spanish. Accordingly he had despatched 'volunteers' in properly organized units from December 1936 onwards and by mid-January the number of Italians in Spain had reached 15 000. Franco, though not over-impressed by them and doubtful of their worth in battle (they were Blackshirt militia and not Italian army) had then agreed to the employment of 6000 of them, jointly with Spanish troops under the Duke of Seville, in an operation in which failure would not matter. The operation was the shortening of the southern front by the elimination of the republican forces in Andalucia and the capture of Malaga.

The part the Italians had played in the successful three-week campaign of January 15–February 7 had been no greater than that of the 3000 Spaniards at their side. The 40 000 Republicans who had given way before them had been the worst equipped and most ill-organized of any of the republican forces. Accordingly the Commander-in-Chief of the force, General Mario Roatta (known in Spain as 'Mancini'), and Ciano now implored Franco to let the Italians act in a more important theatre. As the Jarama offensive lost its impetus, Franco acceded to the demand. By then Roatta had under his command 31 000 men organized as four 'divisions': three Blackshirt and one Italian Army. On paper their fire power was impressive. The force had

Views of the Guadalajara area showing the formidable terrain over which fighting took place.

eighty-six medium and field guns (plus sixty-eight close infantry support weapons)* and a large number of tankettes. The transport was all motorized.

The operation in which Franco was to allow the Italians to display their prowess had as its objective the advance by fifty kilometres of the front on the Madrid–Zaragoza road. It was currently a hundred and ten kilometres away from the capital. With the front brought to within fifty, that is south of Guadalajara, the Republicans would be denied the road to Valencia via Cuenca. Faced with an attack on that sector they might reduce the pressure on the tired nationalist troops at the Jarama front. If the operation succeeded, a further push sometime in the future, past Alcalá de Henares, coupled with a new effort from the Jarama troops up past Arganda, would result in that encirclement of Madrid which Franco had had in mind the previous December, and which the numerous republican brigades together with the International and Pavlov's had thwarted.

The terrain which the Italians were to traverse was a tableland tilted towards Guadalajara. It rolled down from 1100 metres at the points of departure to 700 at the objective. It was covered here and there with shrubs and woods, but it was mostly bare sterile clay; a land without commanding heights but easy to observe from the air; free of natural obstacles – in a word ideal for a rapid advance by motorized troops. In early March the weather to be expected was cold with some rain. Heavy rain would of course turn the ground into a quagmire.

The Italians were not to be the sole participants in the offensive. Holding the front for the Nationalists, from astride the road and westwards right over to Somosierra, were two brigades of their Soria Division, 13 300 men under General Moscardó. Out of them a strike force was formed of some 5–6000 to protect the Italian right flank. They were to advance from the north in phase with the Italians. The river Tajuña was to protect the left flank.

Facing the Soria Division the Republicans had their 12 Division, under Colonel Lacalle: it was nominally of five Mixed Brigades, but somewhat depleted and indeed numbering no more than 10 700. Their

* 65 mm manned by infantry.

morale was high. An attempt by them to drive the Nationalists beyond Sigüenza between January 1 and 11 had not been successful; but the subsequent nationalist counter-attack had established that though they might not have the power to drive the Nationalists back, they could hold ground in defence, and were therefore as 'good' as the enemy. If bravery and valour were all that counted in war then that would have been true. The then Colonel, later Marshal, Rodimtsev visited them at the beginning of March and noted their weakness:

'The lack of camouflage of the trenches jumped to the eye. The earth from them was heaped in little mounds next to them. They were full of water from the recent rains, and one got the impression that the soldiers had just jumped into them when they saw us coming. . . . The defence line was primitive and in no wise based on tactical considerations, done by people with no military knowledge. At its best the sort of work one would expect for hurriedly dug-in advance posts. There was a single or double line of barbed wire 100 to 200 metres in front of platoon or section positions, but the wire was so low that one could clear it easily with a jump . . . the battalions were just strung along . . . no reserves . . . in the event of an enemy attack the front would be broken immediately.'[1]

Given the relative strengths in men and fire power of the Italians and the Republicans, given the naiveté of the defence works and the motor transport available to the attackers, the projected speed of the advance was conservative: ten kilometres on the first day and four days for the sixty to Guadalajara was not much to expect. The danger which the nationalist High Command foresaw was that their troops under Colonel Marzo would not be able to keep up with the motorized Italians and provide protection for their right flank. Colonel Barroso, Franco's Chief of Operations, examined the Italian plan and was at pains to point out to the Italians a major fault: they showed a complete disregard of the security of their left flank. They ignored the use that the enemy could make of the bridges across the river Tajuña in the event of a counter-attack[2]. The Italians were not bothered: they were certain that the impetus of the initial strike could carry them all the

way to Alcalá de Henares. Franco agreed that in the event of such a major breakthrough, then the forces under Orgaz on the Jarama would make yet another effort to cut the Valencia road and try to meet the Italians at Pozuelo del Rey south of Alcalá, but he warned Roatta yet again that after the loss of 6000 men in February, and in the light of the continued presence in the sector of such a concentration of republican and foreign troops, he was not to expect any immediate help from Orgaz.

The date finally fixed for the attack was March 8. The build-up in the Sigüenza–Soria area was duly reported to Miaja. He visited his XII Division, and alerted Pavlov who sent Lacalle a tank company. Unaware of the strength of the Italians, he was confident of the outcome.

Overnight March 7/8 there was snow, sleet and rain in turn. The Nationalists suggested a postponement: the Italian airforce operating from makeshift airfields on clay soil would be in difficulties; 'Douglas's' airforce had concrete runways at Barajas. Roatta would not hear of postponement, and it was in mist and drizzle that the nationalist and Italian artillery opened up at 0700 hours on the appointed day (Map 10A). First tanks and infantry into the attack were troops of the Soria Division which, clearing the enemy from the villages of Castejón and Mirabueno made easy the advance of the Italian 2 'Division' (*Fiamme Nere*, Black Flames) down and south of the Zaragoza road. All went well on the left flank, but a mere 400 Republicans at the village of Almadrones held up into the night 2000 Italians coming down the road – and with that the timetable, indeed the whole plan began to go wrong.

Lacalle ordered the tanks and four infantry battalions which had been rushed up to him by Miaja, to face the most forward of the Italian troops, those in a salient at Hontanares. Before they had reached it Almadrones had fallen to nationalist and Italian troops jointly. The 3 Italian Division (*Penne Nere*, Black Arrows) leap-frogged over the 2, and after the most appalling mix-up of 2 and 3 Division vehicles had been sorted out personally by one of the generals, it proceeded down the Almadrones–Brihuega road but failed to take that townlet before nightfall. Miaja had moved up the XI International Brigade and alerted Pavlov, and the Italians came up against a company of T-26s with which, as before, the tankettes could not cope. The Soviet Colonel Rodimtsev took over command of the defence of the main road with Lister as second-in-command[3]. Lacalle was switched over to the left to cope with the continuing advance of the Soria 2 Brigade, and in counter-attacking lost three of his tanks.

Miaja, realizing now the width of the attack, sent up the Zaragoza road the XII International, Campesino's and other Spanish brigades. They could not reach Brihuega before its fall on the morning of the 10th. Its defenders fell back into the woods off the Torija–Brihuega road, and were joined there by the Italian (Garibaldi) battalion of the XII. The Black Flames, ordered to proceed up the same road since the Black Arrows were being held before Trijueque, ran straight into an ambush. During the rest of the day communist Italian fought fascist Italian in that wood. Other defenders had crossed the river Tajuña. Troops of the 2 Italian Division established a bridgehead, but neglected to take the heights above it from which the Republicans now

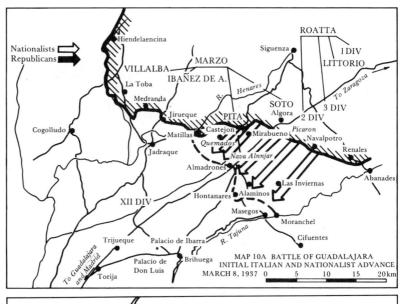

Nationalists ⇨
Republicans ⬛➡

Hiendelaencina

VILLALBA
La Toba
Medranda
IBAÑEZ DE A.
MARZO
R. Henares
Siguenza
ROATTA
1 DIV
LITTORIO
To Zaragoza

Cogolludo
Jirueque
Matillas
Jadraque
Castejon
PITA
Quemados
Nava Alnnjar
Almadrones
SOTO
Algora
2 DIV
3 DIV
Mirabueno
Picaron
Navalpotro
Renales
Abanades

XII DIV
Hontanares
Alaminos
Las Inviernas
Masegos
Moranchel
Cifuentes

Trijueque
Palacio de Ibarra
R. Tajuna
To Guadalajara and Madrid
Palacio de Don Luis
Brihuega
Torija

MAP 10A BATTLE OF GUADALAJARA
INITIAL ITALIAN AND NATIONALIST ADVANCE
MARCH 8, 1937   0   5   10   15   20km

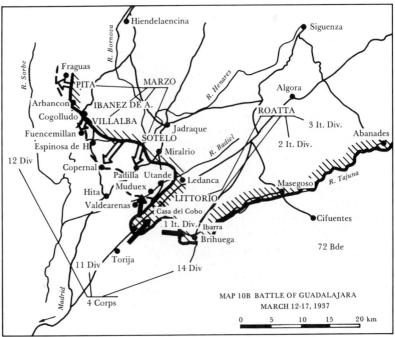

R. Sorbe
R. Bornova
Hiendelaencina
Siguenza

Fraguas
PITA
MARZO
R. Henares
Algora
Arbancon
Cogolludo
IBANEZ DE A.
VILLALBA
ROATTA
3 It. Div.
Abanades
Fuencemillan
SOTELO
Jadraque
R. Badiel
2 It. Div.
Espinosa de H
Copernal
Miralrio
12 Div
Padilla
Muduex
Utande
Ledanca
Masegoso
R. Tajuna
Hita
Valdearenas
LITTORIO
Casa del Cobo
Cifuentes
.1 It. Div.
Ibarra
72 Bde
11 Div
Torija
14 Div
Brihuega
Madrid
4 Corps

MAP 10B BATTLE OF GUADALAJARA
MARCH 12-17, 1937

0   5   10   15   20 km

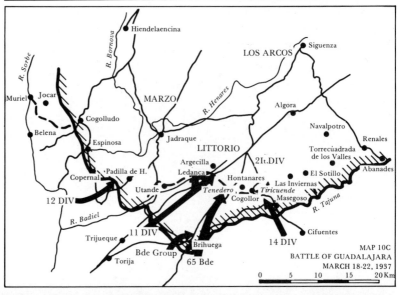

R. Sorbe
R. Bornova
Hiendelaencina
LOS ARCOS
Siguenza

Muriel
Jocar
MARZO
R. Henares
Algora
Cogolludo
Navalpotro
Belena
Espinosa
Jadraque
LITTORIO
Renales
Argecilla
2It.DIV
Torrecúadrada
de los Valles
Abanades
Copernal
Padilla de H.
Ledanca
Hontanares
El Sotillo
12 DIV
Utande
Tenedero
Cogollor
Las Inviernas
Tiricuende
Masegoso
R. Tajuna
R. Badiel
11 DIV
Cifuentes
Trijueque
Brihuega
14 DIV
Torija
Bde Group
65 Bde

MAP 10C
BATTLE OF GUADALAJARA
MARCH 18-22, 1937
0   5   10   15   20Km

began to shell Brihuega. There was worse confusion. That evening two battalions of the 2 mistook each other for enemy; one of them put half the other to flight before the error was discovered. By nightfall the Blackshirts were showing incipient signs of panic. All night long they fired rifles and even guns at shadows.

Their confidence returned to some extent with dawn. The orders now were that the 3 Division should take Trijueque, the 2 Torija while the unused 1 (*Dio lo vuole*, 'God wills it') was to move into Brihuega and, rather belatedly, establish a proper bridgehead on the east flank of the Tajuña. Trijueque fell after stubborn resistance on the part of the brigades under Rodimtsev, and the Italian advance got as far as kilometre 77; but the troops in the woods held the 2, except momentarily when the Italians used flamethrowers. To the right of the Italians, Marzo continued to advance with his cavalry and infantry. On the 10th they had deprived the Republicans of three more tanks, and on the 11th they captured the tactically important village of Cogolludo.

The Republicans now had ten brigades in the area, organized as three divisions, the 11, 12, and 14, and the Russian Tank Brigade. The artillery Lieutenant-Colonel Jurado was given command of the resultant army corps, to the chagrin of his senior, Colonel Lacalle, commander of the 12 Division, which had borne the brunt of the Italian and nationalist attack to the extent that of its five brigades all that was

German troops of the XI International Brigade at rest during the Battle of Guadalajara. In the background is a T-26 tank.

Major, later General
Enrique Jurado.

left were three. Lacalle declared himself ill two days later, and the Italian communist Nino Nanetti took over the 12 Division.

Miaja's orders to Jurado for March 12 were to hold the Italians and Marzo. Marzo continued to forge ahead but the Italians were held (Map 10B). Ever since the 8th it had snowed by night and rained by day, and the Italian airforce had been grounded. Not so the republican operating from runways, and they now began to use their aircraft effectively, strafing the Italian motor transport which was totally exposed. Overnight March 12/13 the Italian regular army Littorio Division relieved the Blackshirt 3 at Trijueque, and the *Dio lo vuole* took over from the 2 at Brihuega. Goriev came down from Madrid to co-ordinate the actions of the republican tanks artillery and infantry: he was not fully satisfied with Jurado's conduct of the battle.

March 13 was the day of determined attacks by the Littorio Division on the one side and on the other by the 2 Republican, the Campesino and XII International Brigades with full support from Pavlov. Once again the Italian flamethrowers mounted on tankettes proved troublesome to the republican infantry. However, the tankettes got bogged in the mud and melting snow and became sitting targets for the powerful guns of the Soviet tanks. The Italians abandoned Trijueque that night, in some disorder and leaving much of their equipment behind[4]. On the following day it was the turn of the Italians on the Torija–Brihuega road to face the onslaught of the Republicans. The Garibaldi battalion of the XII International dislodged their fellow Italians from the ruins of a building known as the Palacio de Ibarra, according to Roatta, by pretending to be friendly troops[5].

The situation was almost static over the days March 15–17. The Italians fell back under pressure from an evergrowing number of republican brigades, and to adjust their front till it ran almost straight from kilometre 83 on the Zaragoza road to Brihuega. General Roatta flew to Salamanca to confer with Franco. He asked that the Nationalists should launch an attack on the Jarama front immediately to relieve the pressure on them; but as Franco had already explained to the Italians before they had embarked on their offensive, General Orgaz's troops were in no condition to attack. He advised that the Italians should take up defensive positions where they were. Among the Italians at the front, however, there were ominous signs: genuine cases of frostbite but also cases of self-inflicted wounds and of men uninjured, but swathed in bandages, trying to board ambulances leaving casualty clearing stations.

Children playing in a Madrid air raid shelter.

The Republicans brought the number of Mixed Brigades in the 'Guadalajara' front up to thirteen. Miaja decided the time had come to launch a counter-offensive. Rojo proposed an attack on a two-to-three-kilometre front northwest of Brihuega, to be spearheaded by thirty tanks and ten armoured cars and followed by the Spanish 70 and Campesino's brigades. This force, Rojo suggested, should make northeast to the thousand-metre heights above Brihuega for about three kilometres, then do a right turn down to the river Tajuña and thus cut off all roads out of Brihuega. The XII International should then attack frontally while the 65 dealt with the Italian bridgehead across the river and the 72 make from across the river for Masegoso fifteen kilometres east of Brihuega. Other brigades could keep busy the Littorio Division astride the main Zaragoza road.

At a meeting on March 17, Miaja, Goriev, Pavlov and numerous amigos,* Jurado and the divisional commanders accepted Rojo's plan. Miaja suggested that Pavlov should be the operational commander: Pavlov proposed Lister. Goriev agreed with Pavlov that it would indeed be politically undesirable that Pavlov's name should appear as in command and that Jurado should sign the orders.[6]

Pavlov gave the order for the offensive to begin at 1330 hours on the 18th. Eighty aircraft attacked the Italians. Fifty-six field and medium guns shelled them. Tanks led the 70 and Campesino's Brigades as planned, and they headed also the frontal attack by the XII International. The Blackshirt 'God wills it' Division cracked and fled in disorder. The Littorio Division was ordered to retreat up the Zaragoza road. It was pursued by nine of Pavlov's tanks, the Spanish 1, and International XI. The Italians withdrew so fast that by the end of the 19th they were at kilometre 97, seven kilometres ahead of the Republicans. The Republicans then turned to attack the Soria Division positions but this they did without success. They were so astonished over the ease with which they had captured Brihuega that they also failed to pursue the routed 'God wills it' Division, and in consequence, the Soria Division's reserve third brigade was able to relieve the Italians with comparative ease during the period March 22–27, and the divi-

* From their contributions to *Bajo la Bandera de la España Republicana* (Moscow 1968) and Marshal Meretskov's in *Voprosi Istorii* 1967 vol 12, it would appear that he, Malinovsky, Batov, Rodimtsev and Voronov were also present.

An Italian-built Fiat-Ansaldo tankette, captured at the Battle of Guadalajara, March, 1937.

sion as a whole stabilized the whole front from the mountains to the Tajuña before the end of the month. The line taken was slightly forward for the most part of where it had been on March 7 (Map 10C).

At Franco's GHQ there was great surprise that the Republicans failed to exploit their rout of the Italians which could have seriously embarrassed the Nationalists.

The Republicans publicized 'Guadalajara' abroad as a major triumph, with references to the capture of 'thousands of prisoners' and of vast quantities of war material, but a subsequent *republican* commission of investigation and collection found only small quantities[7]. If the original claims were anywhere near fact, then the failure of the Republicans to exploit was all the more reprehensible, but if only gross exaggeration, it remained true that the republican leaders and their Soviet advisers had cause to congratulate themselves. Officers and men of the four brigades, three Spanish, one International, involved in the capture of Brihuega had obeyed orders, operated coherently, and shown professional knowledge of tactics down to platoon and section level. They were an army and not autonomously-minded collections of anarchist, communist or socialist militia.

Throughout the Spanish units of the republican army there was overwhelming joy at the fact that a foreign army had been defeated. That was to be expected. It was, however, also the reaction of the equally Spanish nationalist army. There were reports of nationalist officers toasting the victory of the Republicans, and the nationalist rank and file certainly sang most ribald words to the tunes of the Italian Fascist militia. Franco heard the news with equanimity: 'it suits

Republican army officers and men off-duty in Madrid in the spring of 1937.

us well, for we can now mount the strategically important operations in the north'[8]. It had long been the view of Colonel Barroso and other senior members of Franco's General Staff, that the capture of Madrid had no military importance. Barroso went further: he did not believe that the enemy would lose the will to fight with the loss of Madrid, and that its capture before the enemy had lost the power to continue the war could be a disaster for the Nationalists:

'As earlier, the capture of Madrid would have imposed upon us grave difficulties. The city was short of food – had been deliberately kept short of food by the Valencia Government. We hadn't the transport to supply it from our side. We hadn't the food, if it comes to that, without the rich Valencian zone'[9].

Franco now agreed with Barroso, and as far as he was concerned the battle for Madrid was over. Neither side had won, and neither side could win. Madrid would fall when the republican will to fight had been drained away elsewhere.

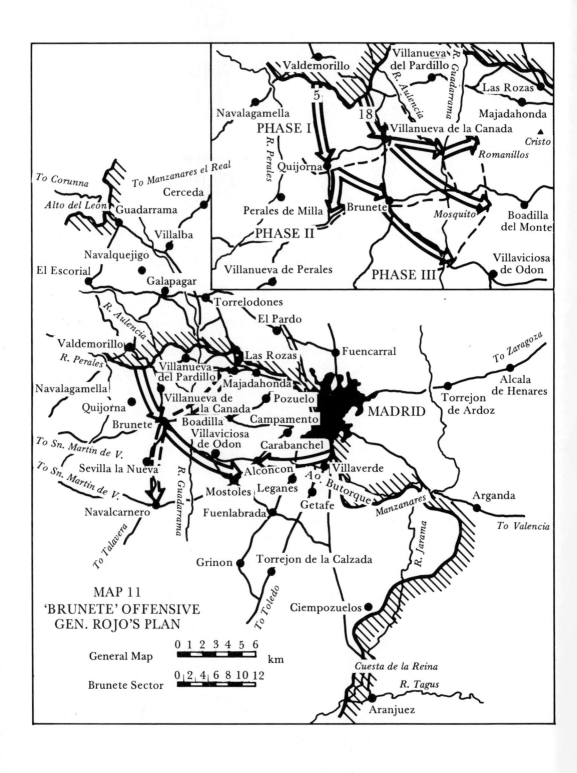

PHASE I

PHASE II

PHASE III

Villanueva del Pardillo

Las Rozas

Majadahonda

Cristo

Romanillos

Valdemorillo

Navalagamella

5

18

Villanueva de la Canada

Quijorna

Perales de Milla

Brunete

Mosquito

Boadilla del Monte

Villanueva de Perales

Villaviciosa de Odon

To Corunna

To Manzanares el Real

Cerceda

Alto del Leon

Guadarrama

Villalba

Navalquejigo

El Escorial

Galapagar

Torrelodones

El Pardo

Valdemorillo

Las Rozas

Fuencarral

To Zaragoza

Villanueva del Pardillo

Majadahonda

Pozuelo

Alcala de Henares

Navalagamella

Villanueva de la Canada

Torrejon de Ardoz

Quijorna

Boadilla

Campamento

MADRID

Brunete

Villaviciosa de Odon

Carabanchel

To Sn. Martin de V.

Sevilla la Nueva

Alconcon

Villaverde

Arganda

To Sn. Martin de V.

Mostoles

Leganes

Ao. Butorque

Getafe

Manzanares

To Valencia

Navalcarnero

Fuenlabrada

To Talavera

Grinon

Torrejon de la Calzada

Ciempozuelos

R. Jarama

To Toledo

Cuesta de la Reina

R. Tagus

Aranjuez

R. Aulencia

R. Perales

R. Guadarrama

**MAP 11
'BRUNETE' OFFENSIVE
GEN. ROJO'S PLAN**

General Map

0 1 2 3 4 5 6

km

Brunete Sector

0 2 4 6 8 10 12

13   Counter-attack

It was at Guadalajara that both sides of the Civil War permitted their foreign allies to help them more than at any other time before or after. Generalissimo Franco, master in his own GHQ, was never again to use the Italians except in roles secondary to his Spaniards, and after Guadalajara Generalissimo Largo Caballero sought freedom for his Spanish generals and staff officers.

There was no reason for subservience to Soviet dictation – or so Largo Caballero thought. As on April 15, the republican army of the centre had over 170 000 men and 224 guns[1] in fifty-two brigades grouped into twenty divisions and six army corps; while they were equipped largely with Soviet weapons, of which substantial quantities had arrived during the past six weeks, the weapons were useless without men, and 90 per cent of the men were Spaniards. Though Pavlov had fought and won the battle he had done so to Rojo's plans. The Soviet tank and International Brigades had played a major role – but so had the brigades of the republican People's Army. Lister and Modesto had shown no less competence than Karel Swierczewski and Janos Galics; and there were many other competent commanders among both the loyal members of the pre-war Spanish army and those schooled since by the experience of war.

In the spring of 1937 Largo was a disillusioned man. He had learnt over the last few months that he was really expected to obey, not merely listen to, the 'advice' on political and military matters given him by the Soviet Ambassador Rosenberg at their frequent and long meetings. He was currently being 'asked' by Stalin himself to amalgamate the Socialist with the Communist Party. That he was not prepared to do[2]. He was in revolt, and as part of his defiance of the Soviet amigos he encouraged his General Staff to ignore Russian advice.

The battle of Guadalajara was hardly over when, on March 22, Miaja and Rojo again put forward the plan for the drive on Brunete, the attack on the rear of the enemy before Madrid.* A victory for Miaja, however, would have been a victory for the communists. Exactly a month later, on April 22, Colonel Alvarez Coque, acting Chief of the General Staff at Largo's own Ministry of War, submitted a much more ambitious plan[3] (Map 2). He recommended a three-pronged offensive – a drive directed at Mérida in Extremadura from starting lines roughly 300 kilometres southwest of Madrid, an attack on Brunete as advocated by Rojo, and a thrust on Oropesa, 150 kilometres along the Madrid–Mérida road. Brunete could trap the troops before Madrid, Oropesa could carve up the rear areas while Mérida

---

* See above pp. 118, 122, 124.

would cut the nationalist area in two. He reckoned minima of nine brigades for Brunete, five for Oropesa and eight for Mérida.

Alvarez Coque's plan was a bold one; the only criticism of it at Largo's GHQ was that Brunete was unnecessary, and that the allotment for Mérida should be seventeen brigades and ten for Oropesa, albeit Franco had reduced to a minimum the forces holding the southern front all the way from Madrid to Mérida in order to give Mola as large a force as possible for the offensive in progress against Bilbao. The new figures and exclusion of Brunete meant that Miaja would have to hand over some of his Madrid brigades – and this he would not do, either because he felt slighted at not having been consulted, or more likely because the Soviet officers at his headquarters would not allow him to obey Largo[4]. Moscow had decided that the 'Spanish Lenin' was now too independently minded in political as well as military affairs. Not only was he still resisting Stalin on the future of the Socialist Party, but also communist insistence that the Trotskyite POUM should be suppressed. Largo had to go. The Extremadura offensive offered a good chance of a spectacular republican victory. Success would exalt Largo to a height from which the communists would have found it difficult to dislodge him. It had to be sabotaged.[5]

May 7 was the original D-day. By that date the concentration of the necessary forces was by no means complete. Miaja had found excuse after excuse not to release his brigades. A new date was determined – May 21.

On May 14 the republican airforce High Command – then wholly under Soviet control – announced that it did not have any fighters available for the offensive, indeed any aircraft, though in fact 'Douglas' had around 200 fighters, 50 bombers and 70 army reconnaissance and co-operation machines in operational condition[6]. At a Cabinet meeting on May 15 Largo was accused of gross political and military incompetence by his communist Ministers. Deserted by his fellow socialists, he resigned the premiership the following day. The much more pro-communist and ductile Juan Negrín took his place as Prime Minister and Prieto as Minister of War. The Extremadura offensive was cancelled. Rojo replaced Alvarez Coque as Chief of the General Staff at the Ministry. Miaja joined the Communist Party to the contemptuous amusement of President Azaña, who with Largo saw in the 'conversion' an insurance against dismissal[7]. There were henceforth to be plenty of dismissals or relegation to desk jobs of officers of proven loyalty to the Republic but resistant to communism[8].

Rojo was of the school which maintained that the object of war is the destruction of the enemy[9]. As the bulk of the enemy on the southern front was concentrated in the immediate vicinity of Madrid, a pincer movement to trap the enemy there – the Brunete operation – was the only answer. Where a strategist of a more modern school might have seen in the capture of Mérida the interruption of the chief supply line for the enemy – the line from Germany and Italy via Portugal, Africa and Cadiz – the deprivation thereby of the enemy's means to continue the war and consequently the undermining of his will to fight, Rojo saw only meaningless territorial gains. Brunete it had to be, and might have been straight away, now that he was Chief of the General Staff, had urgent political considerations not dictated its postponement.

Republican propaganda needed an immediate victory. The Basques were being forced back. They were fighting with the tenacity which has been characteristic of them throughout history, but against odds which the Republicans had encountered neither in the defence of Madrid nor in Catalonia and Aragon. The Republic was under considerable criticism from the friends of the Basques abroad. The German aerial bombardment of Guernica had aroused world-wide sympathy for them. Why was the government of Valencia doing nothing to relieve the pressure on them? Before the Civil War the Socialists – Prieto in particular – had opposed the granting of local autonomy to the Basques and had agreed to its concession only in order to dissuade them from throwing in their lot with the Nationalists. Now that the Basques were autonomous, there was a body of opinion in Valencia that it was up to the Basques to defend themselves; but the criticism from abroad could not be ignored. Besides, the nationalist troops were now threatening Bilbao; and Bilbao, Prieto's home town, was a socialist rather than a Basque stronghold.

The one republican victory since Guadalajara had been the capture of the sanctuary of Santa María de la Cabeza in the Sierra Morena where, early in September 1936, 245 insurgent Civil Guards, 30 members of the armed forces and 840 civilians – 100 men of military age and the rest women, children and old men – had taken refuge. After they had withstood for seven and a half months a siege by a republican force of roughly brigade strength, Largo had despatched three brigades against them. Even then the survivors had held off the attackers for fourteen days before being overwhelmed on May 1[10]. The episode had provided better propaganda material for the Nationalists than the Republicans.

Miaja had a plan at hand – an old suggestion of Rojo's: a drive over Navacerrada (the one major pass over the Guadarramas in republican hands (Map 2)), through the royal park lands of La Granja, to Segovia, the ancient capital of Castile.

The strategic concept was good. With La Granja and Segovia in republican hands, the other passes over the Guadarramas could be turned, and the whole valley of the Duero dominated. Valladolid, Pamplona, Zaragoza, Franco's own headquarters at Burgos would be threatened. The least that could be expected, given enough troops to exploit the initial breakthrough, was the abandonment of the northern offensive.

The Republic could have deployed in the operation the whole of an army corps, and, without endangering their position elsewhere, possibly more than one corps. Seventeen brigades had been allocated to the cancelled Extremadura operation – twenty-seven with its Oropesa offshoot. The offensive, however, was not conceived in such daring terms, but as a limited exercise 'to help indirectly the defence by our forces of the Vizcaya front'[11] and with a ridiculously small portion of the troops at the disposal of the republican High Command.

General 'Walter', that is, Karel Swierczewski, was given command of three brigades (the 69 and 31 Spanish and the XIV International which was then commanded by the Frenchman Dumont) and a squadron of T-26 tanks. He was to attack the Nationalists beyond Navacerrada, and make for La Granja and Segovia. One single brigade (21 Spanish) and a second tank squadron were to move up behind them to

exploit the breakthrough if it occurred. There was to be a diversionary attack by three brigades on the Alto del León pass. In all then, only seven brigades were allocated to the task.

In the event the offensive turned out to be tactically about the most ill-conducted of all operations undertaken by either side. Since the Nationalists had a clear view from the Alto del León of all traffic proceeding out of Madrid, orders stressed the need for all necessary movements to be conducted by night and with no lights. The troops were moved up to their starting points overnight May 29/30 in trucks with their headlamps switched on. The Nationalists received further details of what was afoot from deserters, so that Varela, in command of the Nationalists opposite, was fully informed as to which was the real and which the feint attack, and made the necessary adjustments to his forces which the attackers outnumbered by more than two to one.

'Walter' had thus lost the element of surprise when he attacked at dawn on May 30 after the usual preliminary bombardment by artillery and aircraft. On that day he barely dented the defences. Miaja ordered his reinforcement by the reserve 21 Brigade. On May 31 the 31 Brigade got as far as the gardens of La Granja, but was forced back; however, the 69 took the dominating height called Cabeza Grande. Early on June 1 the 21 Brigade, which had moved up to Cabeza Grande, rushed down towards the Segovia – La Granja road. Varela threw in two battalions which had just arrived to reinforce him. They broke the advance. According to 'Walter' one of the battalions of the 21 then murdered their commander and deserted. The Nationalists regained Cabeza Grande. Dumont had meanwhile attacked the Royal Palace with the XIV International Brigade – to no effect. He and 'Walter' now quarrelled over whether 'French' or 'Russian' infantry tactics were to be used. 'Walter' insisted on frontal attacks. The Brigade suffered heavy casualties in consequence, some at the hands of one of their own officers when they refused to attack frontally a third time.

Communications between the republican brigades now broke down. Miaja ordered Colonel José María Galán to take over command of the 69 and 21 limiting 'Walter's' command to the XIV and 31, and divided between them the 3 Spanish Brigade which he had earlier transferred from the Alto del León sector. In the prevailing confusion there was no advance on June 2, and that night Miaja ordered Galán and 'Walter' 'to take up defensive positions', that is to abandon the offensive. On the 4th the 31 Brigade was left at Navacerrada, and the other four brigades were withdrawn. The 'offensive' was over.

Republican propaganda claimed that the aims of the offensive had been achieved. Varela had indeed received four battalions to reinforce the nationalist brigade in the sector, the two he had used to recapture Cabeza Grande and two which arrived on June 3 when the battle was over. They had been sent to him from a general reserve for the Madrid front, and the Basques did not notice any diminution of the effort against them*.

The XIV Brigade sustained 360 casualties, the other four about 1100 between them: Varela's also about 1100. A small portion of the

---

General Karol
Świerczewski ('Walter').

* The Segovia offensive did, however, affect the war indirectly: General Mola decided on June 3 to discuss the Segovia situation personally with Varela, and with that in mind set out from Vitoria for Valladolid by air. The aircraft crashed into a hillside and Mola, the Nationalists' most meticulous planner, was killed.

enemy army had therefore been destroyed but on balance the Republicans had suffered more. In his despatches and subsequent reports 'Walter' blamed everyone but himself – his own HQ staff and Dumont in particular.

Miaja, Matallana (his chief of staff) and Rojo had looked upon Segovia as a rehearsal for the postponed Brunete. 'Walter's' and Galán's reports were both reassuring and worrying. In defence the infantry had shown at all levels an understanding of tactics which left no doubt that the People's Army was an army: but there was still much to be learnt in attack. Co-operation between tanks, artillery and infantry had left much to be desired. Liaison between brigades and communications generally had to be improved. However, they were all shortcomings which could be made good with training – and an intensive training programme was carried out during the month of June[12].

The reports stressed the lack of firmness in *los mandos*, the officers, but not what must be judged the greatest weaknesses – the inflexibility of the senior officers and the lack of initiative of all. Nor could they suggest that the disciplinary system imposed by the political commissars, and the common interpretation of deviations from or expansion of orders as proof of disloyalty to the cause was not likely to encourage individual initiative. In the case of Segovia, moreover, the greatest inflexibility had been that of the Commander-in-Chief himself. For given the capture of Cabeza Grande and the stubbornness of the resistance at La Granja, a quick change of plan and concentration of forces on the point of breakthrough would have outflanked the defenders of La Granja. That was daring not to be expected of Malinovsky's 'very model of military atrophy'.

Bilbao fell on June 19. The Nationalists still had to capture Santander and Oviedo across mountains even more difficult for an army in attack than those of conquered Vizcaya. To the Government of the Republic in Valencia what remained to them of the north was emotionally more valuable than what they had lost. Oviedo was particularly sacrosanct as the centre of the October 1934 revolt, and there was therefore in Valencia now a greater determination to force the Nationalists to abandon the campaign in the north than there had been when the battlefield had been the last of the Basque provinces. The strategic merits of an offensive in Extremadura were still as high in June as they had been in the spring, but any major offensive other than on the Madrid front was even more out of the question. Prime Minister Negrín had proved himself more accommodating to the communists than Largo: he had murmured over the GPU's suppression of the POUM in Catalonia, but more as a formality than with any hope of saving its leaders from assassination. Madrid was now a fief of the Communist Party. It was there that the Soviet amigos were most numerous. The only place for an offensive had to be the Madrid front because it was there that the Communist Party had the greater concentration of members as commanders of battalions, brigades and divisions. A victory under their leadership could serve to convince the socialists still fighting to preserve the separate identity of their party that their cause was lost.

Colonel Rojo was not obsessively concerned with politics[13]. It was on military grounds that he believed that the destruction of the enemy before Madrid could be decisive of the war, even if his military judgment coincided with his emotional and deep love of the capital, which he explained later:

'Madrid had been the forge of the People's Army: it was there that a motley collection of fighters had been converted into soldiers and an infinite variety of politically motivated groupings into disciplined and properly constituted military formations, long before that had been so much as attempted elsewhere. . . . The Madrid front was still the most critical: it was where we had the most hardened troops, the senior officers with most experience. . . . Madrid was the living incarnation of the spirit of Spanish nationhood in the mass of those bearing arms. . . . It was therefore not surprising that in thinking of the first offensive which aspired to decisive ends Madrid should have been chosen as its venue[14].

Rojo's plan was simple (Map 11).

Fifteen brigades, grouped two or three into six divisions and they into two corps (numbered 5 and 18), with 70 tanks, 20 armoured cars and 130 guns, were to assemble to the rear of the republican lines between the rivers Perales and Aulencia, this last a tributary of the Guadarrama. Through that stretch, ten kilometres wide, the two corps were to proceed overnight D minus 1/D-day, as surreptitiously as possible for the first six kilometres down to a lane joining the villages of Quijorna and Villanueva de la Cañada. There the tanks would overtake the infantry, to shield them over a further four or so kilometres south to the village of Brunete and across the River Guadarrama east and southeast of the village. Tanks and infantry were to be in position to assault the villages and other enemy-held points in the area at dawn. It was expected that Brunete would fall by 1000 hours. With the establishment of the bridgehead over the Guadarrama and the capture of Brunete, the assault force would proceed, as circumstances permitted, eastwards towards Boadilla del Monte thereby outflanking an important fifteen kilometres of the nationalist front, but more importantly southwards and southeastwards to cut at Navalcarnero and Móstoles the enemy's main line of communication to the whole of the Madrid front, the Madrid–Mérida road[15].

A third corps (numbered II bis), of two divisions and five brigades with thirty tanks, ten armoured cars and thirty-four guns, was to assemble on the southern suburbs of Madrid, and after an artillery barrage and aerial bombardment seek on D-day to break through the enemy lines on the southwest outskirts of Madrid, advance through Carabanchel, and work round to link up with the main force at or about Móstoles thus totally encircling the nationalist Madrid front.

There was a reserve of two divisions with five brigades between them, another three independent brigades, thirty tanks, ten armoured cars and twenty-four guns.

The totals for the assault force therefore were twenty-eight brigades with 130 T-26 tanks, 40 armoured cars and 188 guns – not including anti-aircraft. The number of men involved was something between 80 000 and 90 000[16] over and above the 150 000 holding the line. Air support was to be given by 200 aircraft – I-15s (*Chatos*), I-16s (*Moscas* or *Ratas*), SB-2s (*Katiushkas*) and R-5s (*Natashas*). The tank crews were mixed Spanish and Russian, the pilots either Russians or Spaniards recently returned after training in Russia; five of the brigades were International, but twenty-three totally Spanish.

Nothing on such a scale had hitherto been attempted on Spanish soil. To bemuse the enemy there were to be feint attacks on D-day all along the front from Aragon down to Andalucia; and on D minus 1 a particularly intense one in the Jarama.

Valentin González González ('El Campesino').

Shortly before his death, thirty years after the event, Marshal Malinovsky was to claim that Rojo entrusted him with the tasks of working out the details of the operation and of supervising the assembly of the troops selected to take part[17]. Certainly, there were notable differences between this and all previous republican plans for offensives. Far greater forces were to be concentrated on much narrower fronts than ever before. When, back in February, Rojo had first thought of the Brunete operation he had considered seven brigades sufficient. In March he had thought of nine though the nationalist forces before Madrid were fewer. It was now twenty-eight. The starting lines had been narrowed very considerably. However, there was

The Mexican Colonel Alvarez Algrea known as 'The Gypsy' and Chief of Staff to 'El Campesino' is seen on the right of this picture.

nothing exclusively Russian about such a concentration of force. It was a commonplace of the teaching in staff colleges everywhere in Europe in the 1930s, and Rojo had studied in France. The novelty could be explained in this way: as Miaja's Chief of Staff Rojo had never had as many troops to dispose as he had now as Chief of the General Staff. Nevertheless, as Chief of the General Staff he had raised no objection to the paucity of the effort on the Segovia offensive; but again, that may have been because Brunete had long been an obsession with him, and he lacked belief in the value of Segovia. Where Malinovsky may well have had a considerable hand was in persuading Rojo that the senior commanders of the People's Army were already capable of handling such large bodies of men, and in the choice of the units and their commanders: Rojo had his doubts about some of them.

5 Corps to which the most important role was allocated was under the communist Modesto. His divisional commanders were Lister, 'El Campesino' and 'Walter' (Swierczewski), all good Party men. Jurado, commanding 18 Corps, was not a communist but all his divisional commanders were – José María Galán, Enciso and Janos Galics; so were Romero's (GOC II bis) – Bueno and Gallo – and so again the commander of the two divisions in reserve, the Spaniard Durán and the Hungarian Lazar Stern (Kleber). Where, in the case of the twenty-three Spanish brigades the commander was not a communist, his polit-

ical commissar was. There were also Soviet amigos at corps division and brigade HQs. Though Miaja, GOC Madrid Army, was now of the Party, Grygorij Mikhailovich Shtern remained at his side.* What perturbed Rojo most was that in some headquarters there was confusion as to whether the commander, the Soviet advisers or the political commissar had the final word[18]. In a rapidly moving battle there would not be the time for a soviet to deliberate over what should be done – especially at the lower levels. His fears, however, were not as strong as his conviction that his plan would succeed.

* Goriev had gone north to 'advise' on the defence of the north.

14 Stalemate (Brunete)

The terrain chosen could not have been better for either the silent night approach by the infantry or the advance by the infantry behind a curtain of tanks. It is a plain with only a few commanding mounds, sandy but firm soil, almost barren, with vegetation only here and there – small olive groves, vineyards or unfenced fields, small woods or wild shrub. In a hot summer, such as that of 1937, the Perales, Aulencia and Guadarrama run at low levels. The area was typical of so much of pre-war Castile in another way: in the 120 square kilometres over which the 5 and 18 Corps were to advance, there was only one road, and that one unmetalled. It connected Valdemorillo (behind the republican lines) with Brunete via Villanueva de la Cañada. The third village in the zone, Quijorna, was accessible only by bridlepath. Always provided there was no sudden torrential storm there could be no problem, and even then, the going would be good again within a few hours.

Pre-war, Brunete and district had had 1500 inhabitants, Villanueva de la Cañada 800 and Quijorna 400 (Map 11). Almost all of them had fled the previous October before the advance of the nationalist columns. On D minus 2 the occupants of the area were these: at Quijorna a battalion of ex-Falange militia less a company out on a hill to the north of it, Los Llanos. There were two anti-tank guns on the hill and one at Quijorna. At Villanueva de la Cañada there were two anti-tank and two 75mm guns plus another ex-militia battalion, less a company which was away with five more anti-tank and four field guns at the hamlet of Villafranca del Castillo across the Aulencia. Around the village of Villanueva del Pardillo, between the Aulencia and Guadarrama there was a regular army battalion with two anti-tank guns, and at the ruined castle on the confluence of those rivers a company of Volunteers. The OC that sector of the front, a Lieutenant-Colonel Mancebo, had his HQ at Brunete with around sixty combatants and another twenty men belonging to a field casualty clearing station[1].

There were thus no more than 2000 men within the bounds proposed for the first day of the offensive. The Guadarrama was the line of demarcation between the nationalist 7 Corps under Varela and their Madrid or 1 Corps, temporarily without a GOC. Varela had under his command two divisions, the 71 with 26 700 men in the Guadarrama mountains and 72 with 24 700, strung out over a front stretching 150 kilometres westward. The Brunete sector troops were a part of its 2 Brigade. Immediately to their right, that is, across the River Guadarrama, were the left-most troops of the 11 Division under Iruretagoyena, one of the three in the 1 Corps. The other two were the 12 under Asensio and 14 under Yagüe. The three divisions were the ones which

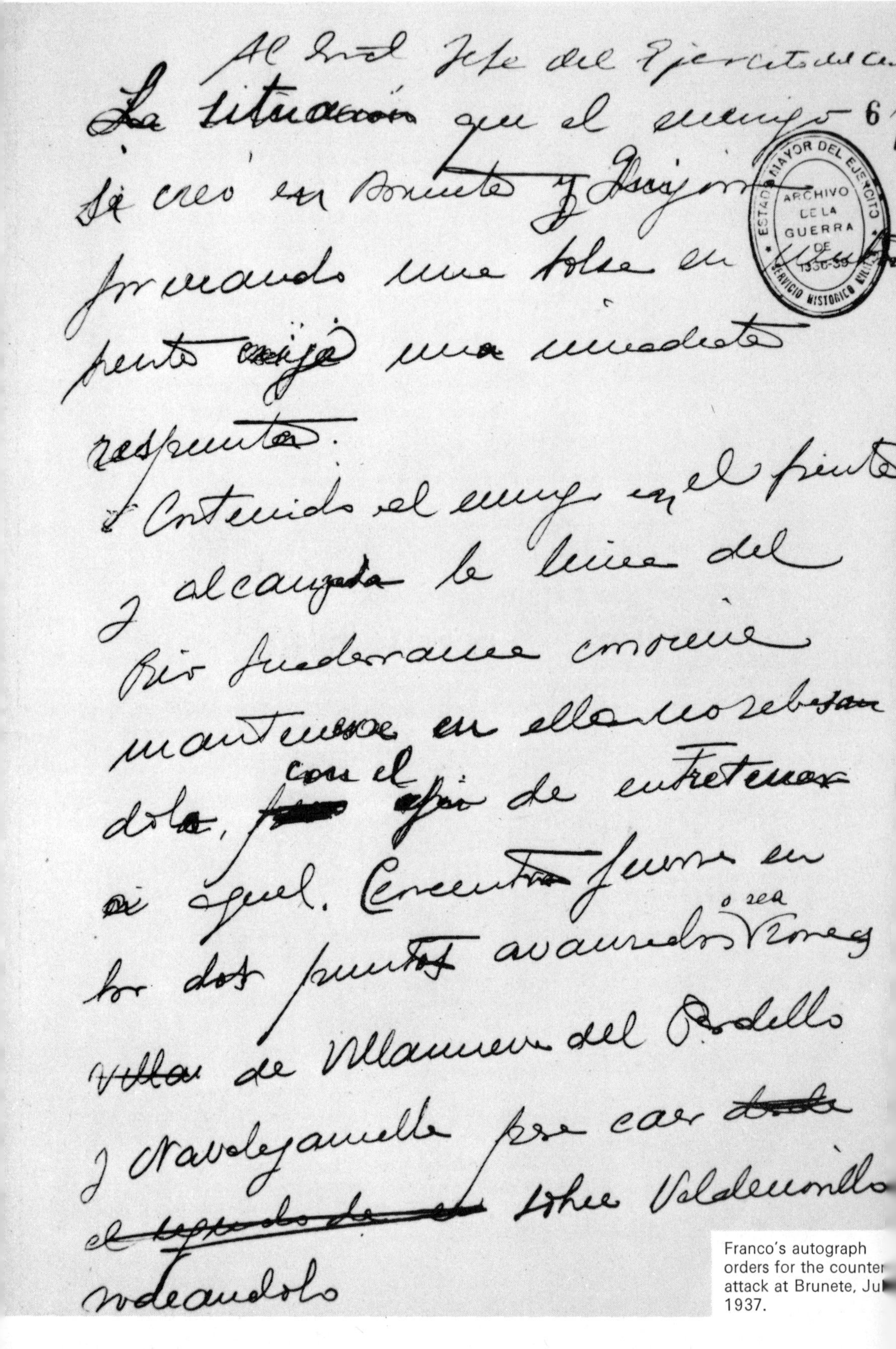

Al Excmo Jefe del Ejercito del Cen[tro]

La situación que el enemigo 6

se creó en Brunete y Quijorna

formando una bolsa en

punto exige una inmediata

respuesta.

Contenido el enemigo en el punto

alcanzado la linea del

Rio Guadarrama conviene

mantenerse en ella no rebasando-

dola, con el afán de entretener

aquel. Concentrar fuerzas en

los dos puntos avanzados o sea Romanillos

de Villanueva del Pardillo

y Navalgamella para caer

sobre Valdemorillo

rodeandolo

ESTADO MAYOR DEL EJERCITO
ARCHIVO DE LA GUERRA DE 1936-39
SERVICIO HISTORICO MILITAR

Franco's autograph orders for the counter attack at Brunete, July 1937.

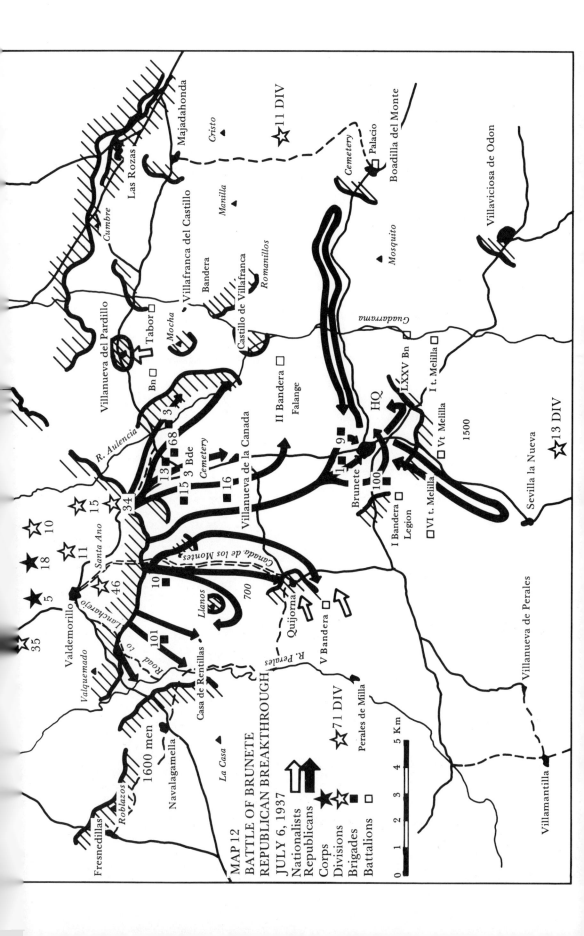

MAP 12
BATTLE OF BRUNETE
REPUBLICAN BREAKTHROUGH
JULY 6, 1937

Nationalists
Republicans

Corps
Divisions
Brigades
Battalions

0 1 2 3 4 5 Km

Fresnedillas

Roblazos

Valquemado

Valdemorillo

1600 men

Navalagamella

La Casa

Casa de Rentillas

Llanos

Santa Ano

Lancharejo

Road rio

700

R. Perales

Quijorna

V Bandera

Villanueva de Perales

Perales de Milla

71 DIV

Villamantilla

35

5

18

10

11

46

101

15

34

13

15 3 Bde

68

3 3

Bn

Villanueva del Pardillo

R. Aulencia

Cumbre

Las Rozas

Majadahonda

Cristo

Manila

Villafranca del Castillo

Bandera

Romanillos

Castillo de Villafranca

Tabor

Mocha

Cemetery

Villanueva de la Canada

Cañada de los Montes

16

II Bandera
Falange

1 9

Brunete

100

HQ

LXXV Bn

I t. Melilla

Vt Melilla

Vt. Melilla

VI t. Melilla

I Bandera
Legion

1500

Sevilla la Nueva

13 DIV

11 DIV

Cemetery

Palacio

Boadilla del Monte

Mosquito

Guadarrama

Villaviciosa de Odon

10

were to be cut off by the republican offensive if it went according to plan. They had 16500, 12300 and 25500 men respectively, so that the total force to be surrounded by the Brunete operation was 54300 men[2]. Together with another corps on the Aragon front, 1 and 7 constituted the nationalists' army of the centre, under General Saliquet whose GHQ was at Valladolid. The army had only one division in reserve, the 13, with 13000 men under Barrón, but as it happened well placed with headquarters at Navalcarnero.

There could be no hope that the republican preparations could be totally hidden from the enemy, but they were so to a praiseworthy degree. When forward observation posts and deserters reported unusual activity in the third week of June, aerial reconnaissance failed to confirm it. It was not till the very end of June that enemy intelligence concluded that there was to be an attack 'between Navalagamella and Las Rozas [villages west of the Perales and east of the Guadarrama], aimed at Quijorna', but they never imagined its scale. The Republicans had had a plan of deception which had succeeded. They had fed newsmen, especially those filing abroad, stories of a pending offensive in the Ebro valley, and nationalist airmen on reconnaissance flight had seen apparently large concentrations of troops and considerable movement there. At Franco's headquarters the conclusion had been drawn that while there would be an attack on Quijorna to provide the Republicans with a springboard for a *future* offensive, the venue of the offensive to make the Nationalists abandon their own against Santander would be along the Aragon front.

On July 5 several of Lister's men deserted, and spoke unanimously of 'an imminent attack designed to wrap up the whole Madrid front'.

A Russian T-26 tank captured by the Nationalists at the Battle of Jarama, February, 1937.

And aimed at Brunete. The feint attack on the Jarama sector had been in progress since 0330 hours that morning. The nationalist high command had no worries that their front there would hold. Still failing to appreciate the scale of the effort on Brunete, they sent a mere one tabor of Moroccans to Quijorna and another to Villanueva del Pardillo, bringing up the numbers who were to come into contact first with those of the republican offensive to 2700.

The following morning those 2700 were to be engaged in battle against a force many times that number whose D-day tasks could therefore, and in consideration of the terrain, hardly have been easier.

The task allotted to the thirds corps, 2 bis, was very different. The nationalist troops opposite the point on the outskirts of Madrid through which they were supposed to break were of Yagüe's outsize 14 Division, well trained, disciplined and manning a system of defence works which they had developed ever since Franco had called a halt in March to any further attempts to capture Madrid. No spectacular results were expected there until, cut off from supplies and reinforcement by the action of the other two republican corps, and worn out by constant artillery and aerial bombardment, the enemy's power and will to resist were weakened; it was 'Brunete' that aroused the expectations of almost all the members of the Government and the troops taking part.

In the afternoon of July 5, Prime Minister Negrín motored through the assembly area in a sort of ceremonial review of the troops, who were lined up along his route and instructed to cheer him. Dolores Ibarruri and Prieto harangued them. The venue of an 'International Writers' Congress' organized by Agitprop was changed from Valencia to Madrid so that the expected great victory should be commemorated in novels, plays and other literary works.

'El Campesino's' 46 Division began to move from Valdemorillo at 2200 hours on D minus 1. One of its brigades (the 101) took up positions on the east bank of the Perales, while the other (the X International) made for Los Llanos and Quijorna. Lister followed up behind with his division (the 11) whose D-day tasks were to surround Brunete by dawn and then storm it, but, as mentioned, more importantly establish a bridgehead across the Guadarrama on the Brunete–Villaviciosa (and Móstoles) road, and push southwards as far as possible on the Navalcarnero road. Modesto kept the remaining division in his 5 Corps (the 35 under 'Walter') in reserve (Map 12).

18 Corps (under Jurado) was to surround Villanueva de la Cañada and hold back any enemy reaction from either Villanueva del Pardillo or Villafranca del Castillo. To this end they were to cross the Aulencia (a minor modification of Rojo's plan). Jurado reckoned that Galán's 34 Division could do both tasks. He expected considerable resistance at Villanueva de la Cañada so he concentrated his tanks on it. Once it had fallen the division was to push on and form a bridgehead across the Guadarrama on the Brunete–Boadilla (Madrid) road; a task which would fall to the two International Brigades (XIII and XV) of the 15 Division if the 34 was too exhausted. The 10 would remain in reserve.

The 34 moved off at 0200 hours. One of the battalions of the 3 Brigade lost its way, but the rest of that brigade and the 16 with the armour reached the outskirts of its objective, Villanueva de la Cañada, safely. At 0530 hours, July 6, the nationalist battalion round and in the vil-

lage was subjected to heavy artillery and at 0600 to aerial bombardment. The infantry moved in to assault behind the tanks.

The assault failed. The two anti-tank and two field pieces brought
the tanks to a halt. Without them the men of the 3 and 16 Brigades,
though outnumbering the defenders about 9:1, made slow progress. At
1400 hours Jurado threw in his corps cavalry, and ordered the 15 Division (XIII and XV International Brigades) into the attack. Miaja,
hearing of the hold up, issued the first of several astonishing orders. He
instructed Jurado 'to take Cañada at all costs, and if the infantry
would not go forward, to place a troop or battery of guns so as to fire
behind our own troops to make them do so'[3]. Even against such overwhelming odds the defenders did not give up Villanueva de la Cañada
till 2115 hours having lost 30 per cent of their number.

On the 5 Corps sector everything went more or less according to
plan overnight but not from dawn onwards. Of the 46 Division's brigades one contented itself with taking up positions on the east bank of
the Perales opposite Navalagamella. The other failed to dislodge the
enemy from either Los Llanos or Quijorna though it tried hard enough
throughout the day, and got generous support from 'Douglas's' airforce.

Lister enveloped Brunete with one of his brigades. The attack on the
eighty men in the village began at 0600 hours. They held out for at
least an hour, and possibly longer[4]. Contrary to orders from the corps,
Lister appears to have held back till 0900 hours his other two brigades
which were supposed to have pushed on along the Navalcarnero and
Móstoles roads without waiting for Brunete to fall. Reconnaissance

A Republican battery in
the torrid heat of the
Battle of Brunete.

then proved that there was nothing to stop them establishing bridge-heads across the Guadarrama or proceeding a long way to Navalcar-nero. One did set out in the latter direction, but after its vanguard had exchanged a few shots with a nationalist patrol, inexplicably it turned back and took up defensive positions only just south of Brunete. The other, preceded by tanks, got only about four kilometres along the Vil-laviciosa route when it too turned back and took up defensive positions one kilometre from Brunete. They were not to be idle for long.

Nationalist reaction to the attack had been rapid. At dawn Mancebo had found his telephone line from Brunete to his own divisional HQ at Avila cut, but he managed to get through to Yagüe, for the time being acting GOC 1 Corps. Yagüe had thereupon instructed a battalion quartered at Villaviciosa to hold the enemy at the bridge over the Gua-darrama to the last man, despatched a tabor of Moroccans to reinforce them and alerted nationalist 7 Corps and army of the centre GHQ. With commendable alacrity Saliquet ordered his one reserve, the 13 Division, to send whatever troops were immediately available to the aid of Mancebo at Brunete (the news of its fall had not yet reached him). One of the officers of the division, Lieutenant-Colonel José Alvarez Entrena, set out on his own immediately for Villaviciosa, took over command of the battalion bivouacked there, organized 320 rear area soldiers and Civil Guard which he found round about into a local defence unit, then led the battalion not to the bridge but right up to a hill dominating Brunete and under three kilometres from it. It was just after 1100 hours. Lister ordered his 9 Brigade and the tanks to dis-lodge them: they failed. The Moroccan tabor sent by Yagüe joined

Republican artillery at the Battle of Brunete.

Entrena. Two tabores arrived from Navalcarnero through Sevilla la Nueva, and established themselves opposite the republican 100 Brigade also one kilometre from Brunete. A bandera of the Legion occupied a similar position on the road westwards out of Brunete. Lister redeployed his three brigades to meet the treble threat from the west, the south and the southeast. He asked for and got air and artillery support. All night long the bandera, the tabores and the battalion were pounded, but they remained immovable[5].

South of Madrid 2 bis Corps had dented the nationalist defences that morning after the heaviest artillery barrage ever recorded in Madrid, but in the evening they retreated to their points of departure in some disorder[6]. There was a renewed attempt at an advance on July 7 when both divisions of the corps suffered considerable casualties and retreated once again. They were to make no serious third attempt. The battle in the Brunete salient required Miaja's full attention.

Saliquet's orders to the 13 Division had of course been only part of a bigger whole. The Guadarrama could no longer be the boundary between the Nationalist 7 and 1 Corps. The 11 Division on the east bank of the river passed out of the latter into Varela's 7, together with the 13. Neither of the republican corps had done as much as had been expected of them on the first day, but there was still plenty of fight in them and Varela could expect several days of anxiety. There was no hope of reinforcements in the immediate future with which to carry out a counter-attack.

During D plus 1, July 7, the 10 Brigade hammered away at Los Llanos and Quijorna. At nightfall Los Llanos was abandoned or, according to Modesto, taken: 'a hundred Moroccans being made prisoner, others committing suicide by shooting themselves in the belly – the classic way among them'[7]. Lister kept up the pressure on the nationalist arc round Brunete. Galics' men tried but failed to cross the Guadarrama due east of Brunete and west of Boadilla, but they did it on the following day when also Quijorna fell after Modesto had thrown his uncommitted division (the 35) into the fight[8] (Map 13A).

Miaja's orders for July 9 had repeated the instruction to cross the Guadarrama by the Brunete–Mósteles road, and if possible 'attack and occupy Villaviciosa'. He dropped the demand in his orders for the 9th, when 5 Corps were told to push down the River Perales and south of Quijorna, and 18 Corps reinforced by the 45 Division with its two International Brigades to occupy Villafranca del Castillo and Villanueva del Pardillo. They were orders which suggest that Miaja was creating for himself an option – the acquisition of territory for its own sake so that 'Brunete' could still be presented at home and abroad as a victory, even if in reality it proved a failure with the non-fulfilment of its primary object as conceived by Rojo.

The secondary object of the operation had however been already achieved. Franco's offensive on Santander had been scheduled to begin on July 10. On hearing of the breakthrough on the 6th he had instructed Kindelan, GOC nationalist airforce, to send the Spanish and Italian squadrons to the Madrid front, asked the German Condor Legion to redeploy a part of its fighter aircraft component, and ordered two infantry divisions out of Cáceres and Galicia to augment Saliquet's resources. Better informed on the 7th of the strength of the enemy effort he had switched south two crack 'brigades' (the 4 and 5 of

Republican troops in Brunete.

ationalist troops after e recapture of Brunete.

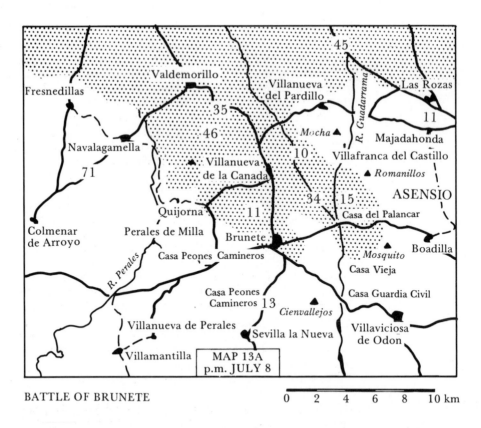

Valdemorillo

Fresnedillas

Villanueva
del Pardillo

45

Las Rozas

11

35

Mocha ▲

Majadahonda

46

R. Guadarrama

Navalagamella

10

Villafranca del Castillo

71

Villanueva
de la Canada

▲ Romanillos

ASENSIO

34 15

Casa del Palancar

Quijorna

11

Colmenar
de Arroyo

Perales de Milla

Brunete

▲ Boadilla

Casa Peones Camineros

Mosquito

R. Perales

Casa Vieja

Casa Guardia Civil

Casa Peones
Camineros 13

Cienvallejos ▲

Villanueva de Perales

Sevilla la Nueva

Villaviciosa
de Odon

Villamantilla

MAP 13A
p.m. JULY 8

BATTLE OF BRUNETE

0   2   4   6   8   10 km

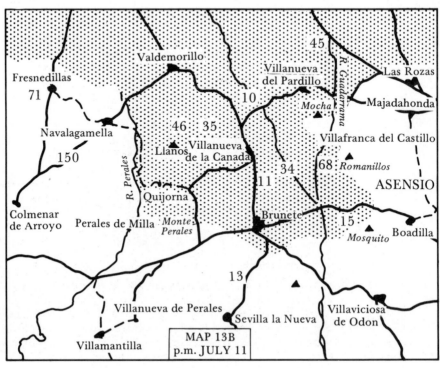

Valdemorillo

45

Fresnedillas

71

Villanueva
del Pardillo

Las Rozas

10

R. Guadarrama

Mocha ▲

Majadahonda

46 35

Navalagamella

Villafranca del Castillo

150

Llanos ▲

Villanueva
de la Canada

68 Romanillos

ASENSIO

R. Perales

34

Quijorna

11

Colmenar
de Arroyo

Perales de Milla

Monte
Perales

Brunete

15

Boadilla

Mosquito

13 ▲

Villanueva de Perales

Sevilla la Nueva

Villaviciosa
de Odon

Villamantilla

MAP 13B
p.m. JULY 11

Navarre, each with fire power greater than that of two republican Mixed Brigades) scheduled for the attack on Santander. On the 8th Franco, accompanied by Barroso, arrived at 13 Division headquarters north of Sevilla la Nueva, and decided that the salient was too dangerous: once the enemy had been contained, the front would have to be restored to approximately where it had been on July 5.

By the 9th the Nationalists had no less than twenty-six battalions in direct contact with the enemy and another twelve in immediate reserve[9]. They had over 100 pieces of artillery, and they were getting some help now from Condor Legion bombers as well as fighters[10].

The speed with which the Nationalists had reacted to the situation was indeed remarkable, and the enormity was now apparent of the failure of the republican divisions – Lister's in particular – to carry out in the appointed manner or fully the tasks allotted to them for the early hours of D-day.

During July 9 the two International Brigades of the 15 Division widened the bridgehead on the east bank of the Guadarrama, while the wholly Spanish 34 and 10 reduced the area held by the Nationalists on the west bank. With help from the 45 they surrounded but could not take Villanueva del Pardillo. It was the turn of Villafranca del Castillo to be surrounded on the 10th. On the 11th the Nationalists succumbed at Villanueva but broke the ring round Villafranca (Map 13B).

Over to the west, 5 Corps had made minuscule gains in three days of bitter fighting, but now the fresh nationalist division from Cáceres was in position, and on the night of July 11/12 Modesto told his divisional

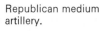

Republican medium artillery.

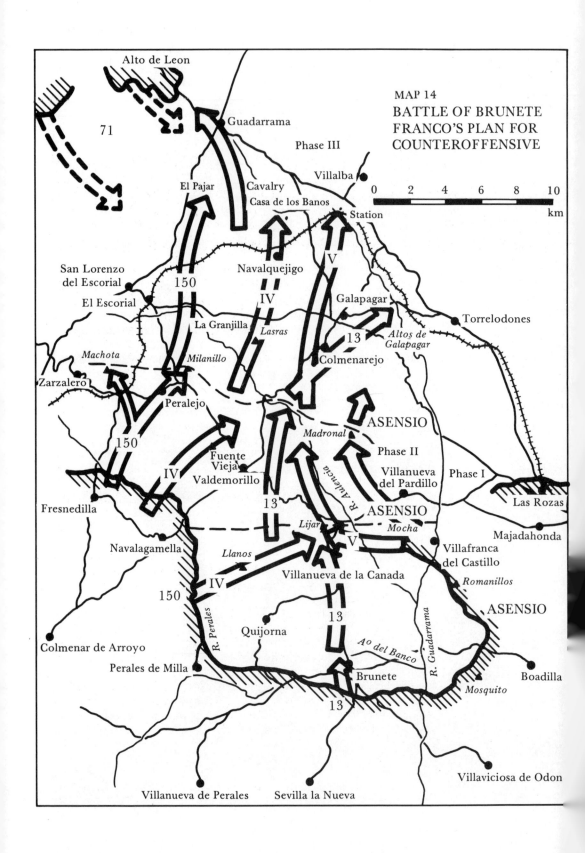

Alto de Leon

71

Guadarrama

Phase III

Villalba

MAP 14
BATTLE OF BRUNETE
FRANCO'S PLAN FOR
COUNTEROFFENSIVE

0   2   4   6   8   10
                    km

El Pajar   Cavalry
           Casa de los Banos
                         Station

San Lorenzo
del Escorial

El Escorial

Navalquejigo

IV

V

Galapagar

Torrelodones

150

La Granjilla   Lasras

13   Altos de
              Galapagar

Machota   Milanillo

Colmenarejo

Zarzalero

Peralejo

ASENSIO

150

Madronal

Phase II

IV

Fuente
Vieja
Valdemorillo

Villanueva
del Pardillo

Phase I

Fresnedilla

13

ASENSIO

Las Rozas

Navalagamella

Llanos

Lijar

Mocha

Majadahonda

150

IV

V

Villanueva de la Canada

Villafranca
del Castillo

Romanillos

ASENSIO

R. Perales

Quijorna

13

Aº del Banco

R. Guadarrama

Colmenar de Arroyo

Perales de Milla

Brunete

Mosquito

Boadilla

13

Villaviciosa de Odon

Villanueva de Perales   Sevilla la Nueva

The University City
Hospital Clínico.

commanders that his orders were 'temporarily' to consider his mission 'one of defence'. The offensive was over for them. Miaja still harboured a lingering hope for 18 Corps. Jurado was relieved of his command 'for health reasons', and Miaja asked of his successor Colonel Casado a major effort towards Majadahonda and Rozas. Nothing came of it except that overnight 12/13 an exhausted XIII International Brigade had to be replaced by a fresh Spanish brigade. It had already suffered barbarously heavy casualties since its entry into the battle on the 9th, and especially on the 11th in the final assault on Villanueva del Pardillo. On the 13th Casado was asked to go for Villafranca del Castillo and eliminate the Nationalists on the west bank of the Guadarrama. Nothing came of that either. Eight days of battle had left the whole corps exhausted. They had been allowed no rest at all for the last four in Miaja's determination that no enemy should be left west of the Guadarrama.

The Condor Legion and nationalist squadrons now had the upper hand in the air. The nationalist anti-tank gunners had taken a heavy toll of the Russian tanks – largely because after the initial attacks they had been used as supplementary artillery, and stationary they presented a much larger target than even a field gun*. Nothing more could be done. On July 14 Prieto ordered the whole of his Madrid Army into the defensive, according to Casado in passing the order to his troops; 'to rest it, to build up reserves to withstand any enemy offensive action in the first place, and in the second to enable offensive action on our part in the near future'[11] – but, Miaja insisted on the 15th, there was to be no withdrawal.

* 'General Rudoft', Soviet OC Tanks in the Brunete sector, reported to Army GHQ that he had only thirty-eight tanks and armoured cars operational at the end of July 11.

A Republican infantryman prepares to throw a hand grenade.

The time had arrived for the Nationalists to move into the offensive. Varela had been for it as soon as the 150 Division arrived from Cáceres, but Franco had told him to wait for the arrival of the two oversize 4 and 5 Navarrese Brigades. Franco's plan, formulated sometime between his arrival at the battle scene on July 8 and the 13th, was the following: Varela was to concentrate forces at Navalagamella and Villafranca del Castillo 'to fall upon Valdemorillo' and thus to trap the whole of the republican 5 and 18 Corps within the Brunete bulge. Once they were mopped up, Varela was to drive north to link up with the Nationalists at the Alto del León, then establish a new front all along the River Guadarrama from its upper reaches to Rozas (Map 14).

On the 13th Franco went into further detail. In Phase I the 5 Navarrese Brigade (or as he called it the *Division Bautista*, after its commander) was to be launched from Villafranca del Castillo towards Lijar, an eminence two kilometres north of Villanueva de la Cañada, and the 4 Navarrese (*Division Alonso*) was to cross the Perales and also make for Lijar through Los Llanos. The 13 Division under Barrón was to take Brunete then fan out towards Quijorna and Villanueva de la Cañada. With the troops thus trapped and finally mopped up, the 150 (*Division Buruaga*) currently holding the front along the Perales and south of Quijorna, and the 11 (GOC Asensio transferred from the 12) currently holding back the republican 18 Corps, would be disengaged. They were to be concentrated one on Fresnedilla and the other on Villafranca del Castillo, and in Phases II and III take part with the Bautista, Alonso and Barrón Divisions in a glorious sweep up the banks of the Guadarrama, the left flank meeting up with the 71 Division up in the Sierra of that name.

Here was as ambitious a plan as Rojo's 'Brunete'. The Republic stood to lose, if it worked, upwards of 60 000 of their best troops, most of the Soviet tank force, their best artillery, and some 4000 square kilometres of territory.

Over the period July 18–23 inclusive, Varela tried to carry out Phase I. The Alonso Division crossed the Perales and got within two kilometres of Los Llanos only to be forced back across the river. The Bautista Division turned the little bridgehead on the west bank of the Guadarrama into a respectable bulge, and Asensio's in support reduced the sizeable Republican bridgehead on the east of the Guadarrama by two-thirds: but that was all. The Alonso Division inflicted such damage on 'El Campesino's' 46 Division that it had to be replaced: the Bautista (which had a squadron of captured Russian T-26s) battered Enciso's but in the process the Navarrese were themselves badly mauled. So also the Asensio Division in reducing the republican bridgehead which was tenaciously defended by the Spanish 68 and International XIII, XV and XVI Brigades.

At 2200 hours on July 23 Galics reported to Casado: 'XIII Brigade completely disintegrated and out of control; am trying to re-establish order in back area'. Called upon to go to the aid of the 10 Division they had refused to move. In an attempt to restore discipline its OC had pulled out his revolver and shot dead one of the mutineers, whereupon some 300 of the 500 men to which the brigade had been reduced in the course of the battle, had taken the road to Torrelodones with the intention of reaching Madrid. Rojo agreed with his successor as Miaja's chief of staff that no attempt should be made to stop them in the battle area 'lest there should be shooting and that were further to demoralize

A group of Republican pilots partake of lunch alongside a I-16 aircraft.

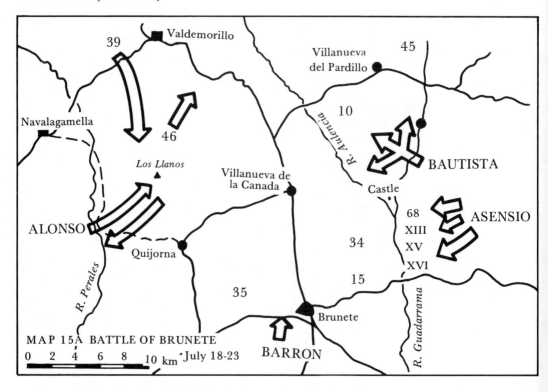

MAP 15A BATTLE OF BRUNETE
0 2 4 6 8 10 km July 18-23

the troops at the front'. Instead he sent out Asaltos in armoured cars to meet them so that 'they could be disarmed and the leaders punished on the spot' at some remote place. They rounded up the mutineers with the help of an army battalion, and took them to Torrelodones. There the brigade was dissolved in August, and those who were not shot were distributed among the other brigades[12].

The XIII Brigade was the only one to crack, but on both sides men were at breaking point. Apart from the normal hardships of battle, aerial and artillery bombardment by day and night, deafening noise, the sickly smell of decomposing bodies, the acrid smoke of burning stubble, the physical effort of attack and hand-to-hand fighting, the sun had beaten down mercilessly day in day out, and the nights had been airless. Neither side's supply columns had been equipped to carry enough drinking water, and there had been cases on both sides of men going mad with thirst[13]. Lister went to see Miaja to ask him to relieve his 11 Division. Barrón opposite him had not attacked, but he had been constantly under bombardment. Miaja asked him to hold out 'for two or three days more'.

Three days more was all that Franco and Varela were to ask of their men – to a new plan with more modest objectives than those first envisaged. As the envelopement of the Republicans had proved impossible with the resources available, Varela obtained permission to try merely to push them out of the Brunete bulge. To that end he disengaged the Navarrese Brigades and brought them round each side of Barrón's Division. All was ready by 0700 hours July 24 (Maps 15A, B and C).

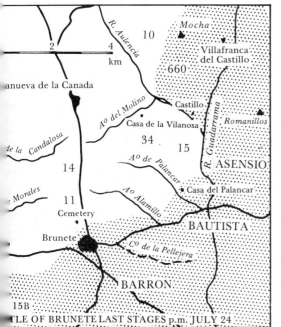

TLE OF BRUNETE LAST STAGES p.m. JULY 24

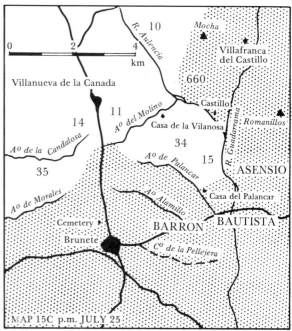

MAP 15C p.m. JULY 25

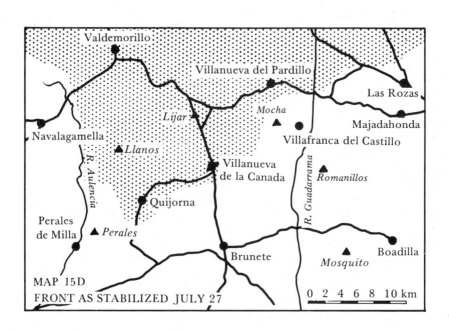

MAP 15D
FRONT AS STABILIZED JULY 27

The Republican 35 and 39 Divisions held Alonso's 4 Navarrese, but Bautista's 5 crashed through the enemy and drove them north of the Brunete–Boadilla road and Asensio cleared the east bank of the Guadarrama. At 1145 hours Barrón forced Lister out of Brunete and as far as the cemetery to the north of the village. The 35 Division went to Lister's aid, and so did a totally fresh 14 Division, which Miaja had ordered to relieve the 11 on that day. This division took up positions in the wood beyond the cemetery. For the rest of that day, throughout that night and into the afternoon the 25th the Republicans counter-attacked repeatedly. Some of their tanks reached the streets of Brunete again. The battle seemed interminable; then, just before 1600 hours, immediately after yet another republican attack, a Spanish sergeant urged his platoon of Moroccans forward. The sight inspired the rest of the tabor and a Spanish battalion alongside, and then the rest of their brigade. At that very moment nationalist aircraft bombed the wood, and the men of the exhausted 11 Division, the frightened men of the 14 and some of the men of the 108 Brigade (35 Division) took to flight in a headlong rush, which neither republican tanks nor cavalry sent to turn them back could stop. Barrón ordered his tanks and cavalry to pursue, and his infantry swept forward before nightfall as far as a hill less than three kilometres from Villanueva de la Cañada[14].

Late on the 25th, Rojo, after referring to the 'disorderly retreat of some units', gave the order that 'all disorderly retreat' would be 'punished with the utmost severity'. Modesto was more explicit: 'machine guns shall be placed behind the front line with orders to open fire on any individual or group which on whatever pretext tries to abandon his post'; and 'Walter' executed several of the officers of the 108 Brigade. The machine guns so mounted did not stop a number of individuals from crossing over to the Nationalists.

Both sides carried out only minor adjustments on the 26th. Franco and Saliquet visited Varela. The Nationalists dug in from one to ten kilometres south of the line of July 6 (Map 15A). Varela was certain from the number of deserters that the enemy was broken, and that with one more push they could be forced right back to the Guadarrama, even to the Alto de Los Leónes. Franco, however, decided, after some deliberation, that there was no point in further action there. The line achieved was one which could be held easily. He wanted his Navarrese Brigades back in the north, and the campaign there to be resumed as soon as possible.

The battle of Brunete was over. There was a plethora of mutual recrimination and accusations among some republican commanders inspired more by political than military considerations; but there were also some acute analyses. Rojo, Miaja's Chief of Staff Matallana, Jurado and his Chief of Staff Ruiz Fornells concentrated on the shortcomings: there had been a lack of co-ordination between the various arms and units; there had been serious breaks in communication and liaison, etc. Thirty years later Rojo was to speak bitterly of 'interference by Soviet advisers at the higher and political commissars at the lower levels'[15]; at the time he noted particularly the lack of initiative among commanders, 'passers on of orders from above' and the inadequacy of the training given junior officers. He was right. In this and this alone had the Nationalists had any advantage over the Republicans: in having men like Varela who was no mere yes-man to Franco,

The Heinkel He 111E-1 bomber was widely used by the Legion Condor and the Nationalist Air Force.

A Messerschmitt Bf 109B-1 of the Legion Condor; this aircraft proved the successful Nationalist answer to the I-16.

the lieutenant-colonel who hurried to Villaviciosa and used his own initiative in deploying his battalion above Brunete and not strictly according to orders, and the sergeant whose action started the avalanche
of the troops which retook Brunete. For the Nationalists had brought
into the battle 87 battalions, the Republicans 119*; the Nationalists
had used 170 guns against 217, some 60 against 100 armoured
vehicles, and 120 aircraft against 200. They had suffered 17000
casualties and the Republicans 23000[16].

Brunete was, as Barroso was to say, 'no model for anyone'. It was a
battle which cannot be justified on military grounds beyond its third
day, and there is some evidence that had Rojo been a free agent and
truly in command he would have ordered the withdrawal of the 5 and
18 Corps back to their line of departure once it had become evident

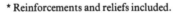

* Reinforcements and reliefs included.

that they were not going to achieve the primary object of the operation. From that moment onwards there was nothing to be gained. The futility of a war of attrition had been proved overwhelmingly in the 1914–18 war – and Rojo knew it, as did Franco. The secondary object, that is to force Franco to abandon the Santander offensive, could have been achieved more effectively had the Republic attacked the Aragon front as it did belatedly. Brunete merely delayed Franco's offensive. It did not stop it – nor, for that matter, did the Aragon offensive, but this was perhaps because so much effort had been squandered at Brunete.

Several aspects of Brunete, nevertheless, deserve careful study. The Republic was forced to continue the battle of Brunete, and both sides to waste lives in the defence and capture of that little village by itself of negligible military value, because the Press of the then influential countries of the world exalted it to the highest pinnacles of importance. There were then and subsequently other distortions, for example the stress which certain writers put on foreign help, or the prowess of their fellow nationals or political co-religionists – Americans, British, communists. Foreign help to one side proves on analysis to have been no greater than to the other, whether in terms of manpower or efficacy of machines and men, and for every foreigner on either side there were at least four Spaniards. This battle, unlike Brihuega, was overwhelmingly between Spaniards; especially at the most important and basic level of all, the infantry private. Notwithstanding the flight of a few on the one side, what the records show when stripped of propaganda and of observations written to correct faults and improve military efficiency at the time, is that the Spaniards of the two sides were equal in their resistance to physical and mental hardship, and equal in self-sacrifice and heroic courage. No other judgment is possible in truth and justice.

15 The End of the Battle

In July 1937 both sides could expect further help from abroad, but there was nothing to warrant the supposition that either could or would get the quantity and quality required for that help to be decisive. For all the Russian, 'International', German and Italian troops, and for all the weapons and munitions imported over the previous twelve months the war was still, and was likely to remain, essentially one between Spaniards armed with Spanish-made weapons. Hence on the one hand the importance of the industrial centres, of Vizcaya, Santander province, Asturias, Catalonia. Hence, on the other the importance of the overrunning of areas which could provide the men for those arms. The day of the volunteer, Navarrese and Castilian on the one side, Madrileño, Catalan and Valencian on the other was over. Both sides were now relying on conscription and the recall of pre-war conscripts to make good losses in battle and to expand their forces. In July 1937 half Spain's population was to be found in the republican and the other half in the nationalist zones.

The Nationalists now had the armaments and munition factories of Vizcaya but not those of Santander province. They could now export iron ore out of Bilbao and so encourage foreign suppliers to provide them rather than than the Republicans with petrol and other essential raw materials, but the Republicans still held the coal mines of Asturias. The bulk of the defenders of Bilbao had escaped into Santander, and 160 000 Basque refugees had gone with them[1], but a far greater number of the inhabitants of Vizcaya had remained behind. Some were actively pro-Nationalist: the others would be given no more choice not to work for the enemy war economy than the pro-Nationalists had been allowed before their 'liberation'. Santander and Asturias were also well-populated provinces.

All those and other factors made the strategic value of the north far greater than that of Madrid. Hence Franco's concentration of force on it. It was even more important to the Republicans that they should deny him the region – or what was left of it to them – for as long as possible. If the Nationalists could be held to mid-October on the edge of Vizcaya the rains and snows of autumn and winter would come to the aid of the defenders of Santander and Asturias. The Republic could reasonably expect over the winter months a greater volume of supplies than their opponents from foreign sources, and so look forward to a chance of a draw, if not victory in 1938.

Simultaneously with the Brunete offensive, the Republicans had carried out a limited operation on the township of Albarracín to the rear of the Nationalist-held Aragonese city of Teruel. It had come to nothing, but it had revealed how lightly the nationalist eastern front

A T-26 tank with Soviet
crew photographed in
October/November 1937.

was being held, and how vulnerable it was even to a minor concentration of force. Accordingly the Republicans now redeployed between 80 000 and 100 000 men[2] (Modesto's 5 Army Corps and other divisions, a total of twenty-two infantry brigades with another nine in reserve, and supporting tanks, cavalry and artillery), for 'a grand offensive on Zaragoza'.

Its object was the capture 'in one day' of that most important centre of communications, not merely to force the Nationalists to give up their northern campaign, but to threaten the whole of their position in Old Castile and Navarre. In the event, it accomplished neither. The Republicans took fifteen days to overcome resistance at the small town of Belchite without possession of which they did not dare advance onward to Zaragoza; the offensive petered out, and they lost most of the ground gained in a subsequent counter offensive. Franco switched three divisions from the Madrid front to stop the original breakthrough, but none from the northern front.

The offensive on Zaragoza began on August 24: the counter-offensive on October 6. Santander city fell on August 26. The Nationalists were through the Peaks of Europe by September 20. Resistance to them in Asturias ended with the capture on October 21 of the ports of Gijon and Avilés. Though hampered by saboteurs and guerrilla activity, the Nationalists had the industries of the north in substantially full production by December.

In retrospect the loss of the north came to be reckoned by republican writers – socialist, anarchist and even some communist – as the heaviest, indeed the decisive, blow against Republic. With the north in his hands Franco had the means to manufacture at least twice as

many guns and shells, and small arms and bullets, as the Republic. By December many of the survivors who had fought for the Republic in the campaign in the north were joining his Army. He had won, and the Republic had lost a population of over two million from which to recruit troops. The odds of a victory in 1938 were now in the Nationalists' favour.

At the end of October Prime Minister Negrín moved the Government from Valencia to Barcelona, and there proceeded in effect to deprive Catalonia of the autonomy which it had been granted in 1931. Catalonia, with its substantial resources, had to be incorporated into the Republic's war economy. As an autonomous region it had looked after its own rather than the Republic's interests. Production in Catalonia, taking January 1936 as 100, had fallen to 64 by August 1936. It was to rise to 70 by January 1937 under Negrín's Government, with the full co-operation of the Communist Party, which considered chimerical the application of anarchist principles to the basically small entrepreneur frame of Catalan industry. The loss of the republican army in the north had also to be made good. From Valencia it had been impossible fully to implement mobilization orders. The call-up was now extended to cover ages 20–28 inclusive, and the loss of the 200 000 strong army in Santander and Asturias was indeed made good.

Franco's Chief of Operations, Colonel Barroso, was already thinking in July 1937 of the next move after the 'liquidation' of the northern front. He advocated an offensive down to the Mediterranean from the Ebro valley, to cut the remaining republican zone in two, then the overrunning of Catalonia and Valencia, in that order and only then the capture of Madrid. 'To take Madrid', he wrote and underlined, '*we should have all the trumps in our hand*'[3].

Rojo's appreciation of nationalist intentions after the fall of Asturias coincided with Barroso's (Barroso considered Rojo to have been one of his best pupils at the Staff College)[4]. On October 27 Rojo wrote: '[The enemy] can consider decisive only two objectives: Madrid, and a thrust on the Aragon front down to the sea . . . [I believe] the enemy has sufficient experience of war to appreciate how bloody the conquest of Madrid would be . . . (hence, and in spite of reports to the contrary) I consider the Aragonese theatre the most likely venue in the immediate future'[5].

Up to November Franco agreed with Barroso's strategy, and brushed aside the insistence of the politically-minded at his headquarters, and of his critics in Berlin and Rome, that the capture of Madrid would yield him international political dividends of greater value than the defeat of the enemy in the field. He then changed his mind. On November 28 he wrote of delays in the provision of artillery for the 'Army of Manoeuvre' which he had been organizing for the offensive down to the sea, a mass of around 250000 men with impressive artillery support. Not to have his troops inactive and for *tactical*, not strategic, reasons (shortening of the front, blow to republican morale since republican propaganda had made its own rank and file believe in Madrid as the key to victory), he decided on yet another attempt to assault Madrid.

The axis of the attack was to be the Zaragoza–Madrid road, via Guadalajara. The Italians were to be given a chance to avenge their defeat at Brihuega. What remained of them (20000 in two 'divisions', and a third reinforced with Spaniards), were scheduled to take part together with thirteen Spanish infantry divisions and one cavalry divi-

A review of troops on the Madrid front in November, 1937 by Azaña, Negrín and Prieto.

sion. Franco still had a low opinion of the Italians as fighters.

The date for the offensive was as yet not fixed when, on December 15 the Republicans struck at the nationalist salient at Teruel, with 77 000 men and two regiments (brigades) of Russian T-26 and BT-5 tanks. The latter, just arrived from the Soviet Union, were heavier and more powerfully armed than any tanks then in service anywhere. Teruel was surrounded. Franco cancelled the Madrid offensive project, and redeployed a part of his forces both to relieve the city and to meet what could develop into a major threat to his communications with Zaragoza.

In temperatures which reached minus 20 degrees centigrade, a terrible battle was fought, and further proof was provided that there was nothing to choose between the heroism of either side. The besieged in Teruel held out till January 8 1938 against great odds, but the Republicans held back the relief force with equal tenacity.

In taking Teruel the People's Army gave evidence that it was now capable of offensive action, and in the defence of their positions against the relief force that it could be driven back only when heavily outnumbered and outgunned. From that it followed that the destruction of the will to fight of the People's Army was unlikely without the destruction of a large part of it.

The kudos that the Republic derived on both sides of the war and internationally from the capture of Teruel, and the degree to which it had lifted republican morale, made it essential that Franco should recapture the city. All thought of an attack on Madrid even for tactical reasons or morale therefore vanished from his mind. In February he outflanked Teruel and the Republicans fell back to

President Azaña, Prime Minister Negrín, Minister of Defence Prieto with officers of the general staff in November, 1937.

avoid being encircled. He now concentrated the whole of his well-equipped 'army of manoeuvre', twenty-five infantry divisions and one cavalry, along the upper Aragon. On March 9 it attacked. The republican front collapsed, and in six weeks the Nationalists overran an area the size of the Netherlands: more, they drove a wedge down to the Mediterranean, reaching it on April 15, thus splitting the third of Spain still in republican hands into two zones.

As the front collapsed Negrín's Minister of War, Prieto, saw the war as lost. So did Rojo; but not Negrín or the Communist Party. Negrín prevailed on Léon Blum of France to allow the uninhibited passage of a substantial quantity of new weapons from the Soviet Union and the arms manufacturers of Europe. Hitler was annexing Austria and no one really believed that that would be his 'last territorial demand'. Negrín harboured the hope that with those arms defeat could be held off for those few months that he reckoned would elapse before Hitler's rapacity provoked a general war in Europe, and that in that war he could persuade Britain and France to look upon Franco as Hitler's puppet, and so intervene to save the Republic.

Franco, instead of going for Catalonia after his drive to the sea, chose now to go for Valencia. To reach it his troops had to go over the marvellously difficult terrain of the Maestrazgo; but he reckoned that with the new weapons in their hands, the republican forces in Catalonia would be better able to resist him than those in the southern region, that the Catalans would be a threat to him as guerrilla fighters after their defeat in the field, that with Valencia in his hands Madrid would be untenable, and that with all of Spain less Catalonia his, France would recognize his Government and so cease to allow the passage of weapons to his enemies. Unseasonal rain upset his calculations. It took his army three months to come within thirty kilometres of the city of Valencia.

All this while Rojo was for striking back at Franco's weakest point, Extremadura. The difficulty of providing the southern region with the equipment necessary diminished the chances of success of his 'Plan P', as it was called. With the Nationalist army advancing inexorably, however slowly, on Valencia, some action was necessary. The storm was not gathering over Europe as rapidly as Negrín had hoped. Rojo therefore had to choose the north for an offensive. On July 25 a strike-force of over 100 000 Republicans crossed the River Ebro on inflatable rubber boats and pontoon bridges bought in France, crashed through positions held by an army corps under Yagüe, and took the heights above the river. In retaking those heights the Nationalists lost 40 000 men, but the Republicans over 70 000 in their defence.

They were losses which Franco could, and did make good, but which the Republicans could not. By December there were over 775 000 Spaniards in the nationalist forces, and at most only 500 000 in the republican. Iron-ore production in Nationalist-held Vizcaya, necessary not only for the production of shells and gun linings but for its sale abroad and the purchase of petrol with the profits, was running at almost six times the 1936 rate. Industry in the republican zones, starved of raw materials, was coming to a standstill.

On December 23 Franco ordered twenty-two of his fifty-two divisions to advance into Catalonia. The republican lines broke. On the last day of the year Negrín appealed to the United States to intervene.

Twenty-three days later he fled from Barcelona to Figueras and on February 5 to France. The Nationalists entered Barcelona on January 26, and occupied the last square kilometre of Catalonia on February 13.

All that now remained of the Republic was the rough square of Valencia, Cartagena, Almeria, Madrid.

On that day Franco had 796000 Spaniards under arms, plus around 15000 Italians and 5000 Germans. On the republican side the International Brigades had ceased to exist as such after the battle of the Ebro: the Russians had been withdrawn over a period stretching even further back: the foreigners in what was left of Republican Spain could not have numbered more than hundreds. There were however four 'armies' comprising sixteen 'corps', and these one armoured and forty-nine infantry 'divisions' – on paper a force as large as Franco's, in fact, and only after the extension of mobilization to youths as young as 17 and men as old as 47* could it have mustered 500000, ill-armed, ill-fed, worse clothed.

North of the Pyrenees there were several million dollars' worth of equipment awaiting transport to the republican zone, but there was little chance that more than a small portion of it could be got there; the smaller nationalist navy had achieved supremacy at sea over the theoretically more powerful republican.

Negrín returned from France to Spain and on February 12 saw Colonel Casado in Madrid. Casado was GOC III Army deployed in the defence of the Madrid front. He described the reality of the situation to the Prime Minister who had come to urge his armies to continue the fight: 'the fire-power of a single enemy battalion is three times that of one of ours. . . . Our air-cover is down to three Natasha and two Katiuska squadrons, plus 25 fighters. . . . Our troops in the desolate moors uplands of Cuenca and Guadalajara are suffering the rigours of this hard winter in rope-sandals [*alpargatas*]; we cannot provide even shoes for them. They haven't had a change of shirt for weeks; they have no other than the ones they have on, and their bodies are covered with sores. Lack of vitamins is wreaking havoc, especially in the Guadalajara sector.'[6] The Other Ranks' rations, consisted of 100 grammes of bread a day, 'coffee' made from toasted barley grains, and a bowl of soup at dinner and suppertime.

Notoriously Spanish soldiers had never in modern history been issued with personal clothing adequate either in quality or quantity: nor had they ever been provided with a plentiful or balanced diet – hence the high incidence of sickness and death on active service of Spaniards in the Riff War, and of Spaniards of both sides from the very start of the Civil War: but a parallel to the situation of the republican forces that winter of 1938–9 could have been found only in the very remote history of Spain. Throughout history, Spaniards had repeatedly distinguished themselves as soldiers capable of withstanding physical discomfort to a heroic degree; but the Civil War was no ancient or mediaeval engagement, and no longer, as in the beginning, of a kind with Napoleonic warfare. It had become a war of trenches, artillery duels, aerial bombardment, attack and counter attack, a war demanding of the participants a high degree of physical fitness. To ask

* Expectancy of life in Spain was then 50 for males.

of those weary, cold, hungry men, short of weapons and equipment further effort was to demand of them a senseless sacrifice.

Yet Negrín did. He was backed only by the communist ministers in his Cabinet (and by the crypto-communist Alvárez del Vayo), by the communist officers in the Army – Miaja (after some hesitation), Modesto, Lister, Barceló and the like – by the Central Committee of the Spanish Communist Party, the Comintern agents in Valencia (Togliatti, Stepanov), and the new chief of the Soviet amigos, General Borov.

Civilians that February were on the whole worse off than the soldiers. In Madrid sixty to seventy were dying of starvation every day, others through the lack of medical supplies, the old of hypothermia. Families huddled in the underground stations, to keep warm rather than to be safe from the occasional shell or bomb. There were few trees left; they had been cut down for fuel. Electricity was severely rationed. There were long queues for the little food available to those, the overwhelming majority, who had neither the hoarded money nor the right party card to buy or sell with impunity in the Black Market. Dogs and cats had disappeared. Rats were on sale in the Plaza Mayor.

In the midst of such misery there were new posters on hoardings and walls. Their purpose was, as before, to strengthen the will of the armed forces to fight on, but use was now made of the force of patriotism. On those posters as also in every issue of the Communist Party daily *El Mundo Obrero*, the war was now presented as one of a national independence against foreign invaders, and not any more as a step in the establishment of a socialist or communist utopia, nor as a defence of democracy or republicanism. People and soldiers were exhorted in such slogans as these: 'Spain is more than ever resolved to fight for her independence. So long as there is a single invader in Spain, the people will remain at war. Long live Free and Independent Spain!' *Viva Rusia!* ceased to be a popular cry.

Several explanations are possible as to why Negrín insisted on the continuance of the war, and why the communists seconded his decision. Such was his belief in himself that he may have decided on it independently of the communists. Such were his sexual aberrations that he may have been in their power, as others have been. If he decided for himself, it may be true, as Alvarez del Vayo alleges[7], that he hoped that continuing resistance would persuade Franco into a negotiated peace with the vanquished. In Figueras, before his flight to France, Negrín had sent Franco, through the agency of the British Foreign Minister Lord Halifax, an offer. The Republicans would surrender if Franco undertook to renounce political reprisals, to have common crimes – murder, rapine, etc. – judged only in ordinary courts, and to allow all those who wished to leave Spain to do so.

That there would be imprisonment and execution on a large scale was a fully warrantable belief, even before Franco's promulgation on February 13 of a decree promising punishment to all whom his military courts found guilty of 'helping to undermine public order' since October 1 1934, or of 'impeding after July 18 1936 the national movement ... by definite acts or by being grievously passive'. The Nationalists had already proved themselves to be as much as the Republicans heirs of the Romano–Visigothic *Lex talionis* in its least Christian aspect.

To accept that Negrín really did harbour the hope that a further show of force would persuade Franco to accept such or any terms would imply that Negrín thought Franco to be ignorant of the parlous state of the republican army, and that Negrín had not studied the character of his enemy, which, given his responsibilities as Prime Minister, he should have done. Franco would never have engaged in negotiations with a man so closely identified with the communists as Negrín had become, and the one hope of mercy from Franco was for someone else to have put the Republic unconditionally at his mercy, immediately, as he was to demand explicitly on February 18. Yet again, Negrín may have hoped from his policy for nothing more than time, time for the escape of the tens of thousands with whom the Nationalists were likely to avenge the deaths of the tens of thousands of their supporters at the hands of the Republicans: but if so it is curious that no such mass escape was planned, nor indeed could it have been possible, given the paucity of the ships and aircraft available. Plans were made for the escape only of a limited number of the prominent political and military leaders.

Whatever the reason, the fact is that Negrín did urge his generals to fight on – on February 12, and after Franco made it known that he would accept nothing less than unconditional surrender. On February 27 any hope that foreign powers would come to his aid became totally unwarrantable: Britain and France recognized Franco's as the *de facto* Government of Spain. Azaña, in Paris at the time, resigned his presidency of the Republic which, in his view, had ceased to exist; in Madrid officially, in fact in a farmhouse near Valencia with the code name *Posición Yuste*, Negrín again said 'fight on'.

It was a curious irony of history that Negrín's 'bunker' should have been named after the place to which the Emperor Charles V retired. There Negrín lived 'as a bandit chieftain', in the words of the most perceptive observer of those latter days of the war, the then anarchist José García Pradas. He was protected by a personal bodyguard of '500 communist guerrillas, of fierce aspect, submachine guns at the ready and handgrenades hanging from their belts'[8] – a remark which suggests a possible answer to the question as to why the Communist Party was so anxious that the war should continue for as long as possible: that the communists wanted time to set up the infrastructure of future guerrilla operations. They did it in certain areas. It is an explanation which complements with another: that they were set on the creation of an image both of themselves as heroes who had never surrendered to the 'fascists', and of the socialists and left Republicans as 'traitors to the sacred cause of anti-fascism'.

In parallel and roughly simultaneously with Negrín's approach to Franco through the British Foreign Office, there had been another, through Franco's military intelligence agents in Madrid. Casado promised Franco to organize a coup against Negrín and the communists and make peace if Franco gave his word that he would 'respect the lives of decent officers and civilians'. The difficulties of communications across the lines, suspicions on Casado's part of whether the men with whom he was in contact were Franco's agents and not agents of the dreaded republican SIM (*Servicio de Investigación Militar*) which was modelled on the NKVD, and doubts on the nationalist side whether Casado had the necessary ability and influence to effect the coup, slowed down the progress of this move to peace begun towards the end of January. It was not till February 22 that Casado received a document (dated February 6) from the hands of two undoubted nationalist lieutenant-colonels, in which Franco gave the promises for which Casado had asked[9]. Franco's agents then understood that Casado would act on February 25.

That very day the official *Gaceta de la República* carried news of Casado's promotion to general in the People's Army. Day after day passed without news of the promised revolt, and Franco became impatient and distrustful. Casado asked for time. He was indeed trying hard to obtain promises of support from his fellow officers, but he had to act warily, and he was not by nature a bold man. He had been under suspicion from at least February 16 when, at an assembly of all the republican senior army, navy and airforce officers convoked at the airfield of Los Llanos near Valencia by Negrín, to hear from him and Miaja, now Supreme Commander of all those forces, that the war was to continue at all costs, Casado had repeated publicly what he had previously said to Negrín privately – that to continue was madness[10].

From that moment onwards in fact Negrín and the Party had been preparing a coup of their own – the removal of Casado and all other non-communists from their positions of military command. The first changes were published on March 4, on which day Negrín invited Casado to 'Yuste' and sent an aircraft to fetch him. Casado declined the invitation. That evening Negrín *ordered* Casado to report to him on the following day. Casado had somewhat naïvely told the Commander-in-Chief of the Republican Air Force, Hidalgo de Cisneros, of his plan to revolt, presumably imagining Hidalgo's espousal of communism insincere.

Casado could delay no longer. He was still by no means certain how many of his own officers and men would follow him in the revolt against Negrín. The one corps commander he could trust completely was the popular anarchist Cipriano Mera, and the one complete unit was a mixed brigade (the 70), resting around Alcalá de Henares. Casado therefore asked Mera to embus that brigade towards evening, and with it to seize the Ministries of War and the Interior, the Telefónica, the GPO and the Bank of Spain, and take up defence positions round the Treasury which he proposed to make his headquarters.

To that very solid building on the Calle de Alcalá, just off the Puerta del Sol, the vaulted cellars of which had provided Miaja with a bomb and shell-proof headquarters during the height of the battle for Madrid, Casado summoned representatives of the Socialist Party, UGT, CNT and Left Republican Parties. Some of those invited arrived two hours late at 2100 hours, but the assembly quickly resolved that as Azaña was no longer President, Negrín's legitimacy as Prime Minister had disappeared; that Negrín was about to betray the Republic to the Communist Party; and that to save Spain from such a fate, they had no alternative but to rise against him. They formed a National Defence Council from among their number.

The 90 Brigade should by now have been in position, but movement control officers had held up its departure from Alcalá until formalities had been complied with, and it did not reach Madrid till 2330 hours. Mera, however, had in the meantime 'neutralized' the communist officers in the whole of his corps.

Just after midnight the most eminent of the socialist intellectuals, Professor Julian Besteiro, broadcast from the Treasury building the news of the formation of the National Council of Defence, and an exhortation to the people to put their trust on the Army of the Republic as represented by those who spoke after him – Casado and Mera. Casado, in the midst of many equivocal statements, called on Spaniards to choose between 'foreigners and compatriots, peace for the good of Spain or war in the service of imperialistic madness'. Mera said 'as from this moment, fellow citizens, Spain has one government, and one mission – peace'.

Reaction to the Casado revolt varied. Negrín and his Cabinet, the remaining Soviet advisers and most of the Central Committee of the Communist Party flew into exile. They were faced not only with the Casado rising in Madrid but with another in the naval base at Cartagena (where eventually troops loyal to them were to succeed and repel a seaborne landing by nationalist forces). General Miaja, in spite of his Communist Party card and previous agreement with Negrín, joined Casado who had offered him the presidency of the Council of Defence, but two of Casado's own army corps commanders, the communist Barceló and Bueno, decided to do battle with Casado and the anarchist Mera. So also a Major Domingo Hungría who took over command of a corps recently organized from crack troops wholly committed to the communist cause, and seemingly destined for special training as guerrillas.

Bueno instructed one of his divisions to occupy Fuencarral on the northern perimeter of Madrid, and take up positions along the east–west avenue now called after General Sanjurjo*. One of Hungría's divisions (the 300) quartered around Alcalá received instructions to secure that town, and to advance on Madrid from the east. Casado despatched a brigade to meet them.

Within Madrid on that March 6 there was utter confusion. Armoured vehicles cruised the streets, and there were battles round the railway terminus at Atocha, the Royal Palace and the Puerta del Sol between detachments of soldiers whose allegiance could be discovered only if questioned by word of mouth, and in fear questions were not always asked before shots were exchanged. Republican aircraft dropped bombs on Madrid, but whether they fell on friend or foe no one could tell.

Hungría's division, reinforced by tank squadrons from the base at Alcalá, advanced inexorably towards Madrid throughout the following day. The brigade sent out by Casado offered no resistance. By nightfall the division was within a hundred metres of Cibeles, and linked up with the anti-Casado forces along Sanjurjo. Barceló took overall command against Casado, whose men, by the morning of the 8th, had been forced out of all but a few blocks north and south of the Calle de Alcalá between Cibeles and Puerta del Sol, and of some isolated buildings elsewhere. The Nationalists in the Carabanchel sector carried out a reconnaissance in force, seemingly in answer to an urgent request from Casado to attack and an assurance from him that no resistance would be offered there or in the Parque del Oeste south of the University City. After suffering 200 casualties the Nationalists with-

* Then Abascal.

drew. The Republicans in the trenches were in no mind to let 'fascists' through even to help them fight communists, or perhaps those troops were communist-controlled.

Help came from another quarter. On that very day a force, gathered together by a pro-Casado colonel, Liberino González, from units in the province of Guadalajara and elsewhere, captured Alcalá de Henares from Barceló's men. It pursued the defeated communists to the very outskirts of Madrid so that for a while any aircraft flying in a straight line west–east over Madrid would have flown over sectors held as follows: Nationalists – anti-Casadists – pro-Casadists – anti-Casadists – pro-Casadists. Two and a half days of very confused fighting followed, with artillery firing at point blank range, and much hand-to-hand fighting. No one knows how many died, but it is not improbable that more men were killed then in the streets of Madrid than in any similar period since November 1936[11]. The victors were the pro-Casadists. The last of the communist troops to surrender were some in the unfinished Nuevos Ministerios, after bombardment throughout the night of March 11/12.

On the 13th the victorious anti-communists executed Barceló and the leading communist Political Commissar Conesa. The communists had previously executed some of Casado's officers. The strong anarchist element in the pro-Casado forces also had old scores to settle with the communists, and they did so.

Casado and the Council, the sole authorities left in the shattered republican zone, now again offered to negotiate peace with Franco, on the basis of 'a peace with honour', outlined under nine headings, the most important points of which were those which Negrín had asked for: no reprisals and liberty of exile for all those who wished it[12].

After ten days of exchanges of views through Franco's agents in Madrid, two republican professional colonels, Antonio Garijo Hernández and Leopoldo Ortega Nieto, were received at Franco's headquarters in Burgos after a flight from Madrid. They carried two documents signed by Casado: the Council did not wish any longer to *impose* conditions on the victors – merely to *ask* of Franco an act of grace for the good of Spain and to make easier the work of reconstruction which lay ahead. If those who wanted to leave Spain were left in doubt as to whether they would be allowed to do so – the colonels in answer to a question estimated their number as 'between 4000 and 10000' – then fear of what might happen to them might provoke them to slaughter the nationalist sympathizers in the republican zone: the Council would do its best to prevent it, of course, but its control of the zone was tenuous.

From Franco the colonels received nothing except Franco's timetable for the rapid surrender of all the republican forces: the airforce was to fly all its machines to nationalist fields on March 25: the whole army was to surrender simultaneously on March 27. Casado had proposed the piecemeal surrender of the army sector by sector over a period of twenty to thirty days[13].

Back in Madrid Besteiro counselled acceptance of the reality of the situation. Casado was all for putting into effect a plan for the withdrawal of the republican army in the southeast corner of Spain before Cartagena, a plan envisaged before him by Negrín. He wrote a personal letter to Franco in which he explained his position: he had committed himself to obtaining the free exodus of those wishing to leave Spain: if it were not granted then the communists who had justified their anti-peace attitude on the assumption that Franco would concede nothing would be proved right, and he would be called a traitor.

Garijo and Ortega took the letter together with two new documents also written by Casado to Franco's headquarters on the afternoon of March 25. When they arrived they were asked whether the republican airforce would be landing on nationalist airfields in what remained of the day. They replied that bad weather was impeding take-off, which occasioned the rejoinder that the same bad weather had not impeded *their* flight from Madrid. In one document Casado reiterated his plea for the piecemeal surrender of the republican forces. In both he now emphasized the need of a signed and sealed guarantee of the promises received through Franco's agents in February.

From all this Franco deduced that Casado was merely playing for time. He instructed his representatives at the conference with the colonels to declare the talks at an end, and decreed the following to be D-day of the general offensive which he had had ready for a month.

At 0240 hours on the morning of Sunday March 26 a message arrived from the National Defence Council. It promised the surrender of the airforce on March 27 and asked 'please fix hour'. At 0320 hours there was a further message: 'we may be able to deliver aircraft later today'. According to plan the offensive began at dawn with a light artillery bombardment in Extremadura. By 0800 hours the front there had broken and whole republican battalions were surrendering. At 0817 hours there was a final threatening and elliptic message from Madrid 'this Council which with the unconditional backing of the people has done everything humanly possible to bring about peace says yet again to [the nationalist] Government that its greatest worry is the reaction that the offensive might provoke, and hopes that to avoid the irreparable damage which surprise [at the offensive] might cause, it will allow the evacuation of those [considered] accountable [for their actions in the war]. If it does not it will be the Council's inescapable duty to resist the advance of [the nationalist] forces.'[14] Burgos replied that it was too late to countermand the orders already given to the nationalist armies to advance, and suggested that republican units in the trenches should show white flags immediately after the preliminary artillery or air bombardment.

That afternoon the nationalist radio stations carried the details of Franco's 'concessions' as given to Casado on February 22. Trust in the broadcasts accelerated the surrender rate.

At 0700 hours March 27 the Defence Council (except for the ailing Professor Besteiro who waited a while longer) left the Treasury building. Miaja fled to Valencia. Casado ordered a member of his staff, Colonel Adolfo Prada Vaquero, to seek out a senior nationalist officer to whom to surrender Madrid. Prada made his way to the University City to find that the republican troops had left their trenches. They were standing on top of them, or dancing drunkenly in the streets. The Nationalists opposite were just looking on.

The nationalist commander asked Prada to come back the following day, and gave his troops orders not to take a step forward. They accepted the surrender of those Republicans who went forward to them – in one place only two metres separated the trenches; but they allowed many more to go their own way – to the nearest Metro station from which they took trains as far as they could from the front, or home where they threw away their uniforms and sought anonymity in the crowds, or hid in their own or friends' houses. Their women tore off the purple band of republican flags, sewed a new red band, and put them out on balconies. Men put on red and gold arm bands, and those that could find any dark blue shirts put them on and burnt their red shirts. There was general revelry and dancing all night long.

The following morning hundreds of civilians made their way through the trench parapets and barbed wire to embrace the nationalist soldiers, while tens of thousands crowded the streets through which they were expected to enter the city. Many had the unnatural pallor of thirty-two months of troglodytic existence.

At 0930 hours or thereabouts on March 28 Colonel Prada hauled down the republican and raised the nationalist flag over the Treasury building. With three regular republican army captains, three Civil Guards and three militiamen he made his way to the University City. There at 1300 hours, among the ruins of the Hospital Clínico, the pride of Alfonso XIII, he formally surrendered the Town of Madrid to the Commander of the Nationalist 16 Division, Colonel Eduardo Losas Camañas.

The streets were packed with civilians, and the progress of the men of the 16 Division through them was slow north and northwest of the city, as was the progress of the other divisions of the nationalist I Army Corps which moved forward of their positions through Carabanchel and other suburbs, across the Toledo and other bridges over the River Manzanares, and into the city denied to the Nationalists since November 1936.

The Battle for Madrid was over.

Trucks and wagons followed the soldiers, bringing food to the starving people of Madrid – *el pan blanco de Franco*, 'Franco's white bread'. Young lads, hunger satisfied, went out to the trenches now empty of soldiers. They came across bodies of men killed on the last day that shots had been exchanged across the lines, March 26. No one had bothered to bury them. More bodies were discovered beneath the rubble of the ruins of the University.

During the two months of the Negrín and Casado negotiations for 'peace with honour', thousands had died of starvation in Madrid, and hundreds had been killed in action. So also all along the long front curving from the Mediterranean north of Valencia round to Extremadura, and round again to the Mediterranean east of Malaga: overall, no one knows how many thousands.

Tens of thousands were yet to die in Spain: from their wounds, from irreversible malnutrition, or tubercular and other diseases aggravated by war conditions, from diseases contracted as they were forced to labour 'in expiation' of their 'faults' in furthering the republican cause, and before nationalist firing squads after being declared guilty of 'criminal responsibilities'.

The Primate of Spain and Archbishop of Toledo, Cardinal Gomá, who in November 1936 had been the first important cleric to declare himself on Franco's side, now wrote a pastoral urging on the victors Christian forgiveness. It was to have been read in the Madrid and all

Victory Parade in Madrid 19 May 1939. General Varela pins on General Franco, Spain's highest military decoration, the Grand Cross of St. Ferdinand.

other churches of his archdiocese. Madrid's conquerors saw to it that it was not.

The material damage of war was gradually made good in Madrid. Truth to tell it was minimal compared with what was to be done over the next few years to cities in the rest of Europe. Carabanchel acquired a large prison, but also good housing. The University City was rebuilt on grander scale. The republican-begun Nuevos Ministerios were not only repaired but completed. A new Madrid developed over the next twenty-five years, three times larger than the old, incomparably more prosperous, and some would say, one of the finest capital cities in the world.

One building was not restored: the Montaña barracks, scene of the bloodiest event in the first week-end of the war. The 'mountain' was turned into a garden; but at the base of it a monument was erected. Before a background of stone fashioned to resemble a wall of sandbags there is in bronze the shattered figure of a man.

That is the reality of war, whatever else it may be as well.

Notes

(L. – London; M. – Madrid)

CHAPTER I

1 Ricardo de la Cierva *Historia de la Guerra Civil española – antecedentes* M. 1969, pp. 463–4 and diocesan archives.
2 *Anuario Militar* 1931, 1932. On the common confusion between *plantillas* (establishment) and true figures of serving officers and men cf. Ramón Salas *Historia del ejército popular de la República* M. 1973, p. 8.

CHAPTER 3

1 Cierva pp. 490–1. J.M.Gil Robles *No fue posible la paz* M. 1968, pp. 232–62 for his own account of his ministry.
2 Salvador de Madariaga *España* Buenos Aires 1955, p. 65.

CHAPTER 4

1 *que se levanten: yo me voy a acostar*, quoted Cierva p. 807.
2 For greater details of the rising based principally on the Republican Army records in the Servicio Histórico Militar (SHM) see Salas pp. 122–38, 174–5, 213–15.
3 Nominal rolls: SHM, AGL–V2–L4–C12 to 14. They contain 2928 names, but as Salas p. 271 points out some names appear to be duplicated.
4 For the to-date most coherent and carefully documented account of the plot see Cierva pp. 761–809.

CHAPTER 5

1 Aurelio Nuñez Mongado *Los sucesos de España*, Buenos Aires 1941, p. 338. Julio Alvarez del Vayo *Freedom's Battle* N.Y. 1940, p. 240.
2 Manuel Azaña *La Velada en Benicarló*, Buenos Aires 1939, pp. 95–6 and 97.
3 Alvarez del Vayo p. 261 *et aliter*.
4 *ABC* etc., July 22 1936.

CHAPTER 6

1 Quoted Salas p. 227 cf. p. 272 n.10 for discussion on various versions of manner of Castillo's death.
2 Official communiqués in SHM, *passim*.
3 Quoted Salas p. 230.
4 *Ibid.* p. 185 updating earlier research in SHM. His figures, however, include those on leave whereas others, myself included (*Franco, the Man and his Nation* L. 1966, p. 246) have worked on figures of those on duty July 18–20. Salas is the first to give the split in the Asaltos.
5 Salas pp. 220 and 492–7 quoting SHM-AGL-L477-C6-B2 ff. 91–109.
6 José Martínez Bande *La ofensiva sobre Segovia y la batalla de Brunete* (*Monografías de la guerra de España no. 7*) M. 1972, p. 23.
7 Enrique Lister *Nuestra Guerra* Paris 1966, p. 62, Dolores Ibarruri in *Guerra y revolucion en España* Moscow 1966, p. 306 and their fellow Communist Luigi Longo *Las brigadas internacionales en España* Mexico 1966, p. 145, all give 70 000.
8 Figures from payrolls. Martínez Bande p. 19.
9 Manuel Azaña *Obras Completas* Mexico 1968, Vol. III p. 495.

CHAPTER 7

1 Principal sources: J.M.Martínez Bande's heavily documented *La marcha sobre Madrid* (*Monografías etc. No. 1*) M. 1968, and Salas pp. 251–63 and 469–72; Vicente Rojo *Así fue la defensa de Madrid* Mexico 1967, the relevant pages in the Soviet *Bajo la bandera de la España republicana* Moscow 1966 (?), Lister op. cit., Segismundo Casado *The last days of Madrid* L. 1939, Hidalgo de Cisneros *Memorias* Paris 1964.
2 *Documents diplomatiques français 1932–9* Paris 1963– Series 2, Vols. III and IV, cf. in particular doc. no. 28. Cf. Salas pp. 425–30, 435–8.
3 *Bajo la bandera, passim*, more than confirming references in Azaña, Casado, Louis Fischer *Men and Politics* N.Y. 1961, W.G.Krivitsky *In Stalin's Secret Service* N.Y. 1939. Cf. Burnett Bolloten *The Grand*

Camouflage L. 1961, pp. 232–3.
4 Hidalgo p. 323.

CHAPTER 8

1 *Docs. dip. français* nos. 374, 405, 407, 504 suggest that Soviet military aid began to arrive in Spain as early as August 15, and that between September 15 and October 3 it included 44 000 tons of fuel and 6000 tons of military 'hardware'. There is a mention of the disembarkation of 5000 men – ? for the International Brigades or already advance parties of the pilots and crews of the aircraft and armoured vehicles which followed? Cf. Krivitsky pp. 98–9.
2 *Diario Oficial del Ministerio de la Guerra* nos. 196, 211, 212, 215, 247. Hidalgo Vol. II p. 361. Ibarruri Vol. II p. 126–7. Cf. Bulloten pp. 228–32.
3 Voronov in *Bajo la bandera* pp. 74–5. Casado p. 77 with an analysis of the inherent inefficiency of the mixed brigade compared with a division as the tactical unit of an army.
4 Cf. Salas pp. 491–511 for a full account of the reorganization of the republican armed forces and the formation of the mixed brigades.
5 Casado p. 53. Ibarruri Vol. II p. 133.
6 Emilio Kleber (usually Klebert in Spanish documents), according to Rojo p. 214 claimed at first that he was a Canadian. For his early life see Hugh Thomas *The Spanish Civil War* L. 1961, p. 302. He appears to have reached the rank of general in the Soviet Army. Stalin had him executed on his return to the USSR. The literature on the International Brigades is plentiful. The republican records in SHM do not substantiate many of the claims to glory and prowess made on their behalf. As we shall see, their role in the defence of Madrid, while important, was nowhere near as overwhelming as the Cominform-inspired propaganda of the time – or the anti-communist Nationalists afterwards – made it out to be.
7 Krivitsky pp. 96–7.
8 Martínez Bande p. 84 for details as in *estadillo* (Returns) for October 7.
9 Franco to Mola orders *ibid.* p. 95.
10 Text *ibid.* note 94.
11 Quotations from *La Voz*, Madrid, October 27 1936.

CHAPTER 9

1 Text in full Salas pp. 546–7.
2 Krivoshein in *Bajo la bandera* pp. 325–6. Lister p. 81. For details and assessment of equipment received from the USSR *vide* Salas pp. 531–8, 563–5, 2534–6, 2568–73, 2584–93, 3418. On pp. 2149–53 Salas pres-

ents an interesting speculative essay on the question 'how many Soviet military personnel served in Spain?' His conclusion '10 000' is at least twice as high as any other previous estimate I have seen. Moscow will have to pull back the curtain on their part in the Civil War before anyone could advance any number 10 000, 5000 or fewer as firmer than speculation; however, 10 000 is not improbable.
3 Barroso to author 1965. Cf. Alfredo Kindelan *Mis cuadernos de guerra* M. s. d.
4 Photostat in Martínez Bande, opposite p. 97.
5 Salas pp. 528–30 makes the total 355 640 as on November 1, but admits reasonably accurate figures are possible only for the TOCE for which he gives 83 566.
6 Operations October 28–November 6 Martínez Bande pp. 105–9, Salas pp. 544–51: Soviet participation Batov in *Bandera* pp. 223–6, Voronov 75–7, Krivoshein pp. 327–33. Cf. Rojo pp. 62–9.
7 Martínez Bande pp. 115–16.
8 Order reproduced *ibid.* opposite p. 117.
9 Salas insists pp. 641–2 *et aliter* that the *amigos* did not have the final say in the defence of Madrid and that Miaja, Rojo, Largo and Pozas did not surrender their independence to them. Perhaps not in these early stages of the battle for Madrid; but their influence certainly grew with the quantity of Russian equipment in Spain.
10 *Bajo la bandera* p. 20.
11 Barroso to author 1965 discussion on this and other battles of the Civil War.

CHAPTER 10

1 For fuller accounts of this stage Martínez Bande pp. 113–45 and documents pp. 177–208 and Salas pp. 569–650.
2 Martínez Bande pp. 123–4.
3 Lister p. 85.
4 Rojo pp. 63 *et seq.*
5 Miaja, quoted by Salas p. 569.
6 *Bajo la bandera* p. 335.
7 Mikhail Koltzov *Diario de la guerra de España* Paris 1963, pp. 224–5.
8 Cf. Luigi Longo.
9 *Bajo la bandera* p. 232.
10 Kindelan p. 33 – a fact relevant to the controversy over the responsibility for the bombing of Guernica in 1937.
11 Salas p. 2522 compiled from Madrid Municipal records.
12 Martínez Bande p. 150.

CHAPTER 11

1 Rojo pp. 56 *et seq.*, 61, 77 etc., wrote of the 'miraculous' saving of Madrid. Given the rela-

tive strengths of men and firepower its capture would have been 'miraculous'. *Vide* Martínez Bande pp. 157–8 and Note 156 for examples of the inconsistency between what he signed as true during the battle and what, on recollection, he wrote in his *Así fue la defensa de Madrid*.

2 For these operations in far greater detail, see Martínez Bande *La lucha en torno a Madrid (Monografías No. 2)* M. 1969, pp. 11–59, and Salas pp. 653–75 and 727–48.

3 Salas p. 673 note 5. As Salas says, their failure before Madrid and at Pozuelo should have made the Nationalists realize that the days of easy victories were over.

4 From a *Guía de Madrid*, published in August 1938.

5 *Bajo la bandera* p. 33.

6 Jesús de Galíndez *Los vascos en el Madrid sitiado* Buenos Aires 1945 pp. 120–1.

7 *Ibid.*, also conversations with survivors 1965–70.

8 Krivitsky p. 8. 'Nikolsky, alias Schwed, alias Lyova, alias Orlov'.

9 On the power of the NKVD over both foreign Communists and Spanish see Bulloten pp. 172–4.

10 Martínez Bande p. 80. Figures rounded off. Battle of Jarama in detail pp. 73–111, Salas pp. 756–78. Voronov adds interesting details in *Bajo la bandera* pp. 110–15. So also Malinovsky pp. 28–30, who significantly still uses Pavlov's code name 'Petrov'.

11 Ibarruri p. 241.

12 Salas pp. 750–1.

13 Voronov loc. cit. for greater detail.

14 Martínez Bande p. 101.

15 *Ibid.* p. 111, figures rounded off. Any breakdown into killed, missing, wounded would be meaningless, since neither side kept accurate records. Certainly, given the medical facilities available the death can be assumed of a substantial proportion of the wounded.

CHAPTER 12

1 Rodimtsev in *Bajo la bandera* pp. 267 and 270.

2 Barroso and Franco to Roatta in Martínez Bande pp. 131–2.

3 Op. cit. p. 272.

4 Rodimtsev pp. 280–308, a most coherent account. Lister is useful but exaggerates his own part. Hidalgo de Cisneros provides much information on the republican air force. Best modern account Martínez Bande pp. 115–75, cf. Salas pp. 861–98.

5 Quoted in Martínez Bande p. 149 n. 169.

6 Minutes of the meeting *ibid.* n. 173. Cf. Salas p. 901 n. 18.

7 Report in full in Martínez Bande pp. 227–30.

8 Barroso to author. Martínez Bande n. 188 virtually discounts the stories of jubilation in the nationalist camp at the defeat of the Italians.

9 Barroso to author.

CHAPTER 13

1 Martínez Bande. *La ofensiva sobre Segovia y la batalla de Brunete (Monografías No. 7)* M. 1972 p. 50.

2 For the political history of the ousting of Largo Caballero, see Bulloten pp. 307–16.

3 Full text in Martínez Bande pp. 239–40.

4 Jesús Hernández *Yo, ministro de Stalin en España* M. 1954 pp. 109–14.

5 Luis Araquistaín *El comunismo y la guerra de España* Carmaux 1939 pp. 13–14.

6 Salas pp. 1075–83 for minute detail.

7 Azaña Vol. IV p. 589. Cf. Bulloten p. 238 n. 53.

8 Partial list Salas p. 1174. On the proselytization among, and the disabilities of, recusant socialists *vide* Largo Caballero *Correspondencia Secreta* M. 1961 pp. 268–71 and Casado pp. 76–9.

9 Conversation with author 1965.

10 Salas pp. 1070–4 for an account of this once famous episode.

11 Full text Martínez Bande pp. 241–5.

12 Martínez Bande on La Granja pp. 63–100. Cf. Salas pp. 1185–95. Texts of reports in full Martínez Bande pp. 246–63.

13 Bulloten pp. 236–7, 241, 285 concludes that Rojo was not unfavourably disposed towards the communists and even helped them. Talking to him I got the impression that he greatly admired their discipline, and that he was guided by the very same principles which were inculcated into Franco at the Spanish military academies of their day (*vide* the author's *Franco, the Man and his Nation* pp. 66–70). His membership of the UME and flirtation with the communists were ideologically equally logical, and Franco seemingly saw in him a kindred spirit in allowing him to end his days in the Madrid he loved so deeply.

14 Op. cit. pp. 97 *et seq.*

15 Texts in full Martínez Bande pp. 264–74. Salas pp. 1217 *et seq.*

16 Salas p. 1226 estimates 125 000, and gives 300 as the number of aircraft available and 200 as that of armoured vehicles.

17 *Bandera* pp. 36 *et seq.*

18 Conversation with author.

CHAPTER 14

1 Martínez Bande pp. 120, 138 and note 157. Principal sources for this chapter: *ibid.* pp.

103–234 and documents pp. 265–318, Salas pp. 1215–85, *Bajo la bandera*, Lister, Rojo.

2 Martínez Bande pp. 111–13 and note 119.

3 *Ibid.* quoting AGL–OR–Ejército del Centro – L 690–C7.

4 Lister (pp. 135 *et seq.*) says one hour, but 5 Corps despatch to army gives 1130 as the hour at which resistance ended. He claims to have captured 250 men there, 3 A/T guns etc., etc., but the brigade concerned reported 60 only and 5 Corps despatch gives 108 as the figure. There is no evidence from the other side that there were more than 80 men at Brunete, including the non-combatant medical corps men. Presumably even in the one hour of artillery and aerial bombardment and assault some of the 80 must have been killed making the original brigade report more likely than Lister's.

5 Alvarez's detailed report in Martinez Bande pp. 275–81.

6 Rojo p. 106.

7 Modesto p. 110.

8 Modesto p. 113 claims the capture of 300 prisoners at Los Llanos and Quijorna, i.e. about 30 per cent of the total of defenders at the start of the offensive.

9 Full details Martínez Bande note 188.

10 HE-111s and Ju-88s. One squadron of 10 ME 109s was now operational and proved as superior over the I-16s as the I-15s had been over the HE-51s.

11 Despatches in Martínez Bande n. 262 and Salas p. 1255.

12 Despatches in Martínez Bande no. 268, cf. Thomas p. 465.

13 Evidence of survivors. Cf. Lister p. 137, though his picture of Prieto drinking champagne with Miaja at GHQ may not be absolutely true.

14 Modesto pp. 117–18 blames the 14 Division for the loss of Brunete but did not do so in his report to Miaja.

15 To author even more explicitly than in his book.

16 Martínez Bande pp. 231–2. Salas p. 1255 puts republican casualties at 29 000.

CHAPTER 15

1 SHM AGL – Ejército del Norte – L. 854 – C. 6. printed in Martínez Bande *Monografía* 8 p. 211.

2 Ibarruri Vol. III p. 272 and Lister p. 165 give the lower figure, but Salas works it out as between 125 000 and 150 000. 80 000 would suggest that the republican losses at Brunete were much heavier than the relevant documents warrant, while 125 000 would suggest a remarkable replacement rate for casualties.

3 Quoted in Martínez Bande *Monografía* 9, p. 14.

4 Statement to author in 1965, when I discovered in separate conversations with the two opposing generals the enormous respect each had for the other.

5 The appreciation in full is printed in Martínez Bande *Monografía* 10, pp. 239–43.

6 Casado op. cit. pp. 113–14.

7 Op. cit. p. 145.

8 *Cómo terminó la guerra de España* p. 33.

9 Copy in SHM. Text printed in J.M.Martínez-Bande *Los cien últimos días de la República*, Barcelona 1973 pp. 297–8. For date cf. references to it in further documents, pp. 310 and 311.

10 The then member of the Communist Party Central Committee, Jesús Hernández, op. cit. p. 221, states that the Soviet officers present dissuaded Negrín from arresting Casado and other doubters there and then.

11 The Socialist historian Antonio Ramos Olveira *Historia de España* – Mexico s.d. Vol. III p. 392 hazards the figure of 1000 casualties between March 6–12.

12 Full text Martínez Bande op. cit. pp. 299–300.

13 Texts *ibid.* pp. 301–13.

14 Quoted *ibid.* pp. 252–3.

Select Bibliography

(L. – London; M. – Madrid)

Abad de Santillán, Diego, *La Revolución y la Guerra de España*, M. 1937.
Alvarez del Vayo, J. *Freedom's Battle*, N.Y. 1940.
Araquistain, Luis, *El comunismo y la guerra de España*, Carmaux 1939.
Azaña, Manuel, *Obras Completas*, Mexico 1968.
Bolloten, Burnett, *The Grand Camouflage* L. 1961.
Casado, Segismundo, *The last days of Madrid*, L. 1939.
Cierva, Ricardo de la, *Historia de la guerra civil española*, Vol. 1, M. 1969.
Coca, Gabriel M. de, *Anticaballero*, M. 1936.
Diario oficial del ministerio de la guerra.
Documents diplomatiques français, 1932–39, Series 2, Vols. III and IV, Paris
    1963–.
Galindez, Jesús de, *Los vascos en el Madrid sitiado*, Buenos Aires 1945.
García Pradas. José, *Cómo terminó la guerra de España*, Buenos Aires, 1945.
Gil Robles, J.M. *No fue posible la paz*, M. 1968.
Hernandez, Jesús, *Yo, ministro de Stalin en España*, M. 1954.
Hidalgo de Cisneros, Ignacio, *Memorias*, Paris 1964.
Ibarruri, Dolores and others, *Guerra y revolución en España*, Moscow 1966.
Kindelan, Alfredo, *Mis cuadernos de guerra*, M.?
Koltzov, Mikhail, *Diario de la guerra de España*, Paris 1963.
Krivitsky, W.G., *In Stalin's Secret Service*, N.Y. 1939.
Largo Caballero, Francisco, *Correspondencia secreta*, M. 1961.
Lister, Enrique, *Nuestra guerra*, Paris 1966.
Longo, Luigi, *Las brigadas internacionales en España*, Mexico 1966.
Madariaga, Salvador de, *España*, Buenos Aires 1955.
Malinovsky and others, *Bajo la bandera de la España republicana*, Moscow
    1966 (?).
Martinez Bande, José Manuel, *Monografías de la guerra de España*
    1   *La marcha sobre Madrid*, M. 1968.
    2   *La lucha en torno a Madrid*, M. 1969.
    3   *La ofensiva sobre Segovia y la batalla de Brunete*, M. 1972.
Martinez Bande, José Manuel, *Los cien últimos días de la República*, Barce-
    lona 1973.
Modesto, Juan, *Soy del Quinto Regimiento*, Paris 1969.
Nuñez Mongado, Aurelio, *Los sucesos en España vistos por un diplomático*,
    Buenos Aires 1941.
Payne, Stanley G., *Politics and the Military in Modern Spain*, L. 1967.
Prieto, Indalecio, *Convulsiones de España*, Mexico 1967.
Ramos Oliveira, Antonio, *Historia de España, Vol. III*, Mexico, s.d.
Rojo, Vicente, *Así fue la defensa de Madrid*, Mexico 1967.
Rojo, Vicente, *España heróica*, Buenos Aires 1942.
Salas Larrazabal, Ramón, *Historia del ejército popular de la República*
    4 Vols., M. 1973.
Thomas, Hugh, *The Spanish Civil War*, L. 1961.

Index

189

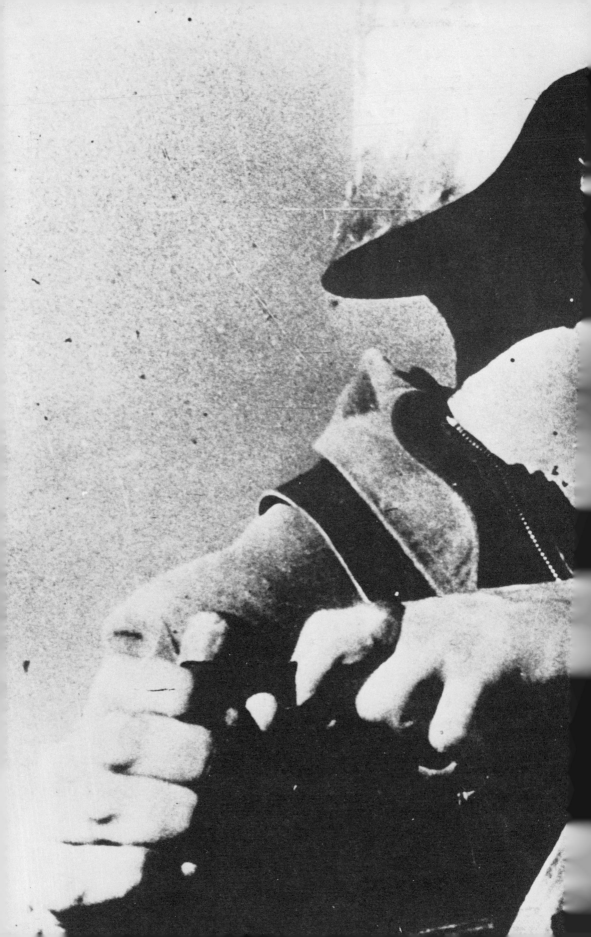